LOST ON BOTH SIDES

DANTE GABRIEL ROSSETTI
Portrait by William Holman Hunt, 1853, courtesy
of the Birmingham City Museum and Art Gallery.

LOST ON
BOTH SIDES

Dante Gabriel Rossetti:
Critic and Poet

Robert M. Cooper

OHIO UNIVERSITY PRESS
Athens, Ohio

Copyright © 1970 by Robert M. Cooper
All rights reserved.
Printed in the United States of America
Library of Congress Catalog Card Number 71-91957
SBN 8214-0069-X

TO MY WIFE
who, in watching me prove Rossetti
a critic, proved herself one as well.

Contents

ABBREVIATIONS

The following abbreviations are used in footnotes for works cited most frequently:

Ashley Catalogue — T. J. Wise (ed.), *The Ashley Library: A Catalogue* (London, 1922-1936).

Collected Works — W. M. Rossetti (ed.), *The Collected Works of Dante Gabriel Rossetti* (London, 1886).

D & W — Oswald Doughty and J. R. Wahl (eds.), *Letters of Dante Gabriel Rossetti* (London, 1965-1967).

L & M — W. M. Rossetti, *Dante Gabriel Rossetti, Letters and Memoir* (London, 1895).

ACKNOWLEDGEMENTS

I am most indebted to Prof. Carlos Baker and Prof. Willard Thorp, with whom I began my pursuit of Rossetti some years ago, and to Prof. John R. Benish, who more recently encouraged me to bring it to a conclusion. I also owe much to all those who have studied and written about Rossetti, especially to Prof. Paull F. Baum, whose studies of the poet-painter remain pre-eminent.

To Professors Oswald Doughty and John R. Wahl, my keen appreciation for their *Letters of Dante Gabriel Rossetti* is tinged with gentle reproach for their not amassing and editing this great collection long since. Their work has proved invaluable to me in checking, updating, and adding to my earlier research. I am indebted to them, and to the Clarendon Press, Oxford, for permission to quote frequently from this collection.

Special thanks are due the City of Birmingham Museum and Art Gallery for permission to use William Holman Hunt's portrait of Rossetti. Finally, I am deeply grateful to Southwestern at Memphis, whose generous research grants made the completion of this book possible.

R. M. C.

AUTHOR'S NOTE

It may seem absurd to call Rossetti a "critic," for he wrote very little formal criticism. Yet from hundreds of comments scattered throughout the poet's extensive correspondence and the records of those who knew him, one can create a body of criticism impressive in bulk, quality, and (for all the apparent contradictions) basic consistency. This criticism, in turn, can prove most useful in illuminating and evaluating his own poetry. This I have tried to do.

In short, I have let Rossetti speak for himself as to what he thought a poet and a poem should be, and what he tried to do as a poet, resulting in an embarrassing—but I thought unavoidable—garland of *ibids*. In addition, I have used this material in the explication of a number of his poems, and in an attempt to explain what I feel was his failure to live up to his potential as a poet.

Experts in Rossetti may wish to skim (or skip entirely) Chapter I; they will find little that is new or startling in this brief review of the poet's family background, his education, early reading, and first attempts at writing and painting. I felt that such a review would be useful to others, however, for it is my hope that this book will prove of value not merely to the student of Rossetti, but to all who are interested in poetry and how it comes into being.

I
The Making of a Poet

Lady. I love thee to excess: oh yield to my desire!
Gabriel Rossetti, Jr., *Sir Hugh the Heron,* 1841 — Age twelve[1]

What makes a poet? Some poets perhaps, like Shakespeare, will not abide our question. But there are others whose boyhood and youth foreshadow and explain to an extraordinary degree the kind of man and poet to be. Such a poet was Dante Gabriel Rossetti.

To the casual reader, the twelve-year-old author of *Sir Hugh* may seem to share only a similarity of name with the poet who wrote *The Blessed Damozel* at nineteen and *The King's Tragedy* at fifty-three. In later life, Rossetti called *Sir Hugh* "absurd trash," saying "It is curious and surprising to myself, as evincing absolutely no promise at all—less than should exist even at twelve."[2] True enough, *Sir Hugh* reveals no signs of potential genius, or even talent. But it, like much of Rossetti's early creative work in both poetry and painting shows a remarkable number of the influences and characteristics that mark the mature poet.

In the same way, a study of the boy with his family, his

education, and his early reading all suggest that the boy
was not only father to the man; in many significant ways,
he *was* the man.

HIS FAMILY

Rossetti was quite aware of important effects of family
background on a poet. He once sternly warned against comparing the genius of two writers who died young, Chatterton
and Oliver Brown, because their family environments were
so different. Oliver, he pointed out, "was the product of the
most teeming hot-beds of art and literature. . . . What he
would have been if, like the ardent and heroic Chatterton,
he had had to fight a single-handed battle for art and bread
together against merciless mediocrity in high places, — what
he would *then* have become, I cannot in the least calculate;
but we know what Chatterton became."[3]

Respectably poor, middle-class professional people,
Rossetti's own family was in its own way as stimulating to
the development of an artist as Oliver's "hot-bed." The
Rosetti's gave Dante Gabriel love, security, education, con-
servative moral training, and encouragement. (He was born
Gabriel Charles Dante on May 12, 1828, but after some experimenting with his name, settled on Dante Gabriel before
he was 21.) Four elements of his family background strongly
influenced the growing boy: literary, Italian, religious, and
urban.

His family was a literary, even an artistic, one. His father,
Gabriele Pasquale Giuseppe Rossetti, was a patriot-rebel
who was forced to flee Italy disguised as a British sailor.
Settling in London, he became a teacher at King's College,
and was a poet, sketcher, musician, and well-known Dante
scholar. Dante Gabriel's mother, Frances Mary Polidori,
who had been a governess, gave him his first lessons, and
remained throughout his life "a constant reader, full of clear
perception and sound sense."[4] Others in the Rossetti and

Polidori families were poets and writers. Gaetano Polidori, the boy's grandfather, owned a private press, which printed the first "published" works of both Dante Gabriel and his younger sister, Christina.

There were four Rossetti children: Maria, a year older than Dante Gabriel; William, a year younger; Christina, two years younger; and Dante Gabriel himself. Christina's success as a poet is well known, but Maria and William also later showed literary ability, Maria with a study of Dante, and William as a critic. From the first, theirs was an artistic environment; books were loved, poetry was written as naturally as a letter, and sketching was a family pastime.

William later wrote: "I cannot, with reference to any one of us four remember any time when, knowing what a verse was, we did not also know and feel what a *correct* verse was."[5] Similarly, he could never remember a time when it was not taken for granted by the family that Dante Gabriel (or Gabriel, as they called him) should be an artist. His brother and sisters, particularly Christina, flattered Gabriel's early attempts in painting with eager imitation, and engaged in spirited *bouts-rimés* sonnets with him. Christina drew sketches most of her life. William expected to become an artist himself when he joined the Pre-Raphaelite Brotherhood, and wrote the introductory sonnet and other poems for the Brotherhood's short-lived magazine, *The Germ*.

From his family, then, Gabriel had every inducement to become a poet and painter. The love of literature and art was there, and as he wrote of Beauty, "I drew it in as simply as my breath."[6] Such an atmosphere had its limitations, however, limitations that were to show up in his poetry and that he acknowledged when he confessed in 1880 that his was a mind "isolated in art."[7]

Rossetti's family was also an Italian family; although born in England, he was only one-fourth English by blood.

Two young men who knew him well in his final years report apparently conflicting statements about Rossetti's opinion of the influence of this Italian background. According to William Sharp, a struggling bank clerk who later became a successful writer, Rossetti considered himself "wholly English."[8] On the other hand, to Hall Caine, also a clerk who was to succeed as an author, and Rossetti's caretaker during his last illness, the poet said: "Our household was all of Italian, not English environment."[9] Rather than conflicting, however, the two statements really suggest another of the many dualities that made Dante Gabriel Rossetti what he was.

As brother William remarked, anyone who reads Rossetti's *Wellington's Funeral* "will perceive there was a good deal of the Englishman in Rossetti. He was even a sort of typical John Bull in a certain unreasoned and impatient preference of Englishmen and things English to foreigners and things foreign."[10] This is certainly substantiated by the almost provincial attitude he displayed during his trip to France and Belgium in 1850 with Holman Hunt, by his rejection of Whistler's French mentors as "simple putrescence and decomposition,"[11] and by his sarcastic advice to such young, French-influenced poets who flocked about him as Morris and Swinburne: "Quit so poor a language as that of Shakespeare, and write entirely in French."[12]

Yet William also said, "for Italy and Italians he had necessarily a fellow-feeling—substantial, though by no means indiscriminate or thorough-going."[13] In fact, said William: "I must always regard my brother—spite of some ultra-John-Bullish opinions and ways—as more an Italian than an Englishman—Italian in temper of mind, in the quasi-restriction of his interest to the beautiful and the passionate, in disregard of those prejudices and conventions which we call 'Philistine,' in general tone of moral perception."[14]

It doesn't matter that the brother ascribes this "quasi-restriction" of interests to the Italian rather than literary part of Rossetti's family heritage. Likely enough, it was both. The important points are that from boyhood on, Rossetti's interests were largely limited to the "beautiful and the passionate," and that this limitation affected his poetry.

There is danger in overstressing the "Italian" in Rossetti. William may be doing so in thus explaining Gabriel's disregard of Philistine prejudices and conventions. After all, it was the Italian Rossetti who warned the wholly English Swinburne to temper his defiance of those very prejudices and conventions, saying of Swinburne's Baudelairean excesses, "I warn you that the public will not be able to digest them."[15] P. F. Baum, in correctly seeing a conflicting "duality" of body and soul in the nineteen-year-old author of *The Blessed Damozel* that was to run "through all is life and poetry," may also go too far when he attributes this to Rossetti's "southern blood."[16] Maria, who became an Anglican nun, had the same three-fourths southern blood; so did the strait-laced William; so did the severe, ascetic Christina.

How far astray this overemphasis of the Italian element can lead one is perhaps best demonstrated by Ford M. Hueffer's statement that Rossetti's "one great gift was *purely* Italian, his great keeness of sight—of insight into life, of power to catch the character of externals."[17] Shades of those great "Italians," Shakespeare and Chaucer!

Avoiding such overstatement, let us just say that the Italian influence on Rossetti was one important factor in the making of the poet. He learned Italian as early and as naturally as English. His father's poetry, perhaps the first he heard, was Italian. William thinks Gabriel's first trifling rhymes were done in Italian.[18] Rossetti's translations of early Italian poets must surely have been an invaluable poetic apprenticeship—the kind of apprenticeship he sorely missed as a painter. Begun when he was eighteen, they show, says brother William, "a keen sensitiveness to whatsoever is poetic in the originals, and a sinuous strength and ease in providing English equivalents, with the command of a rich and romantic vocabulary."[19] Quite likely, too, these translations helped develop Rossetti's habit of hunting out rare and strange words, and his use of near-rhymes, for trying to translate in rhyme is difficult at best.

Rossetti himself proclaims his Italian heritage when he says that his poem *A Last Confession* "was the simple and genuine result of my having passed my whole boyhood among people just like the speaker in the poem. . .this subject, if any, was my absolute birthright."[20] He told Swinburne, "it is the outcome of the Italian part of me."[21] Also almost an absolute birthright was the influence of his Italian namesake, the poet Dante, which dominated much of his poetry and painting. (The heroine of *Sir Hugh,* by the way, was named Beatrice.)

As important in fashioning the poet-to-be as the Italian and literary atmosphere in which he grew up was the earnest, Anglican piety of Dante Gabriel Rosetti's mother—a piety he could never share, yet whose influence he could never completely shake. Maria could escape (if such be the word) to an Anglican sisterhood, and Christina could reject the Pre-Raphaelite Collinson because he was a Roman Catholic. Gabriel could do nothing so dramatic. Instead, he lived out his life wracked by conflicts that had their origin in the struggle to reconcile his basically sensuous, sensual nature with the stern religious and moral training of his childhood.

As a boy he went dutifully to church, "without much liking or any serious distaste."[22] When he was away from home at age fourteen and felt a not-unique urge to play the truant, he found it necessary to explain to his mother: "I do not think that I shall go to church Sunday for in the first place I do not know where I can sit, and in the second place I find that we are stared at wherever we go."[23]

Six years later (1848) he sent his accumulated poems

to William Bell Scott—like Rossetti, both an artist and poet—under the title "Songs of the Art Catholic," but this title hardly heralded any great conversion. For as William Rossetti explains, Gabriel's art was

> in sentiment though not necessarily in dogma, Catholic—medieval and un-modern. He never was, and never affected to be, a Roman-Catholic, nor yet an Anglican-Catholic. All the then excited debates concerning "puseyism," Tractarianism, and afterwards Ritualism, passed by him like the idle wind. . . .Indeed, by this date—so far as opinion went, which is very different from sentiment and traditional bias—he was already a decided sceptic. He was never confirmed, professed no religious faith, and practiced no regular religious observances; but he had (more especially two or three years after this) sufficient sympathy with the abstract ideas and venerable forms of Christianity to go occasionally to an Anglican church—very occasionally, and only as the inclination ruled him.[24]

It was the medieval-Catholic sentiment in Rossetti's earliest poetry *(Ave, Blessed Damozel)* and painting ("Girlhood of Mary Virgin" and "Ecce Ancilla Domini") that made him most responsible for public rumor that the Pre-Raphaelite Brotherhood was pro-Catholic propaganda, rumor so strong that Ruskin at first believed it.[25] Rossetti himself, sensitive to charges of "popery," changed the title of his "blessed white eyesore" from the Latin "Ecce Ancilla Domini" to "The Annunciation."

"There are traces of superstition noticeable in him, none of religion," was the opinion recorded in his diary in 1867 by William Allingham, Customs employee, later poet and magazine editor, and long-time friend of Rossetti.[26] If by "religion" Allingham meant dogma, his remark holds equally true of the young Rossetti. For it was not the dogma or authority of "medieval, un-modern" Catholicism that stirred Rossetti, but the "superstition" or faith that gave flesh and blood to myth, making "real" persons of the Virgin awaiting the Annunciation, the Blessed Mary in heaven or the Blessed Damozel yearning after her lover on earth.

Perhaps it was "superstition," but the fervent desire, at least, for an almost earthly heaven never left Rossetti. When Alexander Gilchrist, who had enlisted Rossetti's help in the writing of the *Life of William Blake*, died in 1861 while the work was still in progress, Rossetti wrote to his widow: "Such terrible partings from love and work must be, unless all things are a mere empty husk of nothing, — a guide to the belief in a new field of effort and a second communion with those loved and lost."[27]

A year later the need to believe in such an afterlife came even more deeply and personally when Rossetti's own wife died suddenly. She was the milliner's assistant Elizabeth Siddal, whom he first met in 1850. From the adored "Guggums" with the stunning hair, subject of endless sketches, she dwindled year by year into a pathetic, complaining consumptive. At last, reluctantly, they married in 1860. There followed the agony of having their only child, a daughter, born dead. On February 11, 1862, Elizabeth ended her wretched life with an overdose of laudanum. Once more Rossetti wrote Mrs. Gilchrist: "Of my dear wife I do not dare speak now, nor to attempt any vain conjecture whether it may ever be possible for me, or I may be found worthy, to meet her again."[28]

It was long believed that the sonnet *Without Her*, written in 1871, referred to Rossetti's dead wife. Now it seems more likely that the poet was moved by the absence of William Morris' wife, Jane, with whom Rossetti was then passionately in love. In either case, there is no gainsaying the poignancy of separation from the loved one expressed:

> A wayfarer by barren ways and chill,
> Steep ways and weary, without her thou art,

  Where the long cloud, the long wood's counterpart,
  Sheds doubled darkness up the laboring hill.

The desire for a physical reunion after death is the "one hope"
of the final sonnet of *The House of Life*, just as it had been
the dream Rossetti created as a youth in *The Blessed Damozel.*
With the death of his wife, the dream became a dreadful
part of his own life, possibly resulting, as K. L. Knickerbocker
has suggested, in revisions of *The Blessed Damozel* that
turned a youthful, imagined work into a poem freighted
with autobiographical detail.[29]

  Rossetti tried again and again to bridge heaven and earth
through spiritualism, attending seance after seance. According to William, his very belief in a future life "depended
partly upon what we call 'spiritualism.'"[30] This was only
one of innumerable indications of how largely he was ruled
by emotion rather than reason, by intuition rather than logic.
Again we have William's corroboration: "For theological
discussions of whatsoever kind he had not the faintest
taste. . . . On the other hand, his mind was naturally prone
to the marvelous and supernatural."[31] Readers of *Sister
Helen* and *Rose Mary* will readily agree.

  Yet the lifelong influence of his mother could hardly
allow Rossetti to avow the agnosticism W. B. Scott thought
he saw. Rossetti's friend Dixon, whose testimony as a
clergyman is significant, told Caine: "I once saw him very
indignant on hearing that he had been accused of irreligion,
or rather of not being a Christian. He asked with great earn-
estness, 'Do not my works testify to my Christianity?'"[33]

  Rossetti had trouble expressing this "Christianity" explicitly, however. The feelings about an afterlife that he strug-
gled to express in *The Cloud Confines* are murky even in his
prose explanation: ". . .it is even a real retributive future
for the special atom of life to be re-embodied (if so it were)
in a world which its own former ideality had helped to fashion for pain or pleasure."[34] He *felt* (for "believed" seems too

strong a word) that there was retribution—in pain or pleasure—awaiting re-embodied souls for what they had done
on earth. For Sister Helen, the soul is "Lost, lost, all lost
between Hell and Heaven!" In *A Last Confession,* the mur-
derer's "soul shall burn." Such retribution is horribly de-
picted in *Vain Virtues,* where the "sorriest thing that enters
Hell" are fair deeds superseded by a soul's sin:

> These yet are virgins, whom death's timely knell
> Might once have sainted; whom the fiends compel
>   Together now, in snake-bound shuddering sheaves
>   Of anguish, while the pit's polution leaves
> Their refuse maidenhood abominable.

To Rose Mary, on the other hand, like the Blessed Damozel,
"the floor of Heaven to her feet forever is given." And even
for the fallen Jenny, perhaps, there is hope:

> And for the body and the soul which by
> Man's pitiless doom must now comply
> With lifelong hell, what lullaby
> Of sweet forgetful second birth
> Remains? All dark. No sign on earth
> What measure of God's rest endows
>   The many mansions of his house.

Caine's own estimate of Rossetti's religion can be ac-
cepted as summary: his emotional approach to life combined
with the influence of his parents to give him a "Catholic"
religious spirit, and unreasoning, unquestioning, intuitive
submission to religious influences. He was not at all touched
by controversies and creeds; he was "naturally incapable
of comprehending differences of belief, and unwilling to
dwell upon them for an instant."[35] In short, the boy who
went to church "without much liking or any serious distaste"
became the poet who said in *Soothsay:*

Let love of all Theology
Be to thy soul what it *can* be:
But know,—the Power that fashions man
Measured not out thy little span
For thee to take the meting-rod
In turn, and so approve on God
Thy science of Theometry.

One other aspect of Rossetti's family life deserves mention: it was a city life. He had short snatches of "'countrifying" at his Grandfather Polidori's house, Holmes Green in Buckinghamshire. "There he loitered about a little, doing nothing in particular. His chief amusement was to haunt a pond in the grounds, and catch frogs."[36] But "these little and never frequent country excursions came to an end in 1839," when the grandfather resettled in London, "and then Dante Rossetti, for two or three years, went out of London not at all."[37]

Thus while growing up Rossetti had little opportunity to know and love Nature as, say, Wordsworth did. He had little preparation for following that basic principle of the Pre-Raphaelite Brotherhood, "truth to Nature," which he was to try to obey in 1848.

The next chapter will examine in detail Rossetti's attitudes toward Nature, and show that critics from Waugh (he "never at any time showed interest in natural scenery")[38] to Grylls (he "hated the country")[39] are inaccurate. True, he was a city boy and a city man, but then, so was Keats. Rossetti's sonnet on Keats showed that he understood the city both they (and the pathetic prostitute of Rossetti's *Jenny*) knew all too well:

The weltering London ways where children weep
And girls whom none call maidens laugh, —strange road
Miring his outward steps, who inly trode
The bright Castalian brink and Latmos' steep: —
Even such his life's cross paths. . . .

Yet Rossetti used Nature often in his poetry, the city seldom —
but Nature in his own way and on his own terms.

HIS EDUCATION

How much formal education does a poet need? Shakespeare
had "little Latin and less Greek"—and so did Rossetti. Yet
the Elizabethan's work shows an astounding breadth of interest
and knowledge; the Victorian was limited in both. Rossetti's
limitations stemmed as much from his own nature as from the
undoubted shortcomings of his schooling.

Rossetti first left the seclusion of his family in 1836 to attend
the Rev. Mr. Paul's school in Foley Street, where he learned
writing, arithmetic, grammar, geography, history and elemen-
tary Latin, and some drawing and composition. For the next
five years, between the ages of nine and fourteen, he went
to King's College School, where as a professor his father
could obtain free tuition for his first son, and reduced rates
for William. When Gabriel left this school, according to
William, he wrote an excellent hand, knew some Latin and
a little Greek, understood French well, and "had some inkling
on subjects of history, geography, etc." He also had some
drawing of a "more or less sketchy kind." But "of anything
distantly tending to science—algebra, geometry, etc.—he
learned nothing whatever."[40] Apparently he couldn't have
cared less.

This was all the formal education Rossetti had, except
for some private lessons in German, and some instruction
in art. He began his study of art in 1842, at Sass's, a drawing
academy, where he "drew from the antique and the Skeleton,
with immense liking for the profession of art, but with only
moderate interest in these preliminaries."[41] Discipline always
irked Rossetti, and his painting, at least, always suffered
in consequence. To the end of his life, for instance, his perspective was often faulty.

In July, 1846, known chiefly for his "chivalric and satiric

subjects," Rossetti left Sass's for the Antique School of the Royal Academy. This was supposed to be only a preliminary to the advanced Life and Painting Schools, but he never advanced beyond it. He lacked, says William, "a resolute sense of duty, firm faith in his instructors, and a disposition to do what was wanted in the same way as other people."[42] Not surprisingly, he failed to profit much from the Antique School. He was aware of his deficiencies, as he admitted to his aunt Charlotte Polidori in 1848, but characteristically sought the quick and easy solution: "Every time I attempt to express my ideas in colour I find myself baffled, not by want of ability—I feel this, and why should I not say it?— but by ignorance of certain apparently insignificant technicalities which, with the guidance of an experienced artist, might soon be acquired."[43] He found his man, one who was experienced but whose charges for instruction were not "exorbitant," in Ford Madox Brown, an obscure twenty-seven-year-old painter he had long admired. He wrote Brown, affirming that aside from "an engraving after that great painter Von Holst." Brown's *Abstract Representation of Justice* was "the sole pictorial adornment of my room." After just six months' instruction, Rossetti concluded, "I feel convinced that I should then have some chance in Art."[44] Brown agreed to accept him as a pupil. Rossetti's school days were over.

Clearly there was little in either phase of his formal education to equip Rossetti for success as painter or poet. In contrast to his painting, however, which always betrayed to some extent the ignorance of "certain apparently insignificant technicalities," even his early poetry (after the unpromising childish scribbles) showed technical skill as well as signs of poetic genius. This difference in degree of mastery of the two arts may be explained partly by their differing demands, partly by differences in Rossetti's talents and temperament. But perhaps the chief reason was that by the time he was twenty, Rossetti had acquired a thorough knowl-

overwhelmed at least temporarily by some new favorite. Shakespeare's *Hamlet,* William thought, was "the very first book my brother took to with strong personal zest," at the age of five, or maybe even four.[46] Soon he knew well *Henry VI, The Tempest, Midsummer Night's Dream, The Merchant of Venice, Henry IV, Romeo and Juliet, Macbeth,* and others. Rossetti wrote no drama as an adult, but his reading of Shakespeare may have added something to the dramatic quality of Rossetti's ballads and influenced Rossetti's own sonnet sequence. Throughout his life Rossetti used Shakespeare as the ultimate measure of poetic greatness.

The next "immense favorite" after Shakespeare was Walter Scott, before Rossetti was nine.[47] "He romped through" *Marmion* "and recited whole pages at a stretch," in an early display of that memory for which he was to be famous among his later friends. With equal delight he went on to *The Lay of the Last Minstrel, The Lady of the Lake,* and *The Waverly Novels; Ivanhoe* being the favorite. Rossetti's first childish attempts at writing, he long afterwards declared, were almost pure Scott.

Even before the Scott phase waned, Rossetti was reading Robert Burns, of whom he had "a kind of idea—but the dialect was a bar to his taking very kindly to the poems,"[48] though late in life he came to describe Burns as "so exceptional a genius."[49] Not at all surprising is William's notation that it was Byron, however, who "supersedes Walter Scott as the boy's prime favorite about 1838."[50] First in his esteem was *The Siege of Corinth,* next *Mazeppa* and *Manfred,* then *The Corsair* and others. In 1842 he was still writing of Byron as "my favorite poet."[51] His "imaginative" (once he went so far as to call it "schoolgirl"[52]) taste held good here. He read *Childe Harold,* but "without special zest."

To the poetry of Shelley, which came next, as to that of Byron, Rossetti seems always to have had contradictory reactions, possibly because his judgement told him that each

was a great poet, while his personal taste found much in both
that was displeasing or boring. When he first discovered
a book of Shelley's in 1843, he "surged through its pages
like a flame."[53] Two statements he made to Caine explain
this ambivalence toward Shelley. On the one hand he called
Shelley, with Shakespeare and Coleridge, one of the three
"Greatest English imaginations."[54] But on the other, he said:
"As to Shelley, it is really a mercy that he has not been hatching yearly universes till now."[55] There was the rub with
Shelley—yearly universes and prophecy getting in the way
of good "imaginative" poetry.

Two poets whom Rossetti discovered about 1845 gave
him no such complaint. Admired to the extreme from the
first, their work never lost its splendor for him. The two
were Poe and Keats. It is important to realize that Rossetti
knew and loved both well before he was eighteen, when
both were far less widely recognized than they are now.
He regarded Keats as almost a personal discovery.[56] He credited Poe with giving him the idea for *The Blessed Damozel.*[57]
From the start, Poe was a "deep well of delight,"[58] and
Rossetti, in his "very earliest days of boyish rhyming. . .was
rather proud to be as cockney as Keats *could* be."[59]

Even so, there was a period beginning in 1847 when
Poe and Keats and all the rest but Shakespeare and Dante
seemed "pale" and "neutral" compared to a new poet—
Robert Browning.[60] Here in Browning was everything
Rossetti sought: "passion, observation, medievalism, the
dramatic perception of character, act, and incident."[61] The
worship of Browning went on and on. In 1850 Rossetti came
across an anonymous poem entitled *Pauline,* recognized it
as Browning's, wrote the poet asking for verification, and to
his glee received it.[62] In 1862, after the two had become
friends, Rossetti was likely to refer to him casually as "dear,
glorious Browning."[63] But after 1871, Browning was among
the many friends who fell victim to the delusions produced

by Rossetti's overuse of the drug chloral. When Browning's *Fifine at the Fair* appeared in print, Rossetti interpreted it as an attack on himself.[64] By 1878, Rossetti was telling Hunt that "Browning and poetry had parted company for ever."[65] It is true, of course, that Browning's poetry had changed.

Curiously, one of the two poets Browning could not supplant, Dante, was not an immediate favorite of the young Gabriel—possibly because the great Italian so dominated the Rossetti household. Dante, said William, was "a sort of banshee in the Charlotte Street houses; his shriek audible even to familiarity, but the message of it was not scrutinized."[66] Gabriel was fifteen or sixteen before he examined Dante for himself, but thereafter "the current of Rossetti's love for the Florentine flowed wider and deeper month by month."[67] In that stream he found mingled many of his deepest interests: the medieval, the Italian, the Catholic, the mystic, and above all the eternal symbol for woman. As soon as he saw it, Leigh Hunt called Rossetti's first good poetry "Dantesque,"[68] an adjective Rossetti hardly liked, but Dante's influence can be seen in poems as various as *The Blessed Damozel* and *Dante at Verona,* as well as in innumerable paintings.

Other poets Rossetti discovered before he was nineteen included three giants, Blake, Tennyson, and Coleridge, as well as a pair of poetic pygmies, Philip Bailey and Charles Wells. Blake is the best single justification for Rossetti's well-deserved fame as a "talent scout." In 1847 he came across a manuscript book of Blake's in the British Museum reading room and bought it for ten shillings, which he characteristically borrowed from brother William. Long a "hearty admirer" of Blake's early poetry, Rossetti now found in this notebook outspoken jeers at Correggio, Titian, Reynolds, and Gainsborough that were balm to his young rebel soul, and grist to the mill of one already unconsciously preparing to help launch the Pre-Raphaelite Brotherhood's revolt. He became a lifelong champion of Blake. Besides aiding Gilchrist's widow in finishing the *Life of Blake* in 1862, Rossetti wrote a sonnet honoring Blake in 1880.

Tennyson's poetry was known to Rossetti as early as 1846. By 1849 he was calling Tennyson's *The Princess* "the finest poem since Shakespeare, superior even to Sordello."[69] Shortly before he died, Rossetti told Caine that the greatness of Tennyson and Browning had kept him from publishing his own poetry between 1853 and 1862.[70] Rossetti apparently never ceased to think Tennyson a great poet, and even (according to William Sharp) "the greatest poet of the period."[71] although he had reservations about Tennyson's later work.

To Coleridge, on the other hand, Rossetti remained unswervingly devoted, possibly because he contented himself with Coleridge's poetry ("six years from sixty saved") and completely dismissed the prose. As early as 1846 he was reading Coleridge with "endless enjoyment."[72]

Bailey and Wells are proof that Rossetti could discover molehills as well as mountains. He stumbled upon both about 1846, reading Bailey's *Festus* "over and over again," and admiring "enormously" Charles Wells's *Stories after Nature* and his poetic drama, *Joseph and his Brethren.* Perhaps because *Festus* came to win a measure of popularity, Rossetti was never quite so interested in it after his first youthful enthusiasm, though he never forgot Bailey. As late as 1880 he was urging Caine to print a Bailey sonnet. But for Wells he fought all his life, a fight that had its dubious reward in 1877 when Swinburne brought about the publication of *Joseph.*

One further poet Rossetti knew in boyhood did not follow the usual pattern of his enthusiasms. This was Thomas Chatterton, whom Rossetti read at first without being swept away, and whom he didn't rank among the great poets until much later. Then, in 1880 and 1881 he found Chatterton to be "absolutely miraculous. . .the true day-spring of modern romantic poetry."[76]

In the main, Rossetti's youthful tastes and favorite authors remained unchanged throughout his life. William Allingham confirms this in a diary entry of 1867, which also supplies the key word "imaginative": "English imaginative literature—Poems and Tales, here lies his pabulum: Shakespeare, the old Ballads, Blake, Keats, Shelley, Browning, Mrs. Browning, Tennyson, Poe being first favorites, and now Swinburne, *Wuthering Heights* is a Koh-i-noor among novels, *Sidonia the Sorceress* 'a stunner.'"[77] Every author or title mentioned by Allingham as pabulum for the forty-year-old poet was a favorite on the reading diet of the young Gabriel, except *Wuthering Heights,* and of necessity, Swinburne.

With reservations to be noted, Sir Walter Scott remained high in his esteem. Parts of *The Fair Maid of Perth,* he wrote in 1871, "can only be compared to the greatest imaginative works existing."[78] Chatterton, Coleridge, and Keats, along with Blake and Shelley, were the five English poets he chose to honor in a series of five sonnets he wrote in 1880-1881. In the last years of his life he had Hall Caine "repeatedly" read Poe's *Ulalume* and *The Raven* to him. On his deathbed Rossetti half-crooned snatches from one of Iago's songs in *Othello.*

Rossetti never lost his habit of excessive praise, either. The boy who could read *Festus* over and over, admire Wells "enormously," find Warren's *Ten Thousand Years* "the most splendid ever read,"[79] call Tennyson's *The Princess* "the finest poem since Shakespeare," became the man who called Keats "the one true heir of Shakespeare."[80] But the mature Rossetti could find heirs to Shakespeare all over the place. Coleridge and Shelley were, with Shakespeare, the three "greatest English imaginations,"[81] although at times he made room for Blake as the fourth. He once even described

Charles Wells to Caine as "another true heir of Shakespeare,"
an encomium few have echoed.[82] Before laughing too much
at this critical bumble, however, one should also remember
the keen insight that led to Rossetti's early discovery of Keats,
Poe, Blake, and Browning, as well as his role in establishing
the reputations of Morris, Swinburne, and *The Rubaiyat*
of Fitzgerald.

A more serious handicap to his development as a poet
than his tendency to overpraise those who were "imaginative" may well have been Rossetti's disdain for writers who
were not. Again, this was a lifelong trait. In describing what
Gabriel read as a boy, William said: "It may be noted that
. . .I have not specified any books of the so-called solid kind—
history, biography or voyages. Science and metaphysics were
totally out of his ken."[83] William also said, "In fact, throughout his life the poetry of sentimental or reflective description
had a very minor attraction for him."[84] This held true even
for poets he generally admired, as shown by his dislike for
Shelley's "yearly universes," and his reservations about
Tennyson. Of Tennyson, he wrote to Swinburne: "I must say
that to have Sir Pelleas turned into a schoolboy deserving
and not getting the birch through pages irrigated with irri-
tation to every poetic sense that one possesses (in spite of
some good verbal passages) is rather too much. . . ."[85]

When Ford Madox Brown was painting his "Chaucer
Reading His Poems" (for which Rossetti posed as Chaucer),
Gabriel was bitter in his tirade against Brown's choice of
poets for the side designs, insisting that "Shelley and Keats
should have been whole-length figures instead of Pope and
Burns."[86] Burns, we noted, was finally seen as an "excep-
tional genius," but for Pope and most of the Eighteenth-
Century writers, "the usual array of nobodies—Addison,
Akenside, and the whole alphabet down to Zany and Zero,"
he had little regard.[87] Characteristically, he called
Christopher Smart's *Song to David* "the only great *accom-*

plished poem of the last century. . .a masterpiece of rich imagery, exhaustive resources, and reverberant sound."[88] (Rossetti does hasten to add that "of course" this doesn't reckon with the works of Coleridge, Burns, and that fourth of the three greatest English imaginations, Blake.)

But aside from Milton,[89] Rossetti's biggest blind spot was Wordsworth. Only he, apparently, of all the Romantic poets escaped the young Gabriel's praise, and the adult Rossetti admitted "I grudge Wordsworth every vote he gets."[90] Caine tells the story of Rossetti's seeing two camels shambling along at the zoo, as if conversing together, and remarking: "There's Wordsworth and Ruskin virtuously taking a walk."[91] Various reasons for this antipathy will be explored later; for now, they can be summed up in Rossetti's damning indictment that Wordsworth lacked "vital lyric impulse." The kind of imagination that Rossetti thought *was* poetry, Wordsworth did not have. Rossetti grew up not only isolated in art, but also in only a part of art. It was to show in his own work.

HIS FIRST WRITING AND PAINTING

"Absurd trash" though it may be, the twelve-year-old Gabriel's *Sir Hugh the Heron* gives fascinating hints of the poet to come. There are the interest in the ballad form, the medieval-chivalric-supernatural subject matter, the experimenting with metre and rhyme (some stanzas have as many as nine consecutive lines of the same rhyme.) There is, too, the use of archaic words like *thane, dight, presage, targe* and *wold.*

Much of this, of course, is Scott, as Rossetti himself said: "when I wrote it, the *only* [*sic!*] English poet I had read was Sir W. Scott, as is plain enough in it."[92] In an absurd, childish way, however, there is much of the Rossetti-to-be. Take the key words of the line:

Lady, I love thee to excess; oh yield to my desire!

"Lady"—how she was to dominate the bulk of Rossetti's poetry. "Love" and "desire"—how they were to become one of his basic conflicts, for the man was to discover they were not identical, try as he might to make them so. And, always, "excess."

Another lesser but nonetheless important characteristic *Sir Hugh* foreshadowed was Rossetti's awareness of the reader, and the need to be completely understood. To this end he wrote three footnotes of explanation, such as: "I have caused the minstrel to commit the mistake of representing Sir Hugh as falling in this battle, in order to apprise the reader that his tale is a fabrication; our hero being in France at the time."[93]

Back of *Sir Hugh* lay seven long years of "apprenticeship": at the age of five Gabriel tried to write a blank verse drama entitled *The Slave,* whose Shakespearian "source" was matched by his painting of Shakespearian characters. From the first, writing and painting were coequal and often interdependent, with similar subject matter. Most often he sketched from imagination or from his reading rather than from direct observation, showing as a child that "invention" which the mature artist was to call his greatest gift. At eight Rossetti was coloring designs for Lewis' *Castle Spectre;* at twelve he sketched four knights and illustrations for *Rienzi* and *The Arabian Knights.*

These early drawings showed no more talent than his writing of the same period, where *The Slave* was followed almost immediately by *Aladdin,* a prose drama illustrated by the author. Only a few lines of the drama were written, but Gabriel carefully listed the actors he wanted: "Mrs. Siddons, Mr. Kemble, Mr. Kean"—all three being not only famous, but also dead. Just before *Sir Hugh* came a chivalric tale, *Roderick and Rosalba, a Story of the Round Table,* again illustrated by himself.

After *Sir Hugh,* the boy's writing continued to be as "imaginative" as what he was reading at the time. At fifteen he wrote a shorter ballad, *William and Marie,* "in a style compounded of Walter Scott and the old Scottish ballads."[94] He submitted it, with his own illustrations, to a magazine. It was rejected. Also in 1843 he began *Sorrentino,* a prose tale whose Mephistophelean Devil provided ample outlet for the author's love of the supernatural. It was later destroyed, but William thought it "spirited, effective, and well-told."[95]

Sorrentino is significant as early evidence of a sensitivity to charges of indecency that should help one to understand Rossetti's collapse during the "Fleshly School of Poetry" controversy. Apparently the first version of *Sorrentino* was somewhat improper, for Maria thought it "horrible" and refused to hear it. After some changes, Gabriel wrote his mother: "The charge of indecency can no longer be laid upon the former portion with any show of reason, since I have purged and purified it most effectually, and burnt up the chaff with unquenchable fire."[96]

The mother's influence, seen here between the lines, made Rossetti ever-sensitive about possible indecency. Moreover, he was innately clean-minded himself. At Mr. Paul's school, Gabriel had reported a fellow student for speaking lewdly. When he was fifteen and thinking of buying the works of Shelley, he was quick to assure an aunt that they were poems "which I should peruse solely on account of the splendid versification, and not for any love of his atheistical sentiments."[97] In 1845 he castigates Lagnon and Touchard's *Les Jolies Filles* as "the highest pitch of disgusting obscenity."[98] When he visited France in 1849, the "can-can" disgusted him. In referring years later to this youthful innocence, Rossetti told Caine that his poem about the prostitute *Jenny* pictured "a world I was then happy enough to be a stranger to."[99] William Rossetti suggests that Gabriel himself was the young schoolboy in this poem to whom an older lad explains Jenny's ancient profession.

Such was the "Victorian," at times almost prudish, sense of morality of the young poet and painter who in 1848, with Hunt and Millais, established the Pre-Raphaelite Brotherhood. Their aim was to promote "truth and justice"; their private lives were equally dedicated. Among themselves the Brothers joked with rough good humor, but profanity was forbidden and even smoking discouraged. Hunt, a model of propriety all his life, paid tribute to the moral purity of Rossetti in the PRB period from 1848 to 1854: "In those days he worthily rejoiced in the poetic atmosphere of sacred and spiritual dreams that then dwelt within him in embryo."[100]

Such was the man who, Evelyn Waugh claimed, had "never been able to simulate a patience he did not feel for the moral prejudices of his adopted country."[101] Would for the man and the poet that he had only to simulate! But the "moral prejudices" were as truly a part of the poet in the making as the fierce sensual passions he was to keep under leash until, at the age of twenty-eight, he met the voluptuous if uncouth Fanny Cornforth. First his model, then speedily his mistress, Fanny was unlettered and unashamedly greedy and grasping, but she embodied the sensual delights that the young Rossetti could only imagine when he wrote in his first version of *Jenny* in 1848:

> When the desire is overmuch,
> And the hands meddle as the lips touch,—
> When the boddice, being loosened therewith,
> Tells the beautiful secret underneath.[102]

How different is the description in the 1870 version:

> For all your wealth of loosened hair,
> Your silk ungirdled and unlac'd

And warm sweets open to the waist,
All golden in the lamplight's gleam.

It was Fanny who, in the words of P. F. Baum, "introduced him to the sins of the flesh."[103] The sonnets of *The House of Life* are eloquent testimony to the raging conflict between the demands of body and soul that ensued.

By 1848, the preparation of the poet—if not the man—was well-nigh complete. Between 1844 and 1846 he had sharpened his talents with translations of Burger's *Lenore*, part of the *Nibelungenlied*, Hartman von Aue's Twelfth-Century *Arme Heinrich*, and the early Italian poets. Two years later he was capable of writing *The Blessed Damozel*, *Ave*, *Jenny*, and *My Sister's Sleep*. At twenty, Rossetti was ready to spearhead the Pre-Raphaelite Brotherhood.

NOTES

[1]Gabriel Rossetti, Jr., *Sir Hugh the Heron, A Legendary Tale* (London, 1843, G. Polidori's Private Press), IV, 23.

[2]*L & M*, I, 85.

[3]T. Hall Caine, *Recollections of Dante Gabriel Rossetti* (Boston, 1898), p. 187.

[4]*L & M*, I, 21.

[5]*Ibid.*, pp. 65-6.

[6]*Soul's Beauty*.

[7]Caine, p. 201.

[8]W. Sharp, *Dante Gabriel Rossetti: A Record and a Study* (London, 1882), p. 37.

[9]Caine, p. 155.

[10]W. M. Rossetti, *Rossetti as Designer and Writer* (London, 1889), p. 135.

[11]*L & M*, II, 180.

[12]G. Hake and A. Compton-Rickett, eds., *The Letters of Algernon Charles Swinburne* (London, 1918), I, 156-57.

[13]W. M. Rossetti, *Rossetti as Designer and Writer*, p. 135.

[14]*L & M*, I, 408.

[15]*Ashley Catalogue*, IV, 115.

[16]P. F. Baum, *The Blessed Damozel* (Chapel Hill, 1938), p. 1v.

[17]F. M. Hueffer, *Rossetti* (London, 1916), p. 85. (Italics are mine)

[18]*L & M,* I, 58.

[19]*Collected Works,* I, xxix.

[20]F. Bickley, *The Pre-Raphaelite Comedy* (London, 1932), p. 85.

[21]*Ashley Catalogue,* VII, 15.

[22]*L & M,* I, 72.

[23]*Ibid.*

[24]*Ibid.,* p. 114.

[25]*Ibid.,* p. 179.

[26]H. Allingham and D. Radford, eds., *William Allingham, A Diary* (London, 1907), p. 162.

[27]H. G. Gilchrist, *Anne Gilchrist, Her Life and Writings* (London, 1887), p. 111.

[28]*Ibid.,* pp. 121-2.

[29]K. L. Knickerbocker, "Rossetti's *The Blessed Damozel,"* *Studies in Philology,* XXXIX (July, 1932), 485-504.

[30]*L & M,* I, 381.

[31]*Ibid.,* p. 380.

[32]*Ibid.,* p. 381.

[33]Caine, pp. 39-40.

[34]*D & W,* III, 989-90. For a detailed discussion of Rossetti's struggle with the last stanza of *The Cloud Confines,* see *inf.* pp. 90-95.

[35]Caine, pp. 140-41.

[36]*L & M,* I, 79.

[37]*Ibid.,* p. 80.

[38]E. Waugh, *Rossetti* (London, 1928), p. 151.

[39]R. G. Grylls, *Portrait of Rossetti* (London, 1964), p. 5.

[40]*L & M,* I, 68-72.

[41]*Ibid.,* pp. 88-9.

[42]*Ibid.,* p. 94.

[43]*D & W,* I, 35.

[44]*Ibid.,* p. 36.

[45]*L & M,* I, 57-110, and I & II, *passim.*

[46]*Ibid.,* I, 58.

[47]*Ibid.,* p. 59.

[48]*Ibid.,* p. 61.

[49]Caine, p. 194.

[50]*L & M,* I, 81.

[51]*Ibid.,* II, 8.

[52]G. B. Hill, ed., *Letters of Dante Gabriel Rossetti to William Allingham, 1854-1870* (London, 1897), p. 137.

[53]*L & M*, I, 100.

[54]Caine, p. 148.

[55]*Ibid.*, p. 170.

[56]*L & M*, I, 100.

[57]Caine, p. 284.

[58]*L & M*, I, 107.

[59]Caine, p. 170.

[60]*L & M*, I, 102.

[61]*Ibid.*

[62]*Ibid.*, p. 115.

[63]W. M. Rossetti, *Ruskin: Rossetti: Preraphaelitism* (London, 1899), p. 301.

[64]*L & M*, I, 308.

[65]W. Holman Hunt, *Pre-Raphaelitism and the Pre-Raphaelite Brotherhood* (New York, 1914), II, 271-72.

[66]*L & M*, I, 64.

[67]*Ibid.*, p. 102.

[68]*Ibid.*, p. 123.

[69]W. M. Rossetti, *Preraphaelite Diaries and Letters* (London, 1900), p. 236.

[70]Caine, p. 40.

[71]Sharp, p. 35.

[72]*L & M*, I, 100.

[73]*Ibid.*, p. 89.

[74]*Ibid.*, pp. 100-101.

[75]Caine, p. 260.

[76]*Ibid.*, pp. 184-5.

[77]Allingham, p. 163.

[78]*L & M*, I, 60.

[79]*Ibid.*, II, 15.

[80]Caine, p. 167.

[81]*Ibid.*, p. 184.

[82]*Ibid.*, p. 167.

[83]*L & M*, I, 102.

[84]*Ibid.*, p. 81.

[85]*D & W*, II, 779.

[86]Holman Hunt, I, 88.

[87]Caine, p. 195.

[88]*Ibid.*, pp. 194-5.

[89]Allingham, p. 162.

[90]Caine, p. 148.

[91]*Ibid.*, p. 148n.

[92]*L & M*, I, 85.

[93]G. Rossetti, Jr., IV, 21.

[94]*L & M,* I, 85.

[95]*Ibid.,* p. 103.

[96]*Ibid.,* II, 19.

[97]*Ibid.,* I, 100.

[98]*Ibid.,* p. 69.

[99]Caine, p. 125.

[100]Holman Hunt, I, 107-8.

[101]Waugh, p. 168.

[102]P. F. Baum, "The Bancroft Manuscripts of Dante Gabriel Rossetti," *Modern Philology,* XXXIX (August, 1941), 49.

[103]P. F. Baum, ed., *Rossetti's Letters to Fanny Cornforth* (Baltimore, 1940), p. 129.

II

Rossetti and "Pre-Raphaelitism"

Madame, I am not an 'ite' of any kind.

Rossetti in 1870[1]

The lexicon of literary criticism contains few words as bedevilled (and bedevilling) as "Pre-Raphaelite." To some it means "strong visual imagination" and "primitive and childlike simplicity." To others it is "lush," preoccupied with "method, effect, technique" and "aureate language." To critics like Grierson and Smith, Christina Rossetti is "the truest Pre-Raphaelite of them all,"[2] while to C. G. Osgood "Christina Rossetti, though by circumstances inseparable from the Pre-Raphaelites, is not to be taken for one herself."[3] It doesn't make things any clearer that to most who use the term, the chief Pre-Raphaelite poet is not Christina, but her brother Dante Gabriel.

J. R. Wahl sums up the confusion succinctly: "The qualities that the word 'Pre-Raphaelite' suggests to the common reader today bear little relation either to the personalities of the leading Pre-Raphaelites or to their finest achievements in art or poetry."[4] But Wahl is not the first to decry the word.

In 1882, the very year of the poet's death, Rossetti's friend William Sharp was saying: "In whatever sense this word may be used [for poetry], whether as signifying archaism or naturalism, it would be a good thing if it now dropped for good from the critical category."[5] In that same year Hall Caine was stressing the difference between Rossetti the "Pre-Raphaelite" painter and Rossetti the poet: "In his pictures Rossetti was first of all a dissenter from all prescribed canons of taste, whilst in his poems he was in harmony with the catholic spirit which was as old as Shakespeare himself, and found revival, after temporary eclipse, in Coleridge, Shelley, Keats, and Tennyson."[6]

Confusion was compounded because "Pre-Raphaelite" was applied not only to two different arts, but also to two different "movements," which in turn were linked with a third. These three movements were: the Pre-Raphaelite Brotherhood, from 1848 to 1854; the so-called "Pre-Raphaelite Movement," from about 1856 to about 1872; and the "Aesthetic" or "Art for Art's sake" movement that budded thereafter and dropped its rotten fruit with the "Decadents" of the Yellow Nineties. Rossetti was the link between the first and second movements; Swinburne, as much as anyone, between the second and the third. A quick look at all three may pave the way to understanding to what extent Rossetti was a "Pre-Raphaelite" in any sense of the word.

The Pre-Raphaelite Brotherhood (or "PRB" as they often called themselves) was formed by seven young men: William Holman Hunt, John Everett Millais, Dante Gabriel Rossetti, James Collinson, Frederick G. Stephens—all struggling painters; Thomas Woolner, a beginning sculptor; and William Michael Rossetti, a clerk of artistic interests who, his brother thought, would become a great proficient in art if he ever tried.

Fellow students at the Royal Academy's art school, Hunt,

Rossetti and Millais met one fall night in 1848 to indulge in a favorite sport—jeering Sir Joshua Reynolds (dubbed "Sir Sloshua") and the "Raphaelite" manner they blamed him for imposing on English art. They thrilled to the freshness and sincerity of a book of crudely reproduced engravings of the Fourteeth-Century Lasinio frescoes at Pisa. If to produce such qualities they had to seek models that predated Raphael, the young rebels would indeed be "Pre-Raphaelite." It was Gabriel who insisted on a "Brotherhood," which the other four were invited to join, William to be secretary in lieu of any actual artistic achievement. Hunt was then twenty-one, Gabriel twenty, his brother and Millais nineteen.

The Brotherhood never did get around to a formal statement of principles, but agreed that contemporary art needed to be rescued from the domination of the Royal Academy and the slough of conventionality and ugliness. They would seek "serious and elevated invention of subject," and bring to their art an "earnest scrutiny of visible facts, and an earnest endeavour to present them veraciously and exactly."[7] This they called "truth to Nature," and promised to "seek inspiration from Nature herself," striving for "frank expression and unaffected grace."[8] Their primary purpose, "left unsaid by reason of its fundamental necessity," Hunt wrote years later, "was to make Art a handmaid in the cause of justice and truth."[9]

In 1849 Hunt, Millais and Rossetti expectantly exhibited their first paintings with the defiant letters "PRB"; the letters aroused no comment at all. Next year, however, Rossetti let slip the meaning of "PRB," and the storm broke. Sensing a concerted attack on the authority of English art, critics fell upon the Brotherhood violently. To the rescue in 1851 came John Ruskin, mightiest art critic of the day, in two powerful letters to the London *Times*. (Ruskin shows that from the start, the real aims of the "PRB" were misunderstood. He had to minimize their realistic detail or "truth to Nature" to identify them with Turner, the hero of his *Modern Painters.* He chose Gabriel as his particular protégé, though Rossetti was, in truth, the least faithful to Pre-Raphaelite tenets.)

Ruskin gave Rossetti a measure of financial security by agreeing to buy the bulk of his paintings, and the two were friends for ten years. But he overwhelmed Rossetti with advice that ranged all the way from urging him to keep his rooms tidy to telling him in annoyingly petty detail how to wrap and mail a picture. This dictatorial criticism, coupled with Rossetti's stubborn, even aggressive, independence, finally ended the friendship.

By the time Rossetti and Ruskin parted in 1865, the Brotherhood itself had long since dissolved, leaving behind as a literary heritage the pathetic little magazine, *The Germ,* which Rossetti had insisted they publish in 1850 to disseminate their ideas by precept and example. *The Germ* died after four issues, with an alarming deficit of £ 50. It did publish some good poems by Dante Gabriel and Christina, some reviews by William (which won him a position as art critic of *The Spectator*), and several poems by Coventry Patmore, who had first interested Ruskin in defending the PRB.

Once Ruskin had sufficiently refuted their enemies, and reassured buyers had begun to grant them a living, the Brotherhood fell to pieces. Woolner left in 1852 to go to the gold "diggings" in Australia. Collinson chose the Church of Rome, giving up both the PRB and Christina's hand in marriage. In 1853 Hunt and Millais went their separate ways— Hunt all the way to the Holy Land to paint in "the cause of justice and truth," and Millais just across the street to the Royal Academy and a career that brought him its presidency and a knighthood. Rossetti gave Hunt a picture with a fond inscription as a going-away gift, and fashioned for Millais an epitaph: "So now the whole round table is dissolved."[10]

Rossetti himself, as Millais put it, "wandered off on his

own exclusive line."[11] Worse, he wandered off with the name "Pre-Raphaelite," which Hunt had come to feel was his own. Beginning in 1856, at Oxford, a group of bright young poets and painters flocked to Rossetti, worshipping him before the throne they themselves created, and revelling in the name critics appropriated from the original PRB and now bestowed upon them: "Pre-Raphaelite." Thus began what, for want of a better name, we may call the "Pre-Raphaelite *Movement.*"

Fundamentally, it was those unique qualities of temperament and talent that Rossetti displayed before he ever met Hunt and Millais, rather than any qualities he may have owed to the Brotherhood, that drew these young people to him. First of these new disciples were William Morris and Edward Burne-Jones. Undergraduates at Oxford, they were wildly enthusiastic about the work of Rossetti, whom they took to be the leading exemplar of the PRB creed. In imitation of *The Germ,* they established *The Oxford and Cambridge Magazine,* which was published monthly throughout 1856. (One of the many ways in which they differed from the PRB was that Morris, at least, had money.)

Rossetti saw the magazine, and with delight wrote his friend Allingham, "Surely this cometh in some wise of *The Germ,* with which it might bind up."[12] The group's aim, too, had a familiar ring: "the sole and only wish to teach others principles and truths which they may not know and which have made us happy."[13] As Rossetti knew well from his own experience with the Brotherhood, however, there could be a wide discrepancy between avowed aim and actual achievement. He correctly located them at once "in — Dreamland."

When, in 1856, Burne-Jones sought out Rossetti at the Working Men's College in London (where Rossetti was teaching a class at Ruskin's request), he found an artist who knew something about him already and was eager to know more. Rossetti was especially interested in hearing about Morris' poetry. Soon the three were seeing each other weekly—the twenty-three-year-old Burne-Jones and twenty-two-year-old Morris dazzled by twenty-eight-year-old Rossetti's talk, stirred by his painting and poetry, and carried away by his characteristically generous praise of their talents. Burne-Jones ("Ned") must make painting his career, and Morris ("Top") must paint, too, much as Rossetti admired his poetry. Rossetti's influence over them and their friends was almost hypnotic. Burne-Jones wrote, "I never wanted to think but as he thought,"[14] and Morris boasted he had "got beyond" the stage of original creation to the superior one of only imitating Rossetti.[15] To their magazine Rossetti contributed *The Burden of Nineveh, The Staff and Scrip,* and a new version of *The Bessed Damozel.*

No doubt Rossetti's vivid, generous, exciting personality was the great thing that bound the younger men to him. But they shared a devotion to Beauty and a love of medieval subject, particularly the Arthurian legends. They also adopted in part "truth to Nature," seeking in their poems and paintings to create tellingly realistic little pictures. Their one joint artistic effort was the painting of murals on the walls of the Union debating room at Oxford in 1857. Morris (who had never painted before) and Burne-Jones acquitted themselves fairly well. But, with typical impatience, Rossetti failed to learn how to prepare the walls for murals. The paintings soon faded. The project was never finished.

From this venture did come public recognition of the group as "Pre-Raphaelites," with Rossetti now undisputed leader, and a new disciple—Algernon Charles Swinburne. Rossetti first seized upon Swinburne as a model because of his mop of flowing hair. Soon the slight, delicate, but fiery newcomer was reading his poems to the group ("grinds," Rossetti casually called them) and receiving the usual lavish praise and counsel. From 1857 to 1872, he and Rossetti were warmest friends, each consulting the other frequently on his poetry, giving and getting critical advice of the highest order.

Rossetti described Burne-Jones's painting as of "the greatest genius,"[16] called Morris "the greatest literary identity of our times,"[17] and said that Swinburne was "certainly destined to be one of the two or three leaders who are to succeed Tennyson and the Brownings."[18] But by 1872 this group, too, had wandered off on their own exclusive lines, demonstrating by their differences the futility of trying to describe them by the single word "Pre-Raphaelite." Rossetti's effect on Burne-Jones was the longest lasting, though the medieval "dream world" often called the province of both belonged more completely to Burne-Jones, who lacked the robustness and intensity that kept much of Rossetti's painting and almost all of his poetry from being "dreamy," however medieval it might be.

Morris progressed rapidly beyond the limits of Rossetti's influence, reacting to the charm of Chaucer, the sweep of the Icelandic Sagas, and finally the demands of contemporary problems and forces to which Rossetti remained largely impervious. Ultimately, Morris was spiritual heir of Carlyle and Ruskin, not of Rossetti. For instance, both Rossetti and Burne-Jones levelled criticism at "Art for Art's sake," for which they were in part responsible. But neither approached the denunciation of Morris: "Its foredoomed end must be, that art at last will seem too delicate a thing even for the hands of the initiated to touch; and the initiated must at last sit still and do nothing — to the grief of no one."[19]

Swinburne, too, felt influences stronger than Rossetti's — influences that made Swinburne — not, as charged, Rossetti — the major link between this second wave of "Pre-Raphaelites" and the Art for Art's sake movement that succeeded them. It was chiefly Swinburne who merged the English struggle of the artist against the Philistines with the French defiance of bourgeois morality pioneered by Gautier and Baudelaire. In Swinburne's *Poems and Ballads* of 1866 (which Rossetti tried to tone down) are the major characteristics of the French esthetes: the overemphasis on form and execution, the deliberately audacious subject matter, the sensuality (as in *Laus Veneris* and *Faustine*) and mingled sensations and satiety (as in *Dolores*). Although in many ways Swinburne later abandoned the principles and practices of the French Aesthetic Movement, his "Englishing" of Gautier and Baudelaire had introduced the full flower of Art for Art's sake, which completely contradicted the Pre-Raphaelite Brotherhood belief that Art should be "a handmaid in the cause of justice and truth."

Thereafter came Swinburne's (and Rossetti's) friend Whistler, and Whistler's friend Wilde, and so on to Symons, Johnson, Dowson, Beardsley and the rest of the "Decadents." The chasm separating them from the earlier "Pre-Raphaelites" is dramatically evidenced by the fact that Wilde was repudiated by the only two masters he acknowledged in poetry, Rossetti and Morris. Rossetti gave his customary generous praise to Wilde's first poems, in 1881. But within a year Rossetti "bitterly resented the way in which Oscar's name was linked with him and his circle, and on one occasion rated his friend Burne-Jones for 'taking up with the man who was posing as the leader of the new aesthetic movement.'"[20] Rossetti's own critical opinions and poetic practices made inevitable his qualified attitude to Art for Art's sake, as recorded by Sharp: "I once asked him how he would reply to the asserveration that he was the head of the 'Art for Art's sake' school, and his response was to the effect that the principle of the phrase was two-thirds absolutely right and one third so essentially wrong that it negatived the whole as an aphorism. In the right sense of the phrase no artist ever did more truly follow out the principle of art for art's sake, but neither as artist nor poet did he forget those limitations as to reticence of inclination or experiment which true Art has ordained in authentic if unformulated command."[21]

ROSSETTI AS "PRE-RAPHAELITE"

As contradictory as the definitions of "Pre-Raphaelite" are the estimates of Rossetti's role in the Pre-Raphaelite Brotherhood. Hunt insisted that Rossetti was no true Pre-Raphaelite, for he "never strictly adhered to the original character" of the Brotherhood.[22] Similarly, Millais complained that what the public took to be Pre-Raphaelite in Rossetti was absolutely alien to the spirit of the PRB.[23] Woolner quarreled with Rossetti over his "preposterous claim" to being the originator of the group.[24] Stephens said that from the beginning Rossetti was in the main independent of Hunt and Millais.[25]

On the other hand, Ruskin, while granting that the creed belonged "to all three of you in right of possession," assured Rossetti that he, rather than Hunt or Millais, was "actually. . . the first who did it,"[26] and once, incredibly enough, called Hunt "Rossetti's disciple."[27] Ford Madox Brown, closely associated with the PRB, said: "Of course it was Rossetti who kept things going with his talking, or it wouldn't have lasted as long as it did."[28] Ford Madox Hueffer, Brown's grandson (later well-known as the novelist, Ford Madox Ford), said Rossetti's "dramatic faculties were so great he could act; speak brilliantly; and even to some extent paint, like a Pre-Raphaelite."[29] Sharp, with no such reservations, proclaimed that Rossetti was truer to the Brotherhood principles than Millais[30] and some later critics, like F. M. Tisdel, have declared that no better statement of these principles exists than in Rossetti's three *Old and New Art* sonnets.[31]

Between these extremes lies the opinion of William Michael Rossetti, the opinion best supported by the record: Dante Gabriel changed as his dual career in art progressed, "but it is not the less true that in 1848 and for some years afterwards he meant a great deal by calling himself Pre-Raphaelite, and meant it very heartily."[32] When, in 1851, William wrote an article about the PRB, Rossetti refused to be given a major role, insisting that Millais be put first, and that Hunt's contributions be detailed. And, he added, don't "defend my medievalisms, which were absurd."[33] The next year he still felt dedicated to the Brotherhood, writing wryly to Brown: "We are but too transcendent spirits—far, far in advance of the age."[34] As late as 1855 Hunt was writing to Rossetti about the latter's painting, "Found": "I could wish we were all employed about such subjects if there be any power in a simple representation by art of such terrible incidents wherein the guilty see the angels sorrowing for them to lead the unstained to guard their innocence. . . . I believe you have designed subjects bearing on every art, science, feeling and virtue that exist in our world."[35] Obviously at this time Hunt felt that Rossetti was carrying out the Pre-Raphaelite aim of "truth and justice." Maybe so, but Rossetti never did finish "Found."

It was just two years later that Woolner objected to Rossetti's claiming to be the originator of the PRB—the very year that Rossetti was being lionized as such by Morris and Burne-Jones. If Rossetti then succumbed to the temptation to pose as chief Pre-Raphaelite, the role was not prolonged. In 1868 he wrote Ernest Chesneau, French writer and art critic, to deny that he was "'chef de l'école' [Préraphaélite] par priorité ou par mérite." The letter goes on to make three other significant points: that "un peintre si absolument original" as Holman Hunt could not possibly be thought of as Rossetti's disciple; that "les qualités de réalisme, émotionnel mais extrêmement minutieux. . .donnent le cachet au style nommé préraphaélite"; and that it was "la camaraderie, plutôt que la collaboration réelle du style, qui a uni mon nom aux leurs dans les jours d'enthousiasme d'il y a vingt ans."[36]

From the time of this letter to the day of his death, Rossetti seems to have tried sincerely and vigorously to rid himself of the Pre-Raphaelite tag. In 1871, when a woman asked if he were a Pre-Raphaelite, he replied sharply: "Madame, I am not an 'ite' of any kind: I am only a painter."[37] Again in 1873 he declined the name, in a letter to Francis Hueffer. Hueffer, husband of Brown's daughter Cathy, sent Rossetti proofs of the memoir he had written to accompany the Tauchnitz edition of Rossetti's 1870 *Poems.* In reply Rossetti wrote: "Really I am not the result of any movement whatever. Many of the most marked things were written before a movement existed." To Hueffer's calling him "the leader" of the movement, Rossetti's response was: "'*The* leader.' Please don't! I have ventured to strike this out bodily. If the thing can be organized by the elements supposed to characterize it as a movement, Holman Hunt is their representative. *I* for one never had anything of the sort."[38]

By 1881, Rossetti thought the whole discussion of this new English school "nonsense." When Caine asked if such a name might not at least be given to the three or four painters who began their careers with Rossetti, he replied: "Not at all, unless it is to Brown, and he's more French than English; Hunt and Jones have no more claim to the name than I have. As for all the prattle about pre-Raphaelitism, I confess to you that I am weary of it, and long have been. Why should we go on talking about the visionary vanities of half-a-dozen boys? We've all grown out of them, I hope, by now." He admitted that "what you call the movement" was serious enough in the beginning, "but the banding together under that title was all a joke. We had at that time a phenomenal antipathy toward the Academy, and in sheer love of being outlawed signed our pictures with the well-known initials."[39]

Note that here Rossetti was denying the very existence of such a thing as "Pre-Raphaelite" painting. The case for "Pre-Raphaelite" poetry is even more slender. Rossetti does not seem to have considered his poetry, or anyone else's, "Pre-Raphaelite." "I should particularly hope," he wrote about 1870, "it might be thought (if so it be) that my poems are in no way the result of a painter's tendencies — and indeed no poetry could be freer than mine from the trick of what is called 'word-painting.' "[40] Yet if there is any such thing as Pre-Raphaelite poetry, its *cachet* should be, as Rossetti suggested of the paintings, "les qualités de réalisme, émotionnel mais extrêmement minutieux." This is the "truth to Nature" the original Pre-Raphaelites sought, the "most literal transcript of fact compatible with the ends of poetry" for which *The Germ* praised Browning.[41] Possibly the best description of such realism is that of Millais's painting, "The Woodsman's Daughter," done in 1850: "Every blade of grass, every leaf and branch, and every shadow they cast in the sunny wood is presented with unflinching realism and infinite delicacy of detail."[42]

Now in Rossetti's poetry it is not hard to find "realism" — before, during and after his "Pre-Raphaelite" period. But his basic and significant use of Nature was not to paint realistic word-pictures, but to serve as symbol. In this sense, his "truth to Nature" and his poetry are not "Pre-Raphaelite"; they are peculiarly his own.

ROSSETTI AND "TRUTH TO NATURE"

> Though as to Nature, Jack,
> (Poor dear old hack!)
> Touching sky, sun, stone, stick, and stack,
> I guess I'm half a quack.[43]

Rossetti wrote this jingle in 1850 during a trip through Belgium and France with Holman Hunt, at a time when his devotion to the Pre-Raphaelite Brotherhood was at its height. Light-hearted as the lines are, they reveal three things: first, that Rossetti could joke about a basic tenet of the Brotherhood; second, that the "Nature" he was poking fun at was sky, sun, stone, stick and stack — the specific objects

of Nature; and third, that he regarded himself in his adherence to "truth to Nature" of this kind as half a quack, but
only *half*.

One could hardly expect the kind of youth Rossetti was
when he joined the PRB to submit wholeheartedly to Hunt's
credo. First, he was too independent, too impatient of authority to submit completely to anyone else's ideas. Second, he
had had little personal experience with Nature. Third, as
William asserted, Gabriel's attitude toward Nature was more
Italian than English: "Italians. . .are not, as a rule, so minute
in observation of scenery, so full of 'gush' over hills and trees,
so Wordsworthian in co-ordinating phenomena and emotion,
as some English have become. . . . To the beauties of Nature
he was not insensitive, but was incurious, and he valued them
more as being so much fuel to the fire of the soul than as
objects of separate regard and analysis. . . . That he cared very
little for descriptive *poetry* is perfectly true—and just on that
account; that it exhibits and extols objects instead of turning
them into the 'medium of exchange' between the material
world and the soul."[44]

Rossetti's attitude toward Nature has been much misunderstood. It may be useful, therefore, to create a "diary,"
as it were, of what he wrote, said and did about Nature.
The very number of entries in the diary will testify to how
much and how often Nature engaged him. The variety will
indicate how much more than mere realistic detail he sought
in Nature. The basic consistency of these entries over the
years will suggest how germane to a study of his poetry such
a record is.

This diary may well begin in 1845, when the seventeen-
year-old Gabriel wrote to William from Boulogne: "I have
bagged a few sketches of Peppino's, with which I am sure
you will be greatly pleased. Certainly, as long as he keeps
to Nature, his powers are perfectly gigantic."[45] Here is evidence of an awareness of the importance of following Nature

before the PRB, as are *The Blessed Damozel* and *My Sister's Sleep* of 1847, two poems most ofter cited as proof of his "Pre-Raphaelite" truth to Nature. So is the early portrait of his grandfather, described by William as "so strongly and exactly realistic as to prove to demonstration that Rossetti, a short while before the Pre-Raphaelite scheme began, required no further prompting from outside as to the artistic virtues inherent in a scrupulous fidelity to Nature."[46]

Examples of "strongly and exactly realistic" detail — like the precise number of stars and lilies in *The Blessed Damozel* and the clicking of the needles in *My Sister's Sleep* — can be culled at random from poems written at almost any time during Rossetti's career. *The Burden of Nineveh* of 1854 included such touches as:

> A human face the creature wore,
> And hoofs behind and hoofs before,
> And flanks with dark runes fretted o'er.
>
> The print of its first rush-wrapping,
> Wound ere it dried, still ribbed the thing.

Rose Mary, written in 1871, has:

> She opened the packet heedfully;
> The blood was stiff, and it scarce might be.
> She found but a folded paper there,
> And round it, twined with tenderest care,
> A long bright tress of golden hair.

The sonnet *Gracious Moonlight,* also written in 1871, has these lines of exquisite detail:

> There where the iris rears its gold-crowned sheaf,
> With flowering rush and sceptered arrow-leaf.

A few lines from *The King's Tragedy,* 1880-1881, show that the poet's mastery of detail endured to the end of his career:

> And the rain had ceased, and the moonbeams lit
> The window high in the wall, —
> Bright beams that on the plank that I knew
> Through the painted pane did fall
> And gleamed with the splendor of Scotland's crown
> And shield armorial.

> But then a great wind swept up the skies,
> And the climbing moon fell back;
> And the royal blazon fled the floor
> And naught remained on its track;
> And high in the darkened window-pane
> The shield and the crown were black.

This is not to say that the PRB influenced Rossetti's attitude toward Nature not at all. In 1848 he was using "truth to Nature" as a handy catch-all phrase (much as he used words like "stunner" and "sloshy") and writing Hunt that he had cast off "a certain want of repose and straining after original modes of expression" in *My Sister's Sleep*, "which. . . seems to me simpler and more like nature than those I have shown you."[47]

The next year Rossetti and Hunt took their holiday on the Continent, during which Rossetti kept a record in verse of places visited and things seen. Here the PRB principle was given full play, and Rossetti demonstrated once and for all his ability to see and record minutely things as they were — when he cared to. Between London and Folkestone, for instance, he saw:

> A constant keeping-past of shaken trees.
> And a bewildered glitter of loose road;

Banks of white growth, with single blades atop
Against white sky; and wires—a constant chain—
That seemed to draw the clouds along with them.[48]

The passage from Boulogne to Amiens and Paris revealed:

. . . . .Sometimes
The ground has a deep greenness; sometimes brown
In stubble; and sometimes no ground at all,
For the close strength of crops that stand unreaped.[49]

Yet even with Hunt at his side, Rossetti succumbed only
partly to Pre-Raphaelite love of detail. Before the trip was
over, the role of rhyming reporter had palled, and he was
writing:

Trees will be trees, grass grass, pools merely pools
Unto the end of time and Belgium—points
Of fact which poets (very abject fools)
Get scent of—once their epithets grow tame
And scarce.[50]

The best poem he wrote on this trip, originally entitled
Upon the Cliffs: Noon, is characteristic of Rossetti, not Pre-
Raphaelitism, in its use of Nature:

The sea is in its restless chime,
Like Time's lapse rendered audible;
The murmur of the earth's large shell.
In a blue sadness beyond rhyme
It ends; Sense, without thought, can pass
No stadium further. Since Time was,
This sound hath told the lapse of Time.

No stagnance that Death wins,—it hath
The mournfulness of ancient Life,
Always enduring at dull strife,

Like the world's heart, in calm and wrath,
Its painful pulse is in the sands.
Last utterly, the whole sky stands,
Grey and not known, along its path.[51]

There is a picture here—a blue, restlessly moving sea, stretching beyond vision beneath a leaden sky. But the picture is important only as it gives concretion to the symbol the sea has become. The poet was well aware of this, for Rossetti once defined poetry as "the apparent image of unapparent realities."[52] This is indeed the important function of symbol in poetry, and in thus defining poetry, Rossetti was in effect asserting the central position of symbol in his own verse.

A brief analysis of *Upon the Cliffs: Noon* will illustrate this. Even in the early flush of enthusiasm for the PRB, earnest scrutiny and veracious reproduction of visible facts are here subordinated to a greater end—the presentation of an "unapparent reality" (Life) by means of an "apparent reality" (the sea).

In this poem, Rossetti is faithful to visible facts, certainly. A picture of the sea is carefully built up on the impressions of sound and sight. The poet makes us *hear* the "restless chime" of the sea, like the "murmur" in a shell, like the swaying of a clock's pendulum (this is visual as well as auditory), and like the beat of a "painful pulse" (again, visual, too, and even tactile). The poet also makes us *see* these "restless" and "always enduring" waves, with their "sad blueness" stretching beyond limit, though bordered on one side by the sand beneath the cliffs, and on the other by the "whole sky" that stands "grey and not known," and stretches—itself unfathomable—along the path of the sea.

But obviously this picture of the sea has gone beyond mere visible facts, and is charged with the emotions of the poet-observer. It is a "restless" chime and a "sad" blueness, with the "mournfulness" of ancient life, and the beat of a "painful" pulse. Even if Rossetti had stopped here, he would have been going beyond the tenet of Pre-Raphaelistic detail. Rossetti did not stop here: the picture is there primarily as symbol.

As symbol, the sea becomes the apparent image of Life itself. This symbol is built up in progressive stages. In line 2, the sea is only *like* Time's lapse, and (lines 5-6) like Time it stretches farther than "Sense, without thought, can pass." But in lines 6 and 7, the sea and Time have become identical, the former serving eternally as the witness of the latter. In the second stanza, the sea now progresses to become the symbol of all existence in Time, which is Life. As the symbol of Life, the sea has not the stagnance of Death (line 8), but the restlessness of Life (line 1), the mournfulness of Life (line 9) always enduring (like Time) at dull strife (line 10). In lines 10 and 11, the "world's heart," which is Life, is equated with the "painful pulse" of the sea, and the "dull strife" is explained as being the always-enduring war between "calm and wrath" in Life. "Last utterly" (lines 13-14) stands the grey sky, symbol now of the "unknown" that stretches beyond the limits of Life. It is this last that fully explains the sadness, the mournfulness, and the pain with which the poet endowed the sea. For the strife between "calm and wrath" that is Life, and the appalling grey unknown that lies beyond Life and beyond man's ability to comprehend, make pain and sorrow inevitable.

Rossetti explicitly announced that his was a symbolic use of Nature, with the concomitant necessity for looking through the surface of things into their heart, in his sonnet *St. Luke the Painter,* also written in 1849, where, speaking of Art, he says:

> Scarcely at once she [Art] dared to rend the mist
> Of devious symbols: but soon having wist
> How sky-breadth and field-silence and this day
> Are symbols also in some deeper way,
> She looked through these to God and was God's Priest.

Hand and Soul, the prose story written in 1850 especially for *The Germ,* suggests again how, at the peak of the Pre-Raphaelite phase, Rossetti conceived of truth to Nature as meaning inner symbolic truth rather than external realistic detail. In this story a young artist is approached by a lovely lady, who urges: "Take now thine Art unto thee, and paint me thus, as I am, to know me."[53] What is to be painted thus realistically is not actually a lady, however, but the artist's own soul, and the resultant picture is a picture-symbol of that soul. The lady's advice is for the painter to look deeply into his own heart, where the hidden truth lies. She tells the youth: "In all that thou doest, work from thine own heart, simply."[54] To this self-given advice Rossetti remained true, repeating it in 1880 in *The Song-Throe:*

. . . . .Magic mirror thou hast none
Except thy manifest heart.

Throughout 1850 Rossetti seems to have tried to treat Nature in the PRB way, painting the Virgin in bed without bedclothes because Palestine would have been too hot for bedclothes, and standing in the rain with Hunt to get background-detail painted accurately. In 1853, he began what he designed to be his greatest realistic picture, "Found." He planned to go to Frome to paint precisely the right brick wall and white heifer. Both his letters and his poetry at this time support the inference that he was completely sincere about the tenet now. He wrote Christina in criticism of one of her poems, for example, that "'dreaming of a life-long ill' (etc.) smack rather of the old shop. I wish you would try any rendering either of narrative or sentiment from real abundant Nature, which presents much variety, even in any one of its phases, than all such 'dreamings.' "[55] In this same year (1853) he wrote *The Hill Summit,* a sonnet affirming his worship of Nature, albeit in elaborate rather than simple style, "a fiery bush with coruscating hair" being as close to realism as the poem comes until the last and best two lines:

> And see the gold air and the silver fade
> And the last bird fly into the last light.

P. F. Baum has pointed out the close and exact observation that went into those last two lines.[56]

In 1854 Rossetti went on with "Found," still trying to paint in the PRB manner, but with effort. Said Brown: "He paints it all. . .hair by hair. . . . From want of habit, I see Nature bothers him, but it is sweetly drawn."[57] In contrast, no such effort is apparent in *The Landmark*, written in the same year but with Rossetti's own typical use of Nature, in which the whole poem is made a symbol of the poet's career. It was in 1854, too, that Rossetti wrote Allingham a brief but vivid description of a scene at Hastings, a description made intense through the poet's personal impressions:

> There are dense fogs of heat here now, through which sea
> and sky loom as one wall, with the webbed craft creeping
> on it like flies, or standing there as if they would drop off
> dead.[58]

Later Rossetti used this very purple patch in a poem, *Even So*, characteristically using the description to symbolize his feelings:

> All such things touch secret strings
> For heavy hearts to hear.

> But the sea stands spread
> As one wall with the flat skies,
> Where the lean black craft like flies
> Seem well-nigh stagnated,
> Soon to drop off dead.

This is only one of several available instances where Rossetti can be seen in the very process of "transfiguring" into poetry something he has seen. It is worth noting that Coventry Patmore, though he understandably disliked these lines as being "scratched with an adamantine pen upon a slab of agate," nonetheless cited them as evidence of what he called Rossetti's "extraordinary faculty for seeing objects in such a fierce light of imagination as very few poets have been able to throw upon external things."[59]

Also in 1854 Rossetti wrote, in a letter to Brown, another casual description that once more proves his observation of Nature at first hand and—much more important—gives in his own words his way of progressing from Nature as Nature to Nature as symbol:

> I lie often upon the cliffs, which are lazy themselves, all grown with grass and herbage, not athletic as at Dover, nor gaunt as at North Shields. Sometimes through the summer mists the sea and sky are one; and, if you shut your eyes, as of course you do, there is no swearing to the distant sail as a boat or a bird, while just under one's feet the near boats stand together immovable, as if their shadows clogged them and they would not come in after all, but loved to see the land. So one may lie and symbolize until one goes to sleep, and that may be a symbol too perhaps.[60]

Obviously, when moved to the point of symbolizing, Rossetti could look upon Nature as a lover. When not so moved, he could be bored. The very next year, he wrote of William's "rambling about the hills, which grow rather monotonous, but I dare say you have longer patience with them."[61] If he was Nature's lover, he was a selfish, unfaithful, independent lover, using her for his own ends, when and how he desired. In consequence, he reaped what is perhaps the inevitable reward of selfish lovers. He failed to obtain complete or lasting satisfaction, the deep content or peace of mind that Nature often gave such poets as Wordsworth.

Theodore Watts-Dunton, a close friend, suggested that "what Rossetti needed. . .was just what he never sought, that close communion with Nature which, with some temperaments, can soothe all sorrows."[62] Watts-Dunton, a solicitor who became the poet's invaluable nursemaid and guardian, can be forgiven the error of saying Rossetti "never" sought communion with Nature, for he only knew the poet in the later, dark days when Rossetti's health kept him largely within his own garden walls. But Watts-Dunton is correct in adding: "It almost seemed that to him, as to Pascal, 'Nature offered nothing but matter of doubt and disquietude.'" At least the doubt and disquietude can often be found in Rossetti's poetry, as in *Upon the Cliffs: Noon*, and in *Autumn Idleness,* where a glowing November day leads the poet to conclude:

> While I still lead my shadow o'er the grass,
> Nor know, for longing, that which I should do.

Nature serves Rossetti similarly in *Woodspurge*, which he wrote in 1856—a poem whose simplicity Wordsworth might have envied, and whose poignacy he never surpassed. Here Rossetti achieves much of his emotional impact from the exact observation, in the throes of great grief, that "the woodspurge has a cup of three." As usual, realistic detail has its primary value as symbol. The memory of the flower serves as symbol for the fact that from a former grief, the poet has remembered nothing else, has learned nothing else, but the detail of the blossom with three cups. There is an extra fillip in this (if E. L. Cary's account be true) in that Rossetti didn't even go out into Nature for this detail. He noticed it while leafing through a book that had a picture of the Woodspurge.[63]

In 1857 he wrote praising W. B. Scott's picture, "in which the surroundings are all real studies from Nature; a great thing to have done. The sky and sea are sky and sea, and the ancient boats are all real as if you got such things to sit to you."[64] A month or two later he wrote Scott about William Morris' first picture: "It is being done all from Nature, of course."[65] *Of course!* In 1857, going to Nature was not simply an "immense advantage"; for a pupil of Rossetti's, it was expected.

Our diary of Rossetti's allegiance to Nature, however, must repeatedly record the qualifications of his loyalty. A letter to William Allingham, dated May 10, 1861, shows that Rossetti always kept his major reservation about the use of Nature. In discussing Allingham's poem *Morley Park,* Rossetti said it was "best where most impassioned, as all poetry is and must be." He objected specifically to "too much dwelling here and there on minute objects in Nature," which diluted the passion.[66]

Between the years 1861 and 1868, the record of Rossetti and Nature is somewhat slender. During this period he was again trying to paint directly from Nature. But a letter to the shy, Calvinist painter Frederick Shields in 1864 shows his continued preference for realistic detail used as symbol: "I have always thought that this subject would be more properly rendered by giving to the Symbolic personation of Christ the character and costume of an actual shepherd rather than an uncertain and somewhat conventional drapery."[67]

In 1867 two items from Allingham's diary show Rossetti disinterested in Nature: "Rossetti takes no interest whatever in the sea, ships, boats, etc."[68] and "He seldom takes particular notice of anything as he goes."[69] Often for Rossetti, a little Nature went a long way—both a long way to satisfy his personal taste for it, and a long way to satisfy the needs of his poetry. *The Stream's Secret*, rich as it is from Nature, was written for the most part (in 1869) in a cave, Rossetti lying with his face to the wall. And in 1870 he wrote C. E. Norton, who had invited Rossetti to be his guest in Florence, that he envied Norton his Italian woods, Rossetti's own English woods being "pleasing, but not very sympathetic."[70]

Yet in 1868, while visiting W. B. Scott, he had described the scenery as "simply paradise. . .the most lovely spot I was ever in."[71] In 1868, too, he declared the Pre-Raphaelite period of realism definitely a thing of the past. Of Brown's painting, "Work," he wrote: "Were its subject a less purely realistic one, I should have no fear of its fate even now, but the epoch of Pre-Raphaelism [sic] was a short one, which is quite over."[72]

In 1871 Rossetti and William Morris took a joint lease of Kelmscott Manor on a backwater of the Thames, where he was equally enchanted with Nature and with Morris' wife, Janey, with whom he was deeply in love. Nonetheless he found time to write letters to his long-time mistress, Fanny Cornforth, one of which shows both his delight in Nature and his powers of observation: "The wild flowers here are wonderfully beautiful, and I think in greater variety than I ever saw before. The other day I found a poor lapwing, or peewit, a beautiful bird that I had never seen before, and which is just the sort of bird I ought to have to paint in that picture of Beatrice. The poor thing had had its beak broken, I fancy, by a fish hook, as they go a great deal by the water."[73]

In another letter to his uncle Henry Polydore he wrote: "The garden, and meadows leading to the river brink, are truly delicious—indeed, the place is perfect; and the riverside walks are most charming in their way, though I must say the flatness of the country renders it monotonous and uninspiring to me."[74] The other features must have more than compensated for the country's flatness, for five of the sonnets in *The House of Life* most dependent upon Nature for imagery were written in 1871: Numbers 12, 19, 20, 30 and 80. In addition, Nature is used powerfully in such longer poems of

1871 as *Down Stream, Cloud Confines,* and especially *Sunset Wings.*

We have Rossetti's own word for the exact observation that went into *Sunset Wings,* for he described the experience that led to the poem in several letters. One to his mother in 1871 said: "I'll send you another little poem done from Nature. I don't know if you ever noticed the habit of starlings referred to, which is constant here at sunsets this season of the year."[75] And again to his mother, two years later, he wrote: "It [*Sunset Wings*] is one I wrote when I first came here, and embodies a habit of the starlings which quite amounts to a local phenomenon, and is most beautiful and interesting daily towards sunset for months together in summer and autumn,"[76] In a third letter, this to W. B. Scott, he repeats that the poem was "done from Nature."[77]

Sunset Wings serves as another excellent example of what Rossetti meant by "done from Nature," as opposed to what Hunt would have meant. The poem begins with three stanzas of vivid description:

> To-night this sunset spreads two golden wings
> Cleaving the western sky;
> Winged too with wind it is, and winnowings
> Of birds; as if the day's last hour in rings
> Of strenuous flight must die.
>
>
> Sun-steeped in fire, the homeward pinions sway
> Above the dovecote-tops;
> And clouds of starlings, ere they rest with day
> Sink, clamorous like mill-waters, at wild play,
> By turns in every copse;
>
>
> Each tree heart-deep the wrangling rout receives, —
> Save for the whirr within,

You could not tell the starlings for the leaves;
Then one great puff of wings, and the swarm heaves
    Away with all its din.

Even if we hadn't Rossetti's word for it, there could be little
doubt that he was here describing, with rich detail, a sight
he himself had seen. The details give color, concreteness,
and vividness. But then comes the transposition into symbol:

Even thus, Hope's hours, in ever-eddying flight,
    To many a refuge tend;

In the fifth stanza, symbol and interpretation are inextricably
mixed with description:

And now the mustering rooks innumerable
    Together sail and soar,
While from the day's death, like a tolling knell,
Unto the heart they seem to cry, Farewell,
    No more, farewell, no more!

The final stanza emphasizes the comparison of the starlings
and the dying day of Hope, thus making the picture of Nature
developed in the first three stanzas a symbol of Rossetti's
sad reflections. Once again, Nature does not soothe his
"doubt and disquietude." It re-enforces them:

Is Hope not plumed, as 'twere a fiery dart?
    And oh! Thou dying day,
Even as thou goest must she too depart,
And Sorrow fold such pinions on the heart
    As will not fly away?

Sunset Wings illustrates precisely what William Rossetti
meant when he wrote that his brother valued the beauties
of nature "more as being so much fuel to the fire of the soul
than as being objects of separate regard and analysis." Writ-

ing to his mother about *Down Stream*, composed in the same year and then entitled *The River's Record,* Gabriel himself makes the technique explicit: "I doubt not you will note in the above [poem] the intention to make the first half of each verse, expressing the landscape, tally with the second expressing the emotion, even to repetition of phrases."[78]

Clearly Rossetti was very much the conscious artist in his use of Nature, carefully arranging the details available to obtain the artistic effect he desired, this effect being predominantly emotional. When on occasion his memory failed to supply a necessary detail, he might go hunting for it, picking other people's memories as he so often picked his brother's for many a piece of quaint, forgotten (or never-known) lore. One example of this was his correspondence with W. B. Scott's devoted friend, Miss Alice Boyd, shortly after his return from a visit to her Penkill Castle estate in Ayrshire. Christina Rossetti's biographer, Marya Zaturenska, has suggested that Penkill's "Romantic landscapes. . .filled Dante Gabriel's mind with dream imagery of water and woods for his poems."[79] Apparently, however, his mind wasn't filled enough, for he wrote Miss Boyd: "I meant to ask you in my note whether you could bring to mind any feature or incident particularly characteristic of the Penkill glen at nightfall. In my poem [*The Stream's Secret*] I have made the speaker toward the close suddenly perceive that night is coming on, and have to give a descriptive touch or two."[80]

This letter has been used to "prove" that Rossetti knew little and cared less about Nature. The wealth of evidence is to the contrary. There is no reason to doubt that Rossetti meant what he said when he wrote Scott in 1871: "If I were at Penkill I know, as you say, that I should do something decided in poetry—to wit, 'The Orchard Pit' poem, which I much want to do; but I find it almost impossible to write narrative poetry in scenery that does not help it, and so have little chance of setting to that here."[81] In 1881, the year before he died, he was writing about the same poem in the same way: "I have a clear scheme for it and believe your scenery might help me much if I could get there."[82]

Another thing that has led some critics to misunderstand Rossetti's relationship with Nature is their reliance on testimony dealing with events that followed Rossetti's desperate illness, in 1872, from the overuse of chloral and his attempted suicide by an overdose of laudanum. Recuperating in Scotland, still shaken in health and worrying about his ever recovering his power to paint (and so to earn a living), he went for long walks for his health's sake. Dr. Hake wrote Watts-Dunton: "Rossetti is rapidly improving in health, stumping his way over long areas of path and road. . .but holding no intercourse with Nature."[83]

Despite the misleading word "all," R. L. Mégroz, a perceptive Rossetti scholar, is basically correct when he says "the personal records of Rossetti's indifference to natural scenery all have reference to the period after his health had begun to fail, when nervous strain and insomnia were opposed by chloral and alcohol. The mind of the artist was then following its dangerously powerful tendency to turn in upon itself, avoiding fresh points of contact with the external world, and breaking the old Egyptian commandment: 'Consume not thy heart.' "[84]

Here the diary of Rossetti and Nature may well end with, appropriately, a statement about his brother by William Rossetti: that works of art "should convey their message in a suggestive way he thought fully requisite; that they should be rigorously realized by scientific rule or naturalistic presentment he did not care; and, if under a system of that sort they usurped the place of the main idea or of human emotion and expressional force, he wished them well away."[85]

In sum, the *cachet* of fidelity of natural detail is at best a minor aspect of Rossetti's poetry, and no more stamps him as "Pre-Raphaelite" than any poet with clear vision, such as Chaucer, Shakespeare, or Keats. The important thing is not that precise detail is used, but how it is used. Rossetti's way was his own, not Hunt's, not the Brotherhood's. If his way is to be used by critics to identify a certain kind of poetry, such poetry should not be described by so ambiguously confusing a label as "Pre-Raphaelite." It should be described as what it is: Rossetti poetry.

NOTES

[1]Sharp, p. 37.

[2]H. J. C. Grierson and J. C. Smith, *A Critical History of English Poetry* (New York, 1946), p. 495.

[3]C. G. Osgood, *The Voice of England* (New York, 1935), p. 539.

[4]J. R. Wahl, ed., *Dante Gabriel Rossetti: Jan Van Hunks* (New York, 1952), p. 3.

[5]Sharp, p. 72.

[6]Caine, p. 63.

[7]*L & M*, I, 127.

[8]Holman Hunt, I, 91.

[9]*Ibid.*, p. 118.

[10]*L & M*, II, 120.

[11]J. G. Millais, *The Life and Letters of Sir John Everett Millais* (London, 1899), I, 216.

[12]*D & W*, I, 293.

[13]G. Burne-Jones, *The Memorials of Edward Burne-Jones* (London, 1904), I, 124.

[14]*Ibid.*, p. 139.

[15]J. W. Mackail, *The Life of William Morris* (London, 1899), I, 111.

[16]Burne-Jones, I, 159.

[17]*L & M*, I, 199.

[18]E. Gosse, *The Life of A. C. Swinburne* (London, 1917), p. 87.

[19]W. Gaunt, *The Aesthetic Adventure* (London, 1945), p. 84.

[20]T. Hake and A. Compton-Rickett, *The Life and Letters of Theodore Watts-Dunton* (London, 1916), I, 175-6.

[21]Sharp, p. 414.

[22]Holman Hunt, II, 266-8.

[23]Millais, I, 52-5.

[24]Holman Hunt, II, 106.

[25]F. G. Stephens, *Dante Gabriel Rossetti: A Record and a Study* (London, 1894), p. 15.

[26]W. M. Rossetti, *Ruskin: Rossetti: Preraphaelitism*, p. 12.

[27]J. Ruskin, *The Art of England* (London, 1886), p. 6.

[28]F. M. Hueffer, *Ford Madox Brown* (London, 1896), p. 63.

[29]Hueffer, *Rossetti*, p. 19.

[30]Sharp, p. 69.

[31]F. M. Tisdel, "Rossetti's *House of Life*," *Modern Philology*, XV (September, 1917), 77-78.

[32]*L & M*, I, 136.

[33]*Ibid.*, II, 94.

[34]*D & W*, I, 117.

[35]J. C. Troxell, *Three Rossettis* (Cambridge, 1937), pp. 39-40.

[36]*D & W*, II, 672.

[37]Sharp, p. 71.

[38]*D & W*, III, 1232.

[39]Caine, pp. 219-20.

[40]*D & W*, II, 850.

[41]*The Germ*, Ed. facs. W. M. Rossetti (London, 1901), p. 201.

[42]Millais, I, 109-10.

[43]W. M. Rossetti, *Preraphaelite Diaries and Letters*, p. 20.

[44]*L & M*, I, 410-11.

[45]*Ibid.*, II, 32.

[46]*Ibid.*, I, 123.

[47]*D & W*, I, 45-6.

[48]*L & M*, II, 56.

[49]*Ibid.*, p. 58.

[50]W. M. Rossetti, *Preraphaelite Diaries and Letters*, p. 13.

[51]*L & M*, II, 57-8. (Revised and published in 1870 as *The Sea-Limits*.)

[52]*Collected Works*, I, 511.

[53]*The Germ*, p. 33.

[54]*Ibid.*, p. 32.

[55]Troxell, *Three Rossettis*, p. 140.

[56]P. F. Baum, ed., *The House of Life* (Cambridge, 1928), p. 173.

[57]W. M. Rossetti, *Ruskin: Rossetti: Preraphaelitism*, p. 21.

[58]Hill, p. 22.

[59]*L & M*, I. 436.

[60]W. M. Rossetti, *Ruskin: Rossetti: Preraphaelitism*, p. 9.

[61]*L & M*, II, 138.

[62]T. Watts-Dunton, "The Truth About Rossetti," *The Nineteenth Century*, XIII (March, 1883), 418.

[63]E. L. Cary, *The Rossettis* (New York, 1900), p. 190.

[64]W. B. Scott, *Autobiographical Notes* (London, 1892), II, 35-6.

[65]*Ibid.*, p. 39.

[66]Hill, pp. 256-7.

[67]*D & W*, II, 532.

[68]Allingham and Radford, p. 161.

[69]*Ibid.*, p. 162.

[70]*D & W*, II, 839.

[71]W. M. Rossetti, *Rossetti Papers, 1862 to 1870* (London, 1903), p. 370.

[72]Hueffer, *Ford Madox Brown*, p. 227.

[73]Baum, *Rossetti's Letters*, p. 32.

[74]*D & W*, III, 993.

[75]*Ibid.*, p. 981.

[76]*Ibid.*, p. 1171.

[77]*Ibid.*, p. 977.

[78]*Ibid.*, p. 976.

[79]M. Zaturenska, *Christina Rossetti* (New York, 1949), p. 141.

[80]*D & W*, II, 818.

[81]Scott, II, 134.

[82]Caine, p. 274.

[83]Hake and Compton-Rickett, *The Life and Letters of Theodore Watts-Dunton*, I, 69.

[84]R. L. Mégroz, *Dante Gabriel Rossetti; Painter Poet of Heaven and Earth* (London 1928), pp. 204-5.

[85]*L & M*, I, 159-60.

III

Rossetti and the Critic

*The men of imagination in England have always been
a persecuted sect.*

Rossetti in a letter to Frederick Shields[1]

Rossetti shares with his idol Keats the legend of having
had his "life snuffed out" by hostile critics, in particular by
Robert Buchanan's attack on the *Poems* of 1870, Rossetti's
first published volume of original poetry. William Rossetti
says, "It is a simple fact that, from the time the pamphlet
[Buchanan's "The Fleshly School of Poetry"] had begun to
work into the inner tissue of his feelings, Dante Rossetti
was a changed man, and so continued to the close of his
life."[2] In his life of Rossetti (1887), Joseph Knight said:
"Shocked and pained Rossetti accordingly was, and his
early demise is due indirectly to the disturbance thus
caused."[3] In 1949, Marya Zaturenska shows the legend
still alive: "Buchanan's attack gave him the psychic wound
for which he was waiting. It proved mortal."[4] In his herculean
biography of Rossetti, Oswald Doughty speaks of Rossetti's
health as being "fatally affected, and largely through
Buchanan's foulness."[5]

Yet Zaturenska and Doughty are themselves among the many who have realized that such a man as Rossetti could not have been mortally wounded by the attack of one critic, however vicious. Something had sapped his strength and resolution *before* the attack. To Zaturenska it was a sense of guilt in connection with his wife's death — rumored a suicide — and the recovery from the grave of the poems he had dramatically placed in her coffin in 1862: "He waited with hidden fear and guilt for some disaster — some secret blow from the dead hand in Highgate Cemetery."[6] To Doughty, ultimately, it was Rossetti's frustrated love for Jane Morris: "'Love's Fatality!' — was not that, rather than a belated repetition of a contemptible literary criticism, the basic cause of Rossetti's breakdown. . .?"[7]

William Rossetti recognized a host of factors that paved the way for Gabriel's collapse, flatly denying that Rossetti was "snuffed out by an article."[8] Among these were his wife's "early and shocking death, with. . .anxieties and conflicts ensuing; partial failure of eye-sight; insomnia, only combated by perilous palliatives."[9] Beyond this, though, William saw that the basic cause might lie not in external events, but in Gabriel's very nature: "Mental trouble and a too active and unappeased imagination had long ago brought on insomnia; insomnia had brought on chloral; chloral had brought on depression, agitation, and a turmoil of fantasies."[10]

Doughty as well, when he isn't obsessed with the Rossetti-Jane Morris affair, sees that the poet's make-up and background furnish significant explanations for his breakdown: "in truth invulnerability was hardly to be expected in one who had all his life avoided public exhibition through fear of criticism, and who, but a few months before, had taken measures of such meticulous completeness to defend his poems from possibility of attack."[11] One wishes that Doughty had made more of this fear of criticism, for it was part and parcel of Rossetti. . .boy, youth and man.

It stemmed from an innate self-mistrust, a mistrust that profoundly affected his poetry. Speculating about whether Rossetti was to blame to some degree for his wife's death, or whether his affair with Jane Morris was ever consummated, may be titillating. But an understanding of his attitude toward critics and criticism may well be more helpful in trying to understand the kind of poet he was, and how and why he came to be that kind of poet rather than the greater poet he might have been. . .and why he collapsed when his kind of poet was challenged.

ROSSETTI'S FEAR OF THE CRITIC

As a boy, it will be recalled, Rossetti was acutely sensitive to criticism. When his family objected to the "indecency" in his *Sorrentino,* he purged it. When his aunt questioned the propriety of his reading Shelley, he hastened to reassure her. Fear that his picture would be rejected caused him to send his first "PRB" painting not to the Royal Academy—as did Hunt and Millais—but to the so-called Free Exhibition, where a small fee guaranteed that it would be hung. As William said, "he must have contemplated with revulsion the mere possibility of being rejected at the Academy."[12] Rossetti later rationalized this desertion of his P-R Brothers, but he had in fact shown the same trait six years earlier (in 1843) when he wrote his mother that he might submit a painting to the Academy with his application for admission, and added: "The next opportunity for so doing will be at Christmas, when I may probably try, though certainly not unless I feel sure of success, for a rejection is a thing I should by no means relish."[13]

The key to Rossetti's fear of criticism is supplied by brother William, who called Gabriel "a singular compound of self-reliance and self-mistrust. He relied upon himself so far as the working impulse and the actual work were

concerned. He mistrusted himself with regard to the effect
of his work upon other minds."[14] Quite probably this mistrust of the effect of his work caused him, in 1848, to send
Aunt Charlotte only certain of his poems, holding back
others to save "a heavy postage for things of such little
value."[15] Apparently among the poems too heavy was the
first draft of *Jenny*, whose possible effect upon the minds
of others was to concern him all his life. He also begged
his aunt not to allow the "verses to be seen by anyone but
yourself, as I think an unpublished poet is always a rather
ridiculous character to appear in before strangers."

One suspects that what Gabriel really feared was ap-
pearing as a bad poet, rather than as an unpublished one,
for he sent similar warnings throughout his life to such
friendly critics as Scott, Swinburne, and brother William.
Like a mother fearing lest her children appear in public
half-dressed, Rossetti insisted that if his artistic offspring
appear at all, they be resplendently attired. As he wrote
the Leeds Committee in 1868:

> Only a thoroughly well-considered and sufficiently impor-
> tant appearance in public, after all these years of partial
> reputation, could do otherwise than greatly damage me;
> and this could only be obtained by my having full control
> and selection. In short at present nothing would be so
> discouraging to me as to be forced before the public in a
> sudden and incomplete way, and I am most anxious to do
> all I can to prevent it.[16]

Small wonder that Rossetti showed such interest in the
printing and binding of his first volume of original poems,
worrying about the accuracy of the typography and the
order in which the poems appeared, creating a special
design for the book's covers, and fussing about details of
color and cloth.

The critics' rather favorable reception of his first PRB

painting, "The Girlhood of Mary Virgin," (before they knew what "PRB" meant) seems temporarily to have encouraged Rossetti to pursue an orthodox career in art, winning his way by critical and popular approval. He wrote his aunt in May, 1849: "As my picture this year has created some interest, it is desirable that I should come before the public next year as prominently as possible, so as to succeed in establishing at once some degree of reputation."[17] Then came the unmasking of the Brotherhood, the critics' attacks on his "Annunciation" (the "face of the angel is insipidity itself"),[18] and Rossetti's vow never again to exhibit to the general public.

The fault was the public's, not Rossetti's, he explained to his aunt: "I find unluckily that the class of pictures that has been my natural preference is not for the market."[19] Next year he was writing of his despair of finding a purchaser for "Annunciation":

> Even were it only a *little* less peculiar, I would have done so [sent it off for inspection] for the sake of the chance; but, as it is, I know by experience that you might as well expect a Liverpool merchant to communicate with his Chinese correspondent without the intervention of someone who knows the language as imagine that he could look at the picture in question with the remotest glimmering of its purpose.[20]

Here spoke the "too transcendent spirit—far, far in advance of the age." The youth who grew up too independent, too stubborn to yield to authority became the man who—to a degree astounding in one who was to win solid success in two arts—avoided the public eye. He did so by selling his paintings to private individuals, and by keeping his poetry restricted, for the most part, to his closest friends until the *Poems* of 1870.

The years did little to build up Rossetti's trust in critics.

Even after the 1870 *Poems* had been generally well received, and his income from paintings had soared above £ 2,000 a year, he had no love of critics. In one of his few published art criticisms, a review of "Maclise's Character-Portraits," Rossetti thundered:

> Here too are the kings of slashing criticism, chiefs of that phalanx of rampant English and blatant Scotch mediocrity: insolent, indolent Maginn; Lockhart, elaborately at ease; Croker, tasteless and shameless; and Christopher North, cock of the walk, whose crowings have now long given place to much sweet singing that they often tried to drown, and who, for all his Jove-like head, cloud-capped in Scotch sentiment and humour, was but a bantam Thunderer after all. Not even piteous inferiority in their unheeded successors can make such men as these seem great to us now.[21]

After all, hadn't the *Saturday Review* flayed Morris as a "Pre-Raphaelite" who was devoted to a "false principle in art" that led to "morbid study" and "insufferable affectation"?[22] Hadn't the same publication fulminated against Swinburne's *Poems and Ballads* of 1866 for their "feverish carnality" and "spurious passion of a putrescent imagination"[23]—with the *London Review* adding such choice phrases as "utterly revolting" and "raving blasphemy"?[24] And wasn't Rossetti identified by most as the mentor of Morris, Swinburne, and company? As early as 1860, one John Parker was writing to John Skelton: "For myself, I am sick of Rossetti and his whole school. I think them essentially unmanly, effeminate, mystical, affected and obscure."[25]

Rossetti bitterly resented these attacks, not only because they were directed against his friends (and so, indirectly against him), but also because he thought them so unfair. To this same John Skelton, Scottish barrister and a whist-playing companion, Rossetti wrote in 1864 of Swinburne's *Queen Mother:* "No doubt you, with me, are astounded that with all its faults, it should have hitherto had no justice whatever done to its beauties."[26] In 1866, much as he personally disapproved of the more questionable elements in *Poems and Ballads*, Rossetti was again defending Swinburne to Skelton: "The attack in the press has been stupid, for the most part, and though with some good grounds, shamefully one-sided."[27] Even when the reviewers were kinder, Rossetti was unhappy. Said he of Morris' *Gudrun* in 1869: "Hearty as is the praise with which critics are greeting the book from their own point of view. . .I do not think justice is yet being done by them to this most remarkable poem."[28]

All might have been well if Rossetti had been able to say, like Byron in *English Bards and Scotch Reviewers*, that he had

> Learned to deride the critic's starch decree,
> And break him on the wheel he meant for me;
> To spurn the rod a scribble bids me kiss,
> Nor care if courts and crowds applaud and hiss.

But if Rossetti might try to spurn the critic's rod, he could not spare the crowd's applause. As William delicately put it, "to general recognition he was not indifferent."[29] Despite the critics, Morris and Swinburne had won such recognition. So must he. Yet the apprehension was there, in 1869, when he finally began to prepare for publication of his poems. W. B. Scott wrote: "He would not publish. There cropped up the fear of a public ordeal of miscellaneous criticism, which had prevented him from exhibiting his water-colour pictures, and had shut him up exclusively in his own studio."[30]

Even so, Rossetti began to polish and repolish his old poems, often agonizing over the choice of a single word, and appealing to William and to Swinburne for their advice. He braced himself for the ordeal of having his old manuscript book recovered from his wife's grave, because without three or four important poems (especially *Jenny*) that the book contained, his appearance in public would be incomplete. And he wrote new poems, each "as perfect as in me lay."[31] He tried a dress rehearsal or two. In 1868, he had three sonnets published as a "feeler," in William's words. In 1869 he had a number of his poems printed privately in "trial books" to be sent to intimates like Scott, Swinburne and brother William for their comments, and then took the braver step of having sixteen sonnets appear in the *Fortnightly Review*.

With his poems ready for publishing, however, and despite the reassurance of his friends and the quiet acceptance of the *Fortnightly* trial balloon, Rossetti remained mistrustful of his poetry's effect on the public mind. Therefore he "worked the oracle," as Scott put it, by lining up his friends in advance to rush favorable reviews into print before the expected hostile critics could get to work. Swinburne and Morris led the claque, followed by such critical luminaries as Sidney Colvin and Buxton Forman. To his publisher, Ellis, Rossetti frankly confessed his fear of bad reviews, adding that he only wanted to "appear when I know a few friendly reviewers are ready, to keep spite at bay and leave it gaping and goggling without a chance of a good snarl."[32] He wrote to Skelton, asking for a review and saying that Swinburne and Morris had promised, too. His purpose in asking for such reviews, Rossetti told Skelton, was so that "spite. . .in at least one quarter" might be scotched.[33]

What Rossetti was doing was neither unique in his time nor is it unknown today. Furthermore, he did have good reason to expect spite from at least one quarter: Robert Buchanan. A minor poet and critic, Buchanan had been among those attacked in William Rossetti's defense of Swinburne. And now, Gabriel feared, he lay waiting to wreak vengeance upon the innocent brother. "Bye the bye," he wrote Swinburne, "I expect the B-B-Buchanan to be down upon me of course now in *The Athenaeum,* and am anxious to time my appearance when it seems likely that friends can speak up almost at once and so just catch the obscene organ of his speech when it is hitched up for an utterance, and perhaps compel the brain of which it is also the seat, to reconsider its views and chances."[34] Rossetti had made this crude reference to Buchanan even more explicit in his letter to Ellis: "I fancy Mr. Buchanan probably has his natural organ of speech hitched up for an utterance. It would be nice if he had to make it a silent emanation and got nothing but the smell to enjoy."[35]

On April 25, 1870, the *Poems* of Dante Gabriel Rossetti at last reached the public. Promptly came the appointed paeans of Swinburne, Morris, and the others. There were a few discordant notes, such as reviews in *Blackwood's Magazine* in England and *The Nation* in America. But Rossetti was surprised to "find such things producing a much more transient and momentary impression of unpleasantness than he would have expected — indeed he might say none at all."[36] When an attack on the poems called the "The Fleshly School of Poetry" by a Thomas Maitland appeared in *The Contemporary Review* for October, 1871, Rossetti wrote to his publisher, Ellis: "Have you seen our contemptuous *Contemporary*? What fools we must be! For it seems that we are even greater fools than the writer, and even I can see what a fool *he* is. For once abuse comes in a form that even a bard can manage to grin at without grimacing."[37]

Then came a startling bit of news: "What do you think?" Gabriel wrote his brother. "Ellis writes me that Maitland is — Buchanan! . . . If it be, I'll not deny myself the fun of a printed Letter to the Skunk."[38] Rossetti still seemed to be composed about the matter when he wrote Ellis for confirmation, adding that if the news were true, "By God. . .I'll give myself a treat and write and print a Letter on Lying (to Thos. Buchanan Esq.)"[39]

But Rossetti was hardly as composed as the words "fun" and "treat" would suggest. He dashed off a limerick that gives some hint of his real emotional state:

As a critic, the Poet Buchanan
Thinks Pseudo much safer than Anon.
  Into Maitland he's shrunk,
  Yet the smell of the skunk
Guides the shuddering nose to Buchanan.[40]

More indicative of how upset Rossetti was would be the first draft of the letter he prepared as a public refutation of Buchanan's attack, did we have it. Says Ellis: "It was a very angry letter and in the opinion of Rossetti's best friends was not worthy of publication—a lawyer who was consulted gave it as his opinion that it was actionable. It was put in type, and a slip proof was printed. One copy was sent to Rossetti and one I kept by me for some years, but as it had been the author's wish to suppress it I did not think it right to preserve it and so destroyed it."[41]

Such a letter would hardly have supported Rossetti's statement that he was "frankly amused at some remarks by Mr. Buchanan upon certain rhymes in his volume."[42] In a note to Hake, Rossetti makes light of "the effect which adverse criticism has on me," and asserts that "the first form in which I had put my reply was one of pure banter and satire, having for its central part only a serious reference to the critic's mis-statements. However, my friends seem scandalized at the satirical side of the reply, and this induced me to give up the idea of printing it as a pamphlet which a sense of fun had chiefly suggested."[43] But the unanimity with which his friends urged him not to print this first reply, the advice of the lawyer that it might be "actionable," the very vehemence and vulgarity of his feelings toward Buchanan (even before Buchanan's attack appeared!) all suggest anything but a reaction on Rossetti's part of "pure banter" and a "sense of fun."

The fact is that in place of his original reply, Rossetti did heed the advice of his friends and sent instead a dignified, telling rebuttal to *The Athenaeum* called "The Stealthy

School of Criticism." Meanwhile his *Poems* prospered: the entire first issue of 1,000 copies sold within a month; three months after publication he was £ 450 richer for having braved the public. Still, Buchanan's charges rankled, hurt, gnawed at Rossetti's perilous balance of mind.

Nor was Buchanan through. In 1872 he enlarged upon his first article, made it even more abusive, and published it as a pamphlet. After hitting at Swinburne and Morris but admitting they were capable of better things, Buchanan struck his heaviest blows at "the head of the school," Rossetti.[44] He had already linked all three to Gautier, the Marquis de Sade, and Baudelaire, whom he called the "godfather. . .of the modern Fleshly School."[45] Moreover, he charged that the new school viewed art only as a means of sensation: "The fleshly gentlemen have bound themselves by solemn league and covenant to extol fleshliness as the distinct and supreme end of poetic thought, and by inference that the body is greater than the soul, and sound superior to sense."[46]

The effect of this expanded attack on Rossetti was devastating. Rossetti thought he saw a league of conspiracy against him. He broke down utterly, mentally and physically, in June, 1872, and attempted suicide by an overdose of laudanum, the same drug that had killed his wife ten years earlier. June 2, 1872, said his brother William, "was one of the most miserable days of my life, not to speak of his."[47] Rossetti recovered remarkably; by autumn he was again doing excellent work in both poetry and painting. But the curse of insomnia grew worse, the doses of chloral (and whiskey to mask the drug's bitter taste) grew larger. His recluse habits became settled; he saw little or nothing of many of his oldest friends; he broke with Browning over an imagined slight; he began to leave his Cheyne Walk house only after dark.

It was not Buchanan's attack in itself that did this: it was the confirmation that the attack provided of all Rossetti's old distrust of critics and the public. "His fancies now ran away with him," said William, "and he thought that the pamphlet was a first symptom in a widespread conspiracy for crushing his fair fame as an artist and a man, and for hounding him out of an honest society."[48]

Today we would patly say that Rossetti had a "persecution complex." But one need not be a psychologist to see that the root of his suspicions of others was his mistrust of himself. The record of *The House of Life* sonnet sequence alone, so much of it devoted to frustration, regret, and a sense of inadequacy, is evidence enough of what Rossetti called elsewhere his "lifelong feeling of dissatisfaction which I have experienced from the disparity of aim and attainment in what I have all my life produced as best I could."[49] He did strive always, at least in his poetry, for the best he could produce, but there was more than mere banter beneath such self-depreciation of his poems as "a howling canticle,"[50] and "lackadaisical things,"[51] and "bogies,"[52] as if he were begging to be refuted. The wrong-turning expressed in *The Land-Mark* could not be denied. The neglected opportunities of *Vain Virtues* could not be forgotten. The *Lost Days* of his youth continued to ask accusingly, "I am thyself, — what has thou done to me?"

Doubting himself as he did, how could Rossetti help but doubt the critics, especially when these "kings of slashing criticism" were so different from what Rossetti tried to be as a critic? To see the qualities that Rossetti displayed as a critic is to see why the likes of Buchanan could breed nothing but contempt — and fear.

ROSSETTI AS A CRITIC

Coleridge once wrote: "To the young I would remark, that it is always unwise to judge of anything by its defects; the first attempt ought to be to discover its excellencies."[53] To an uncanny degree, this could stand as the cardinal principle behind what Rossetti thought a critic should be and his own

performance as a critic. He declared forcefully to Frederick
Shields: "The man who, on seeing a work with claims to
regard, does not perceive its beauties before its faults, is a
conceited fool. I am ashamed to belong to a profession in
which the possession of intellect is rather a disqualification
than an advantage. The men of imagination in England have
always been a persecuted sect."[54] To James Douglas he wrote:
"A miscreant who in kind of meanness and infamy cannot
well be beaten, [is] the man who in an anonymous journal
tells the world that a poem or a picture is bad when he knows
it to be good. That is the man who should never defile my
hand with his touch."[55]

To perceive the beauties before the faults, Rossetti advocated considering a work on its own merits: "studied work,
where unity is specially kept in view, suffers I think by the
associated plan of criticism, and the comparative treatment
seems to me never quite a sound one."[56] As with Morris'
Gudrun, Rossetti would say, any worth-while work of art
"can only be dealt with by detailed analysis."[57] Not that a
microscopic search for possible flaws was desirable or useful.
To Caine's assertion that a certain metaphor of Coleridge's
was scientifically inaccurate, Rossetti replied: "Your geo-
logical strictures [are] but too just. . . . But I would fain think
that this is 'to consider too nicely.' "[58] (Truth to Nature
could go too far!) What mattered was the over-all conception,
not picayune details, he said in this statement that unfortunately is more widely known than understood: "You have
too great a habit of speaking of a special octave, sextette, or
line. Conception, my boy, *FUNDAMENTAL BRAINWORK*,
that is what makes the difference in all art."[59] This fundamental brainwork is frequently misinterpreted to mean intel-
lectualizing in poetry. What Rossetti really meant was what
he said: "Conception, my boy". . .that is, the awareness of
the over-all intent of the artist, and the appreciation of how
that intent is realized in a given work of art.

Even when Rossetti analyzes a poem in detail, therefore, it is in accordance with the principle of finding this fundamental brainwork in action. There, ultimately, as the sum of all the parts, lay the full beauty contributed by each of the various elements. For the most part, Rossetti as critic was a poet writing to poets. Much of his criticism was a practical, practicing criticism, intended to be applied. Aside from a few art reviews written for brother William, and critical remarks for the Gilchrist *Life of Blake*, Rossetti published only three critical essays — two reviews of poems by his friend Dr. Hake in 1871 and 1873, and "The Stealthy School of Criticism."[60] Throughout the hundreds of letters he wrote, however, he set down critical opinions of scores of poets and their poetry, ranging from flashing phrases to carefully worded statements of considerable length. These, together with acounts of his comments recorded by those who knew him, when collected, organized and analyzed, show a basically consistent attitude toward poetry, and prove of great value when one applies them to Rossetti's own poetry. The "critic" Rossetti that emerges is of great help in understanding the poet Rossetti.

The nature of Rossetti's critical comments, scattered and disconnected as they were, makes the creation of any formal dialectic impossible. It is unlikely that the young Gabriel of Chapter I — intuitive, imaginative, impatient of restraint and dogma, so one-sided in the kinds of things he read — would have become a formal critic in any case. Caine describes Rossetti the critic with considerable accuracy:

> A critic, in the sense of one possessed of a natural gift of analysis, Rossetti assuredly was not. No man's instinct for what is good in poetry was ever swifter or surer than that of Rossetti. You might always mistrust your judgement if you found it at variance with his where abstract power and beauty were in question. . . . But here Rossetti's

function as a critic ended. His was at best only the criticism
of the creator. Of the gifts of ultimate classification he had
none, although now and again, (as where he says that
Chatterton was the day-spring of modern romantic poetry),
he seems to give signs of a power of critical synthesis.[61]

Although Rossetti may have rarely displayed a gift for
(perhaps more precisely, an interest in) "critical synthesis,"
his criticism reveals that he had a sure knowledge of the basic
ingredients of good poetry. More clearly and completely than
such a critic of "ultimate classification" as Matthew Arnold,
for instance, Rossetti knew and described the necessary
elements of poetry, for he was concerned only with poetry as
poetry. He was not led away from a poem, as Arnold often
was, by the need for something to "rest upon," nor by concern
for social, political or economic systems, nor by the conflict
of Hebraic duty and Hellenistic beauty. For none of these
had he cared as a youth; none concerned him closely as a
man. Thus, in a limited yet illuminating way, Rossetti's
comments lay bare the very heart of poetry as he saw it.
There is much truth in Arthur Symons' too generous words:
"Certainly no modern poet ever had anything like the same
grasp on whatever is essential in poetry as Rossetti's; for
all that he wrote and said about Art has in it an absolute
rightness of judgement; and with these, as absolutely, an
intellectual sanity."[62]
Within his limits and granted his blind spots, Rossetti
was a consistent critic working from definite and clearly
defined ideas of what poetry should be. A. M. Turner's opinion that "Rossetti depends on sudden intuitions, on insight,
for his judgements"[63] has been shared by many, but is misleading. Guiding the intuition and insight were those basic
critical principles, as A. C. Benson realized:

[Rossetti's] criticisms all seem to me to show the hard
intellectual force, so distinct from the dreamy character

with which Rossetti is generally credited, which he brought
to bear on his art. There is no vagueness or looseness about
them; he goes straight down to fundamental principles.
Nothing proves more conclusively the sanity and sense
of Rossetti's critical power than his discussion of particular
authors.[64]

Turner is equally misleading when he speaks of Rossetti's
"strong personal bias," and declares sweepingly: "When a
writer does not harmonize with his well-marked preferences,
he neglects him altogether. When, on the contrary, he finds
one who chimes with them, Rossetti's enthusiasm runs away
with his judgement, and, as in the case of Chatterton or
Wells, he exalts them to the skies."[65] Yes, the tendency
toward over enthusiasm and the blind spots of prejudice
that characterized the young Gabriel were never really out-
grown. But numerous examples of his sympathy for poetry
that did not "essentially harmonize with his well-marked
preferences" are available. Although he "grudged"
Wordsworth every vote he got, Rossetti gave a "special and
unique homage, as a thing absolutely alone of its kind among
all greatest things" to Wordsworth's *Intimations Ode.*[66] He
admitted that "Tennyson's new volume [*The Holy Grail*]
does not enlist my sympathies, except a second 'Northern
Farmer,' which is wonderful"; then he continued: "and of
course there is much high-class work throughout."[67] A man
who heard Rossetti speak, the art critic J. W. C. Carr, goes
so far as to say:

> It was indeed the breadth of his sympathy both in literature
> and art, no less than the fineness and delicacy of his taste,
> that most impressed me. . . . His talk was assuredly more
> inspiring than that of any man I have ever known; most
> inspiring, certainly, to a youth who had ambitions of his
> own, for, although intolerant of any utterance that was
> merely conventional, and quick to detect the smallest lack

of sincerity, he was ever patient with the expression of any
enthusiasm however crude, and was as ready to listen as to
reply. . . . He ranged widely over the fields of literature
and art, always trenchant, always earnest, yet now and
again slipping with sudden wit and humor into a lighter
vein.[68]

Sympathy was the quality that Rossetti most earnestly
desired in other critics, and most strikingly displayed in his
own criticism. He obeyed his own dictum: "The true artist
will first perceive in another's work the beauties, and in his
own work the defects."[69] To this, William Sharp and Dr.
Hake, among others, attest. Said Sharp: "An ardent and
appreciative critic, he seldom failed to select the peculiar
excellences of any poem by a contemporary writer he might
be reading, irrespective of the author's celebrity or insigni-
ficance."[70] And Hake, whose admiration for Rossetti was
qualified, paid this tribute: "He had a very just mind. When
an author was discussed, whatever might be said against
him, he would insist on his merits being remembered."[71]

Those who loved Rossetti never tired of testifying to the
sympathy and greatness of heart that won him the fealty of
such young disciples as Morris, Burne-Jones, Val Prinsep,
and P. B. Marston. Burne-Jones may speak for all when
he says: "Towards other men's ideas he was decidedly the
most generous man I ever knew. No one so threw himself
into what other men did—it was part of his enormous imagination. The praises he first lavished on me, if I had not had
a few grains of inborn modesty, would have been enough
to turn my head altogether."[72]

When Rossetti discovered a writer or painter of promise,
moreover, he went beyond mere encouragement. He sought
art commissions for Burne-Jones, and repeatedly offered
direct financial aid as well as advice and opportunities for
art work to Frederick Shields. He wrote publishers in behalf
of Swinburne, Morris and others. His rare venture into pub-

lished criticism was to help Hake, and the year before Rossetti died he said of Thomas Dixon, "If I live, I mean to write something about him in some quarter when I can."[73] Ironically, Dixon died before Rossetti did, apparently from overexertion occasioned by a triumphal trip to London during which he met a number of literary celebrities in addition to Rossetti. Dixon was only a humble cork-cutter, but in reporting his death to Christina, Rossetti called him "a man of real genius. . . . He was a worthy man; indeed, I never knew of any one individual in any walk of life—even a much higher one than his—who was so entirely devoted to promoting intellectual good among those within his reach."[74]

Force was another basic quality in Rossetti's criticism. Burne-Jones, who at his first meeting with his hero heard him "rend in pieces" someone who spoke disrespectfully of Browning, testifies to the power of Rossetti's opinion.[75] "He never harangued or persuaded," Burne-Jones said, "but he had a gift of saying things authoritatively. . . . I never wanted to think but as he thought."[76] That there was danger in such power Burne-Jones came to see. "He taught me practically all I ever learned," he once wrote Carr, but "Afterwards I made a method for myself to suit my nature."[77] Young as he was, Brown's gifted son "Nolly" perceived this danger clearly: "He has had several long discussions with me on the subject of novel writing, from which I see that he has a great facility of expression, but that he would be a dangerous preceptor."[78]

Rossetti's forcefulness came in part from a conviction about the works of others that was in curious contrast to his frequent uncertainty about his own. The adolescent who unhesitatingly called Warren's *Ten Thousand a Year* "the most splendid ever read,"[79] carried over into the man who flatly contradicted Brown's assertion that Longfellow and Smith were the best poets after Tennyson. Rossetti clinched the argument by saying that he had "studied the matter all his life and should know best."[80] Caine says, "in matters of taste in art, or criticism in poetry, he would brook no opposition from any quarter."[81] Yet Caine was able to distinguish these sudden gusts of opinion from the prevailing winds of basic belief, and Caine's way was to sit back and wait for Rossetti's abrupt enthusiasm to pass. "He was a man of so much impulse," Caine wrote, "impulse often as violent as lawless—that to oppose him merely provoked anger to no good purpose, for as often as not the position first adopted with so much pertinacity was afterwards silently abandoned, and your own aims quietly acquiesced in."[82]

One must remember that when Caine knew him, Rossetti was a sick and broken man, hence the violence and lawlessness of these outbursts. But Rossetti was hardly a moderate man at best. The forcefulness also came in part from the not uncommon process whereby argument momentarily carries a man beyond a calm and precise statement of his views. Rossetti realized this when he explained Blake's neglect of color as "the misleading things he wrote about colour, carried away at the moment, after his fiery fashion, by the predominance he wished to give to other qualities in some argument in hand."[83] This is a good explanation of Rossetti's own fiery fashion of tossing out superlatives, first one quality being the *sine qua non* of poetry, then another, then another. The argument in hand produced the moment's superlative. The seeming contradictions of his individual comments largely vanish when one analyzes the whole body of his criticism. The extremes, Rossetti would say (as he did say of Blake) are

> the impatient extremes of a man who had his own work to do, which was of one kind, as he thought, against another; and who mainly did it, too, in spite of that injustice without which no extremes might have ever been chargeable against him. And let us remember that, after all, having greatness in him, his *practice* of art included all great aims, whether they were such as his antagonistic moods railed against or no.[84]

Rossetti modified his own extremism in two important respects. One of these was a keen awareness of the need for historical perspective. The other was an acknowledgement of his own fallibility as a critic. In urging historical perspective, he warned Caine curtly against letting admiration for a contemporary blind him to the full merits of a predecessor: "There are few indeed whom the facile enthusiasm for contemporary models does not deaden to the truly balanced claims of successful efforts in art."[85] This would seem, perhaps, to be only another instance of Rossetti's insistence that each poem be criticized on its own merits. But Rossetti went further than that in his championing of the art of the past. He urged that due consideration be given the circumstances of the age in which the poet lived when *ability* (as contrasted with performance alone) was in question. As he phrased it, "the nett [*sic*] results of advancing epochs, however permanent on accumulated foundation-work, are the poorest of all tests as to relative values."[86] Moreover, neither the value of a given work nor the ability of a given poet, he thought, could be definitely established until time had made historical criticism possible.

In his review of Maclise, Rossetti said: "There is much in the function of criticism which absolutely needs time for its final and irreversible settlement." With the passage of years, he continued, criticism of a work of art can improve in the light of "clearer grounds for decision."[87] It was this light that enabled Rossetti to see Chatterton as "The true day-spring of modern romantic poetry."[88] It was this same light of historical perspective that justified much of his praise of Blake. Thus he admires Blake's lyrical power as being "startlingly in advance of the time at which he wrote."[89] He praises his "astonishing merit" in "relation to Blake's youth. . .or the poetic epoch in which they were produced."[90] And he described "exquisite metrical gift and rightness in point of form" as Blake's "special glory among his contemporaries." These qualities, Rossetti continued, can be found in poets before and after Blake's own day, "but he alone (let it be repeated and remembered) possessed them *then*, and possessed them in clear completeness."[91]

As for Rossetti's fallibility as a critic, Rossetti was well aware of it and often acknowledged it—Caine's "he would brook no opposition from any quarter" notwithstanding. (Anyone who has read Caine's *Recollections* of Rossetti will agree that Caine stands somewhat this side of infallibility himself.) Rossetti was quite willing to affirm that Swinburne knew more about the ballad,[92] and Watts-Dunton more about the sonnet,[93] than he. When he found himself in error, he could admit it, as he did in a letter to Henry Buxton Forman, a critic who was among the first to appreciate Rossetti's poetry, and who had stoutly defended him against Buchanan's attack. After discussing the superstition that Keats planned to use in his unfinished *Eve of St. Mark*, Rossetti continued: "By the bye, I was too sweeping in what I said of Keats's Sonnets. I perceive there are fourteen in my opinion more or less worthy of him."[94] Often, too, Rossetti paused in the very act of emphatic criticism to acknowledge that he might be wrong. When objecting to Swinburne's diction, for example, he wound up by suggesting, "perhaps this is only [my] morbid Bohemian fancy."[95] After criticizing Watts-Dunton's lack of subtlety of execution, he confessed to personal foible with: "perhaps [it seems so] through habits of my own, which some may think too fine-strung."[96] Similarly, he qualified his objection to Nolly Brown's "finish" with the phrase, "if it strikes others as it does me."[97]

Strong as were his convictions, Rossetti never pretended that the secret of either poetry or criticism was his exclusively or even outstandingly. If his advice were asked, he gave his honest opinion, marked most often by the force of generosity rather than the slash of censure. When the young would-be poet Theodore Marzials lashed back at Rossetti for calling his work "crude and immature," Rossetti's quiet response was, "if work sent to me is weak, I prefer silence; but if it is not, I take it the author can only wish for one's real opinion either way."[98]

Such were Rossetti's ideas of what a critic should be. It is time now to watch the critic Rossetti in action, to see what he thought a poet and a poem should be, and to use his own criticism as a guide to understanding Rossetti the poet.

NOTES

[1]*L & M,* I, 414.

[2]*Ibid.,* p. 307.

[3]L. C. Knight, *Life of Dante Gabriel Rossetti* (London, 1887), p. 143.

[4]Zaturenska, p. 176.

[5]O. Doughty, *Dante Gabriel Rossetti* (New Haven, 1949), p.503.

[6]Zaturenska, p. 176.

[7]Doughty, *Dante Gabriel Rossetti,* p. 541.

[8]*L & M,* I, 326-7.

[9]*Ibid.,* pp. 303-4.

[10]*Ibid.,* p. 304.

[11]Doughty, *Dante Gabriel Rossetti,* p. 508.

[12]*L & M,* I, 145.

[13]*Ibid.,* II, 17.

[14]*Ibid.,* I, 276.

[15]*Ibid.,* II, 38.

[16]E. Mills, *The Life and Letters of Frederick Shields* (London, 1912),pp. 118-9.

[17]*L & M,* II, 47.

[18]Doughty, *Dante Gabriel Rossetti,* p. 101.

[19]*L & M,* II, 47.

[20]*Ibid.,* p. 91.

[21]*Collected Works,* II, 510.

[22]*Saturday Review,* VI (November 20, 1858), 178.

[23]C. K. Hyder, *Swinburne's Literary Career and Fame* (Durham, 1933), pp. 37-8.

[24]*Ibid.,* p. 41.

[25]J. Skelton, *The Table Talk of Shirley* (Edinburgh, 1896), p. 79.

[26]*Ibid.,* p. 80.

[27]*Ibid.*, pp. 84-5.

[28]*D & W.* II, 773.

[29]*L & M,* I, 304.

[30]Scott, II, 116-7.

[31]Skelton, p. 89.

[32]*D & W.* II, 794.

[33]Skelton, pp. 88-9.

[34]*D & W,* II, 793.

[35]*Ibid.*, p. 794.

[36]*L & M,* I, 291.

[37]*D & W.* III, 1017.

[38]*Ibid.*, pp. 1017-18.

[39]*Ibid.*, p. 1018.

[40]*Ibid.*, p. 1020.

[41]*Ibid..* p. 1019, fn. #2.

[42]*L & M,* I, 299.

[43]*D & W.* III, 1043.

[44]R. Buchanan, *The Fleshly School of Poetry* (London. 1872), p. 31.

[45]*Ibid.*, p. 2.

[46]*Ibid.*, p. 32.

[47]*L & M,* I, 307.

[48]*Ibid.*, p. 305.

[49]*Ibid.*, p. 352.

[50]*Ibid..* II, 43.

[51]Scott, II, 143.

[52]*L & M,* II, 17.

[53]S. T. Coleridge, *Shakespearian Criticism,* ed. T. M. Rayson (Cambridge, 1930), II, 122.

[54]*L & M.* I, 414.

[55]J. Douglas, *Theodore Watts-Dunton* (London, 1904), pp. 210-11.

[56]Skelton, p. 90.

[57]Compton-Rickett. p. 315.

[58]Caine, p. 162.

[59]*Ibid.*, p. 249.

[60]"Hake's Madeline and Other Poems," printed in *The Academy,* Feb. 1, 1871; "Hake's Parables and Tales," printed in *The Fortnightly Review.* April. 1873; and "The Stealthy School of Criticism," printed in *The Athenaeum,* Dec. 16, 1871.

[61]Caine, p. 191.

[62]A. Symons, *Studies in Strange Souls* (London, 1929), pp. 19-20.

[63]A. M. Turner, "Rossetti's Reading and Critical Opinions," *Publications of the Modern Language Association.* XLII (June, 1927), p. 489.

[64]A. C. Benson, *Rossetti* (New York, 1904), p. 170.

[65]Turner, pp. 489-90.

[66]Caine, p. 150.

[67]Mills, p. 139.

[68]J. C. Carr, *Some Eminent Victorians* (London, 1908), pp. 65-6.

[69]*Collected Works*, I, 510.

[70]Sharp, p. 35.

[71]T. G. Hake, *Memoirs of Eighty Years* (London, 1892), pp. 220-21.

[72]Burne-Jones, I, 137.

[73]Caine, p. 258.

[74]*D & W*, IV, 1794.

[75]Burne-Jones, I, 129

[76]*Ibid.*, p. 149.

[77]Carr, p. 72.

[78]J. H. Ingram, *Oliver Madox Brown* (London, 1883), p. 149.

[79]*L & M*, II, 15.

[80]W. M. Rossetti, *Ruskin: Rossetti: Preraphaelitism*, p. 20.

[81]Caine, p. 13.

[82]*Ibid.*, p. 245.

[83]*Collected Works*, I, 445.

[84]*Ibid.*, p. 466.

[85]Caine, p. 187.

[86]*Ibid.*

[87]*Collected Works*, II, 506.

[88]Caine, p. 185.

[89]*Collected Works*, I, 458.

[90]*Ibid.*, p. 459.

[91]*Ibid.*, pp. 464-5.

[92]S. C. Chew, *Swinburne* (Boston, 1929), p. 40.

[93]Sharp, p. 29.

[94]*D & W*, IV, 1712.

[95]Compton-Rickett, pp. 314-5.

[96]*Ashley Catalogue*, IV, 134-5.

[97]Ingram, pp. 83-4.

[98]Scott, II, 194.

IV

Rossetti and the Poet, I

*I can never get over the weakness of making a thing as
good as I can manage.*

Rossetti in 1853 — age twenty-five[1]

To separate the poet and the poem may seem absurd.
It may also be useful. For the poet has certain aims — and
certain gifts — that may or may not be realized in whole or
in part in the poetry he produces. This is precisely the distinction that Rossetti had in mind when he said in his reply
to Buchanan, *The Stealthy School of Criticism*, "I speak
here, as does my critic. . .of *aim*, not of *achievement*."

A distinctive poet is likely to have aims that are peculiarly
his own, and his own unique view of the ideal poet. Yet if
one has only the poet's work to go by, he may be badly misled
in guessing what those aims and ideals are. With Rossetti,
we are singularly fortunate in not having to guess. He expressed, often and forcefully, his ideas about the relationship
between poet and reader, the ideal toward which the poet
should strive, and the gifts or talents necessary to the good
poet. He demanded much, and it may be that when this recit-

al of Rossetti's ideas about the poet is finished, the reader may cry with the prince in *Rasselas:* "Enough! thou hast convinced me that no human being can ever be a poet." But such is the stuff of this and the following chapter.

THE POET AND THE READER

To what extent, as he creates, should the poet keep the reader in mind? Dr. Sam Johnson's succinct answer was: "That book is good in vain, which the reader throws away." Surprisingly—at least for a poet so often identified with "Art for Art's sake"—Rossetti fundamentally agreed with Johnson, and tried to shape his work accordingly. He might claim, as he did to Shields, that aside from making his poetry as nearly perfect as possible, he had "taken little trouble" about winning an audience.[2] He might threaten to omit *My Sister's Sleep* from the 1870 *Poems* because "I feel so sure the British fool will greet it with congenial sympathy, and I do so hate to please him."[3] But the facts support William Rossetti's exquisite litotes: "To general recognition he was not indifferent."[4]

Rossetti's first review of Hake's poems, "Hake's Madeline, and other Poems," begins with a flat statement of the poet's need to have the reader in mind in the very act of production:

> Above all ideal personalities with which the poet must learn to identify himself, there is one supremely real which is the most imperative of all; namely that of his reader. And the practical watchfulness needed for such assimilation is as much a gift and instinct as is the creative grasp of alien character. It is a spiritual contact, hardly conscious yet ever renewed, and which must be part of the very act of production.[5]

Few indeed, Rossetti continues, are the poets who have this

spiritual contact with the reader "in pure perfection." He
names only five English poets so gifted: Chaucer,
Shakespeare, Byron, Burns, and (the only contemporary)
William Morris. On another occasion, he called Morris "the
greatest literary identity of our time. . . .chiefly on the ground
of that highest quality in a poet — his width of relation to
the mass of mankind."[6] Even if few could perfectly relate to
the mass of mankind, said Rossetti, "some degree, entire
or restricted, must be the test of every poet's vocation, and
has to be considered first of all in criticizing his work."[7]
True to his dictum of first finding the virtues in a poet's work,
Rossetti does concede that Hake has qualities "which no
true reader can regard with indifference," and prophesies
that "he will not fail to be welcomed by certain readers for
his manly human heart, and genuine if not fully subjugated
powers of hand."[8] Still, there is the implication that "certain
readers" are not enough: "With all his peculiarities, and all
the obstacles which really stand between him and the reading
public,"[9] Hake's "faculty of rapport seems on the whole
imperfect."[10]

In his own work, always mistrustful of its effect on the
minds of others as he was, Rossetti did all he could to minimize the public's objections. As he changed the subject matter
of his painting in 1851 in response to public taste, and
flinched in 1853 when the public voice accused him of "popery," so in 1869 he hesitated to publish Ave lest the same
charges be repeated. Within two months of the publication
of the 1870 Poems, he was writing Swinburne, "I think of
omitting Dennis Shand, as rather chargeable with triviality,
and its objectionableness strengthening those who will rail
at the more important Jenny."[11]

On rare occasions, Rossetti foresaw objections from
some particular segment of the public, as when he withheld
the Mulberry-Tree sonnet from the 1870 Poems lest it offend
"some sensitive member or members of the tailoring craft."[12]

The offending line was the last line of the sonnet, which first read "Some Tailor's ninth allotment of a ghost." Rossetti changed "Tailor's to Starveling's" when the poem was published in *The Academy* in 1871. Most often, however, his efforts to forestall or overcome criticism were directed at making his poems easier for the reader to understand, and at avoiding the risk of unduly shocking the reader, especially with the treatment of sex.

As a critic, Rossetti pounced upon anything that seemed to make it difficult for a reader to understand a poem. Obscurity was anathema — a number of his own poems notwithstanding. Hence his disapproval of the "baffling involutions of. . .treatment and diction" in Hake's work, "rendering it, we fear, inaccessible to most readers."[13] Hence, too, his feeling that Blake was "so far removed from ordinary apprehensions in most of his poems."[14] According to brother William, Rossetti "took a prejudice to *Tiriel*, said it must be heavy, and would scare readers away from the rest: he would not adventure its perusal himself."[15]

The twelve-year-old author of *Sir Hugh* was never to outgrow his fear of being misunderstood by the reader, although he usually managed to find ways less awkward and obvious than footnotes to make his intentions clear. For a number of his paintings — among them "Cassandra," "Pandora," "Astarte Syriaca," and "Mnemosyne" — he wrote explanatory sonnets, and planned to write "concise mottoes" to explain his Llandaff pictures.

For his poems, he actually did use introductory mottoes for *Jenny* and *Dante at Verona,* and planned mottoes for *Sister Helen* and *The Card Dealer* which were ultimately discarded. There is something almost ludicrous in the lengths to which he went to explain to Holman Hunt the meaning of *The Card Dealer* (originally entitled *Vingt-et-un*): "[I had] intended to indicate that state before death when the forms of things may supposed to be lost, while their colours throb, as it were, against the half-closed eyelids, making them to ache with confused lights." Adding wryly that it is dangerous to describe death if one hasn't died, Rossetti goes on to explain that the game of twenty-one in the last line is a game of cards which the lady of the picture is playing, that the lady symbolizes intellectual enjoyment, and that "twenty-one is the age at which the mind is most liable to be beguiled for a time from its proper purpose."[16] One can hardly fault Rossetti for adding that this "lengthy explanation" was "scarcely worth elucidating."

Similar to the mottoes are the introductory notes that Rossetti affixed to *The White Ship, The King's Tragedy,* and *A Mulberry-Tree,* and that he also contemplated for *Troy Town* and *Sister Helen*—again to help the reader. He asked Swinburne about *Troy Town:* "I had put an explanatory note to *Troy Town,* which I cut because the authority (in Pliny) did not quite meet the case. . . . Do you think some explanation absolutely necessary to prepare the reader for so outlandish a notion as a cup resembling a bosom?"[17] For *Sister Helen,* written but never printed, was this explanation of why he had added a new incident and eight new stanzas to the poem after its original publication in 1870: "It is not unlikely that some may be offended at seeing the addition made this late to the ballad of Sister Helen. My best excuse is that I believe some will wonder that such a climax did not enter into my first conception."[18] He even worried about the reaction to this change from so devoted a friend as Hall Caine: "Your hair is on end, I know, but if you heard the stanzas, they would smooth if not curl it. The gain is immense."[19] Delighted as he was to learn that Swinburne was "battling with the British Dragon" on the subject of obscurity in Rossetti's sonnets, Rossetti all the same considered writing an "exposition" of *The House of Life* sequence—a service finally rendered by William.

From a single line to entire poems, Rossetti revised and

revised his work with the reader in mind. Typical are these comments in a letter to his brother:

> I remember I had made additions (now lost) at points which I thought abrupt in *Stratton Water* and *Staff and Scrip.* In S[*tratton*] W[*ater*] some stanzas were inserted after "The nags were in the stall" (p.48) to give the gradual impression of his recognizing the girl whom he thought dead. Do you think it necessary to write something of the sort again?

> In S[*taff*] and S[*crip*] there was something added where the damsel gives her relics to develop this incident and help the transition. Does this seem necessary? Or is there any other point in any of the poems which seems to want working out? I have added a first stanza to *Sister Helen,* as Scott said the impression of what was going on was not perfectly distinct.[20]

Troy Town, too, got a new first stanza to meet the objection that the reader wouldn't realize that Helen was in Sparta, not in Troy.[21] The very first line of *Eden Bower* bothered Rossetti, as he wrote Swinburne:

> It rather troubles me that the first verse is readable in an inflexion not intended, and may set the reader on a false tack of sound, i.e. if he does not at once emphasize the first *it*. Do you think this a decided defect? I *might* make it run thus or somehow:—

> 'Twas so with Lilith the wife of Adam (etc.)
> That not a drop of her blood was human', etc.

> But this weakens it in value. Give me your opinion and don't damn me.[22]

Rossetti finally settled for his original line:

It was Lilith the wife of Adam.

He was equally concerned about *A Last Confession*, as he confided in another letter to Swinburne:

> There are various slight changes throughout — notably I have tried to make less emphatic the passage at the end of the *Confession* about the whore laughing, as I found someone to whom I read it actually thought the heroine herself was the whore! Not that this *ought* to have been thought by anyone, but I think the slight change has bettered the passage.[23]

Clearly, Rossetti would do all he could to help his readers understand, feeling as he did that this understanding was primarily the responsibility of the poet, and only secondarily that of the reader. This was an important distinction, for Rossetti's poetry — with its frequent use of implied metaphor, its compact and often crowded lines, and its unconventional symbolism — demands considerable co-operation from the reader. Rossetti truly did wish to make this co-operation as easy as possible. Therefore, as he wrote Coventry Patmore, symbolism must "bear its meaning broadly and instantly," must be "really inherent in the fact" and not "having had the fact made to fit it."[24]

Great was his glee when his butcher-boy model instantly guessed the subject of his painting, "Found": "Now I know the picture is right. If the subject of a picture cannot tell its own story, but has to be explained, that picture is a failure."[25] (Ironically, "Found," like so many other paintings, had a sonnet written to explain it.) As early as 1849, Rossetti was agreeing with Hunt that art should be intelligible to *all*, not merely the initiated few.[26] Unmistakably, that "all" meant the butcher-boy as well as the Liverpool merchant patron.

One poem is particular that shows Rossetti struggling

desperately to make his meaning intelligible to all is *The Cloud Confines.* Part of his problem may well have been that he was trying to be "contemplative, not to say philosophic," as Franz Hueffer put it.[27] The topic was one of the most baffling that man can face, the yearning to solve the riddle of his very existence, here and in the world to come. As Rossetti wrote his brother, the poem was "not meant to be a trifle."[28] Tracing the development of this poem from its inception in August, 1871, to its final form provides a fascinating glimpse into the mind of a poet at work.

Rossetti sent the first version of the poem to William Bell Scott on August 9. The opening stanza states the theme and explains the title:

> The day is dark and the night
>   To him that would search the heart;
>   No lips of cloud that will part
> Nor morning song in the light.
>   Only, gazing alone,
>   To him wild shadows are shown,
>   Deep under deep unknown,
> And height above unknown height.
>   Still we say as we go, —
>   'Strange to think by the way,
>   Whatever there is to know,
>   That shall we know one day.'

Succeeding stanzas ponder the mysteries of the past and of death, of hate and war, of love "that bleeds," and finally of what happens to man after death.

Each of the poem's five stanzas except the last concludes with the same refrain:

> Still we say as we go, —
>   'Strange to think by the way,
> Whatever there is to know,
>   That shall we know one day.'

In the final stanza of the original version, however, Rossetti attempts an answer other than "That shall we know one day":

> Our past is clean forgot,
> Our present is and is not,
> Our future's a sealed seed-plot,
> And what betwixt them are we?
> Atoms that nought can sever
>   From one world-circling will, —
> To throb at its heart forever,
>   Yet never to know it still.[29]

What he was trying to say in these lines, he wrote Scott, was this:

> I cannot suppose that any particle of life is *extinguished,* though its permanent individuality may be more than questionable. Absorption is not annihilation; and it is even a real retributive future for the special atom of life to be re-embodied (if so it were) in a world which its own former ideality had helped to fashion for pain or pleasure.[30]

Rossetti immediately went on, however, to admit one obvious difficulty: "But I believe I am of opinion with you, perhaps, that it is best not to try to squeeze the expression of it into so small a space. . . ."

Although he does not say so, perhaps Rossetti also felt that besides being obscure to the reader, he might shock his Victorian sensibilities. In addition, the final four lines broke the pattern of the repeated refrain in all the other stanzas, and there was a contradiction between the basic refrain's "That shall we know one day" and the final line's "Yet never to know it still." The rest of the poem satisfied him, and remained intact throughout four revisions to come. But he worried and wavered over these last four lines like a Nine-teenth-Century Prufrock with "decisions and revisions which a minute will reverse."

Toward the end of the month he wrote Scott, "What do you think of this as a change in the last four lines of *Cloud Confines*:

> Oh never from Thee to sever
>   Who wast and shalt be and art,
> To throb at Thy heart for ever
>   Yet never to know Thy heart."[31]

Gone are the atoms and the vague "world-circling will," replaced by an eternal "Thee" that suggests a conventional and wholly acceptable Victorian deity. This bothered Rossetti: "Does this not seem as if it meant a personal God? I don't think it need do so."

Meanwhile the contradiction of "Yet never to know it" remained, as well as the discrepancy between Rossetti's own vague theory of the hereafter and that of a personal God. And so the atom-answer of the first version and the personal God-answer of the second both must go. Rossetti confesses that the latter was "a thought of the moment," and claims that he has "since made it fit better:—as thus—

> And what must our birthright be?
> Oh, never from thee to sever,
>   Thou Will that shalt be and art,
> To throb at thy heart for ever,
>   Yet never to know thy heart."[32]

The world-circling "will" of the first version is restored, but now capitalized, as if in partial compromise to convention, but the "thee's" and "thy's" are not capitalized.

Rossetti then proceeds to reopen the whole matter in this very same letter to Scott with yet another version: "However, I now incline to reject this and adopt the other plan. . . . I should propose to end thus—

What words to say as we go?
What thoughts to think by the way?
What truth may there be to know?
And shall we know it one day?"[33]

Now Rossetti has given up the attempt to solve the riddle,
and questions replace answers. Now, too, there is an echo,
at least, of the refrain of the first four stanzas, and the contradiction of knowing vs. not-knowing is partly resolved by the
final question.

The poet has come a long way toward settling the problems posed by his first version of the close. Yet the decisions
and revisions continued. On September 2 he wrote Hake:
". . .I propose probably to alter the five lines thus. . ." and
proceeds to quote lines almost identical to those in version
3, previously rejected in his last letter to Scott.[34] Just eight
days later, however, he sent brother William a copy of the
poem, saying "the form of the four last lines there given is
the one I incline to adopt—thus, you see, leaving the whole
question open," and *reverts to version* 4! Significantly, he
tells William that he is adopting these lines "as the *safest*
course."[35] On September 11, he writes Hake, "I fancy I've
resolved now to leave the whole question open," and again it
is version 4 that he chooses.[36]

And so at last the conclusion of the poem seemed settled
upon. Not so! The final version of the lines, as published in
Ballads and Sonnets, 1881, is:

And what betwixt them are we?
    We who say as we go,—
    "Strange to think by the way,
    Whatever there is to know,
    That shall we know one day."

Thus Rossetti found solution to all the problems that had
confronted him in version 1, by using the same refrain that

had ended the first four stanzas in every version of the poem—a device that he had already considered while hesitating between versions 3 and 4, and had rejected because "to wind up with the old refrain would hardly be either valuable or artistic."[37]

Yet valuable and artistic it was indeed. The several barriers to rapport between poet and reader are gone. The retention of the refrain gives us the symmetry of structure we have a right to expect. The cramped, confused, and (to some, at least) perhaps unacceptable concept of an atomic hereafter no longer puzzles the will. There is no contradiction between knowing and not-knowing now; rather, there is the comfort that was implicit from the start of the poem: "Whatever there is to know, / That shall we know one day."

Nothing can serve better than the revisions and revisions of these four lines to illustrate the indecisiveness, the wavering between opposites, the self-mistrust that so marked Rossetti as man and poet.[38] But in this instance he won through. "By the bye," he wrote Caine, "you are right about *Cloud Confines,* which *is* my very best thing."[39] Of its sort, it is.

The desire for a larger circle of readers, for such a rapport with "the mass of mankind" as Morris enjoyed, also underlay Rossetti's fear of shocking the reader's sensibilities. He may have wished to be bolder, but in face of the "British Dragon," he often retreated. Again and again he advised, even begged, Swinburne to do likewise. To prepare the reader for the alarming *Poems and Ballads,* he urged Swinburne first to publish the more acceptable *Atalanta:* "It is calculated to put people in a better humour for the others, which, when they do come will still make a few not even over-particular hairs to stand on end." If Swinburne persisted in his Baudelairean excesses, "I warn you that the public will not be able to digest them."[40]

Rossetti was seriously perturbed about Swinburne's *Songs Before Sunrise,* and wrote the publisher, Ellis:

I think the *Crucifix* on the whole less objectionable perhaps
than the sonnets, though its last stanzas are startling. . . .
The "Christ" anathematized in the *Crucifix* is the priests'
corrupted and falsified God,—not the true one. But still
this might not appear clearly to everyone to whom the
phraseology would give a shock.[41]

Rossetti felt so strongly that Swinburne had a duty not to
alienate the larger circle of readers in this way that he risked
an open break with his friend. In a remarkable and moving
letter, after praising Swinburne's "glorious pieces of poetic
diction," he wrote:

But they resolve me to risk even your displeasure, by one
earnest remonstrance as to their publication. I cannot but
think absolutely that a poet like yourself belongs of right
to a larger circle of readers than this treatment of universal
feelings can include. . . . You have no right to imperil your
sacred relation to the minds of many men worthy to profit
by your mind, by using one form of metaphor rather than
another when its use involves such disproportionately
grave issues. . . . Do, do, my dear Swinburne, withdraw
these sonnets. . . . This is my birthday, by the bye. Do
make me the birthday gift I ask of you.[42]

Let those who think Rossetti a complete Art for Art's sake
poet ponder this letter.

Young Nolly Brown was another to whom Rossetti urged
"any modifications thought necessary for the circulation of
the book," and he was pleased to be able to say, "from what
I saw of it in its first form, I think you have managed so well
that the situation is retained, while much is abated of what
is unavoidably repelling in it."[43] The same reasoning evoked
this comment on Keats's *Eve's Apple*: "Of course I do not
consider that sexual passion, if nobly expressed, should be
excluded from poetry for any reason except that of not
restricting its circulation."[44]

So far as he could, Rossetti tried to practice what he preached, from the careful ordering of his poems to lure the reader on, to incessant revision to lessen or eliminate reader-shock, to outright refusal to publish a possibly offensive piece. As late as one month before the publication of the 1870 *Poems*, he wrote his publisher:

> I have all of a sudden been strongly advised, I think from a specially trustworthy quarter, that my book would begin very much better and please a much larger class of readers at the outset if it opened with the *Blessed Damozel* and not with *Troy Town*, which latter is supposed (and I think rightly) to be likely to please a smaller class.[45]

He had already written Swinburne: "I think of omitting altogether *Dennis Shand*, as rather chargeable with triviality and its objectionableness strengthening those who will rail at the more important *Jenny*. . . ."[46] Those who read *Dennis Shand* today may wonder what all the fuss was about, but the poem was not published in Rossetti's lifetime, and when it finally appeared in print nearly a quarter of a century later, William Rossetti thought it necessary to explain:

> If the public agree with me, they will say that the 'reprehensible' quality in the ballad, though not absolutely 'nil,' is really slight; and that Rossetti's action in with-holding it, while commendable on the ground of dignity and scrupulosity, went beyond any positive requirement in the case. If he had in fact been a member of a 'Fleshly School' of Poetry or of Poets, he would have 'made no bones' of publishing 'Dennis Shand.' His preference would have been in the direction of publication.[47]

It is easier to understand why Rossetti also banned the publication of *After the French Liberation of Italy,* in which the sexual act serves rather tastelessly as the basic image.

Such was the fate of poems that could not be revised into

a publicly acceptable form, for butchering a poem to "excise objectionabilities" was "unpardonable. Much better leave the whole out."[48] But if skillful editing or revising could save the work, Rossetti was all for it. Thus he wrote Mrs. Ann Gilchrist about the publishing of Blake's *Everlasting Gospel*, "if there is anything to shock the ordinary readers, it is merely the opening, which could be omitted."[49] And thus he revised his own poems, both before and after their publication. These somewhat unpleasant lines in the original version of *Jenny* were dropped before publication,

> When the hot arm makes the waist hot
> And the shaken breath fails and is not, —
> When the desire is overmuch,
> And the hands meddle as the lips touch, —
>
> (ll. 14-17)

as were also

> Thine arms are bare and thy shoulders shine,
> And through the kerchief and through the vest
> Strikes the white of each breathing breast,
> And the down is warm on thy velvet cheek,
> And the thigh from thy rich side slopes oblique.[50]
>
> (ll. 112-116)

After Buchanan's attack on "fleshliness," the sonnets *Vain Virtues* and *Love's Redemption* in *The House of Life* both underwent revision. Reacting to Buchanan's charge that *Vain Virtues* "pursues the metaphor to the very pit of beastliness," Rossetti changed

> Of anguish, while the *scorching bridegroom* leaves
> Their refuse maidenhood abominable.
> Night sucks them down, the *garbage* of the pit.

to

Of anguish, while the *pit's pollution* leaves
Their refuse maidenhood abominable.
Night sucks them down, the *tribute* of the pit.[51]

Love's Redemption was given both a new title and a change
in basic imagery, one change obviously requiring the other.
The original title and basic imagery of the octave echoed
Christ's redemption of man:

O thou who at Love's hour ecstatically
  Unto my *lips* dost ever more present,
  The body and blood of love in sacrament
Whom I have neared and felt thy breath to be
The inmost incense of his sanctuary;
    Who without speech hast owned him, and, intent
    Upon his will, thy life with mine has blent,
And murmured *o'er the cup, "Remember me!"*

With the changing of the word in the title, "Redemption"
to "Testament," the crucial part of the original octave's imagery is also dropped. The new octave reads:

O thou who at Love's hour ecstatically
  Unto my *heart* dost ever more present,
  Clothed with his fire, thy heart his testament;
Whom I have neared and felt thy breath to be
The inmost incense of his sanctuary;
    Who without speech hast owned him, and, intent
    Upon his will, thy life with mine has blent,
And murmured, *"I am thine, thou'rt one with me!"*

With his revisions, Rossetti may have lost both the charge
of blasphemy—and the poem. Certainly, in the second, 1881,
version, "testament," "incense," "sanctuary," and the blent
lives no longer make much sense. The sestet, too, which
remained unchanged, fits badly with the new octave.
    Title changes were among the easiest and most frequent
ways in which Rossetti sought to counter possible objections.

Most notable was the change of *Placata Venere* to *Nuptial Sleep*, "which I think will help it stand fire."[52] Vain hope! *Nuptial Sleep* was one of Buchanan's prime targets—despite a title change that suggested the lovers were now legally entitled to make love—and Rossetti removed it completely from the next edition of *The House of Life.* In particular, as Grylls and others have noted, in the revised titles of many sonnets in *The House of Life*, "Love" is played down. *Love's Compass* was changed to *Heart's Compass, Love's Pageant* to *Beauty's Pageant, Sleepless Love* to *Sleepless Dreams, The Love-Lamp* to *The Lamp's Shrine, Love's Antiphony* to *Youth's Antiphony, Love-light* to *Soul Light,* and so on.

Grylls and Doughty are among recent critics who suggest that these changes were made to mask the fact that the sonnets were inspired by the poet's love for Jane Morris. This may be so, for they were all written during the 1869-1871 period when his passion for Janey apparently waxed hottest. And when, in 1881, Janey worried lest she be recognized in the sonnets, Rossetti reassured her, "Every new piece that is not quite colorless will be withdrawn and the book [*Ballads and Sonnets*] postponed."[53] (Part of the new colorless-ness came from changing references to dark hair, which Janey had, to fair.)

If the theory be right, these changes were made to forestall a very special objection: Rossetti's illicit passion for a woman who was not only married, but married to a man who had been for years one of his closest friends. If a mask, these title-changes represented a rather transparent one. Whatever the new title, the theme remains Love. *Heart's Compass* still asks, "and is not thy name Love?" *Beauty's Pageant* is "Love's very vesture and elect disguise." *Sleepless Dreams* asks, "would love feign in thee. . .?" *Lamp's Shrine* still declares "at Love's shrine/ Myself. . .will set. . .thy heart." And so it goes with the others.

Rossetti, it seems, would go only so far in mollifying the

reader. If the "mass of mankind" demanded too much, the
artist (at least so he claimed) must remain true to himself.
"He taught me," says Burne-Jones, "to have no shame of my
own ideas. . .to seek no popularity, to be altogether myself."[54]
But who can truly know oneself? Surely not a man of so many
inner conflicts as Rossetti. Despite the great success of his
1870 *Poems,* he ruefully wrote Scott: "I fear I have no more
of the popular element than yourself."[55] What solace
remained he may have found in viewing his work as he
viewed Blake's : "While anyone who can here find anything
to love will be the poet-painter's guests, still such a feast is
spread first of all for those who can know at a glance that
it is theirs and was meant for them."[56]

THE IDEAL OF THE POET

There is nothing unique about Rossetti's expressed "lifelong dissatisfaction. . .experienced from the disparity of aim
and attainment."[57] Such is the lot of the artist whose ideal
is perfection. Nor can one question Rossetti's assertion that
peering over the shoulder of the poet as he works must be the
"double of himself, the self-critic, who should always be one
with the poet."[58] A "searching self-criticism," as he says, may
lead to such a remolding of a work "as to give the readers the
best possible guarantee of its being worth his while to follow
the author in his future course."[59] In this vein, he scolded
James Smetham, a rather unsuccessful painter and essayist:

> I am afraid that you will think no better of me for pronounc-
> ing the commonplace verdict that what you lack is simply
> ambition, i.e. the feeling of pure rage and self-hatred when
> any one else does better than you do. This in an ambitious
> mind leads not to envy in the least, but to self-scrutiny on
> all sides, and that to something if anything can. You com-
> fort yourself with other things, whereas art must be its
> own comforter or else comfortless.[60]

This echoed Rossetti's belief that just as the true artist will first perceive in another's works the beauties, so he must first seek "in his own work the defects."[61]

But what if the self-critic be a man of deep, innate self-mistrust? And what if the aims he considered ideal be so conflicting as to be irreconcilable? What if he sought "arduousness" and "intensity" *and* "momentousness" *and* "fulness"—and yet compactness? These are among the dilemmas that faced Rossetti as self-critic. It is not, as E. B. Burgum has suggested, that only after the Buchanan attack did Rossetti "dismally. . .[begin] to feel that something was wrong with his work."[62] He had forebodings of failure as early as the *Hand and Soul* of 1849. In 1854, when he was only twenty-four, he was asking in *The Landmark*:

> Was *that* the landmark? What,—the foolish well
>   Whose wave, low down, I did not stoop to drink,
>
> But lo! The path is missed, I must go back,
> And thirst to drink when next I reach the spring.

In *Lost Days*, written perhaps as early as 1858, when he was thirty, he wondered sadly:

> The lost days of my life until today,
> What were they, could I see them on the street
>
> Each one a murdered self, with low last breath.
> "I am thyself,—what hast thou done to me?"

In 1853, Rossetti had said, "I can never get over the weakness of making a thing as good as I can manage."[63] He may have meant to be wry; he was certainly right. For with him, this effort proved often a weakness. Prophetically enough, in 1858 he was lamenting: "I find no shady hill or vale, though, in all these places and pursuits which I have to do with. It seems all glare and change, and nothing well done. Another man might do better, no doubt. . . . It is always to be thus with me."[64]

At times he believed he had actually captured the chimera. Then he would write exultantly of a picture or a poem that it was "the best I have done!" Soon, however, the glow faded. In painting, picture after picture was hailed as his best work, only to yield to another—without the steady march toward perfection that this would imply. In 1848, it was "Genevieve"; in 1849, "Annunciation"; 1853, a sketch of Aunt Charlotte; 1855, "The Nativity"; 1866, "Lilith" (later redone with a new model's head replacing that of Fanny Cornforth); 1870, a head of Mrs. Morris; and 1873, "Proserpina." His own evaluation of his poems shifted similarly. He told Sharp that *A Last Confession, Dante at Verona,* and *Nineveh* were his masterpieces.[65] Later he thought *The King's Tragedy* his magnum opus, a position once held by *Troy Town.*[66] The year before his death, he was calling *Cloud Confines* "my very best thing."[67]

Particularly as he neared publication of his *Poems* in 1870 did Rossetti assert his desire for perfection. In 1869, he boasted to Shields that he had done no "pot-boiling" in poetry.[68] He wrote to Swinburne, "I want to make all quite perfect if I can"[69] By the end of the year he again wrote Shields: "It is all very close and careful work. . . . It is certainly the best work of my life."[70] Early in 1870, the same emphasis appears in a letter to Skelton: "Did you see some sonnets of mine in the *Fortnightly* nearly a year ago? I had tried to make them as perfect as in me lay."[71] If he protested too much about his efforts, he could not help it. Shortly before his death he was still proclaiming his high level of attainment to Caine: "But in truth, if I have any distinction as a sonnet-writer, it is that I never admit a sonnet which is not fully on the level of every other."[72]

Rossetti frequently censured "unequal" artists, those

who could approximate perfection in a poem or two, but who refused to limit their publications to only their best. Thus he wrote Arthur O'Shaughnessy, "Will you excuse my saying this. I cannot but think that you write far too much and too rapidly to develop your best resources."[73] He also said of Morris: "The fact is Topsy writes too much both for his own sake and for that of his appreciators."[74] He had much the same objection to such literary luminaries as Hake, Charles Whitehead, Fanny Kemble, William Davies, and John Payne. Rossetti's attitude toward them all can be summed up in the following comment: "One younger poet among them, Philip Marston, has written many sonnets which yield to few or none by any poet whatever; but he has printed such a large number in the aggregate, and so unequal one with another that the great ones are not to be found by opening at random."[75] It was one of the virtues of Keats that *Cap and Bells* was "the only unworthy stuff Keats ever wrote except an early trifle or two."[76] (Here Rossetti conveniently ignores his reservations about some of Keats's sonnets.)

If O'Shaughnessy and Morris wrote far too much, Rossetti wrote too little. In bulk alone he is too slight. There is a measure of justice in Matthew Arnold's calling Wordsworth a great poet because he gives us "so much to rest upon." Rossetti might have retorted that the "rest" too often turned to slumber. But Rossetti gives us too little to rest upon. Not only are his poems too few in number; they are also too restricted as to theme and subject matter, too slight in scope, even too limited in length. The reputations of neither Dante, Shakespeare, nor Milton depend upon their sonnets. Whether or not Rossetti could have written more poems, longer poems, and greater poems can only be guessed at. The fact is, he deliberately did not try. Late in life he both reproached and consoled himself in a single, significant statement: "Sloth, alas, has but too much to answer for with me; and it is one of the reasons (though I will not say the only one) why I have always fallen back on quantity in the little I have ever done."[77] In discussing a sequel to *The Bride's Prelude,* he said, "I suppose I must set to and finish it one day, old as it is." But then he added, "I hate long poems."[78]

Rossetti felt, as he said in a letter to a young poet, Théophile Marzials, that "a poem of six lines, made perfect, adds something to one's permanent work; but a poem of 6000 adds nothing to that, if left imperfect."[79] Striving for "arduousness" and "intensity" as he did, Rossetti would no doubt have agreed with Poe, whom he admired so much, when Poe wrote: "A poem must intensely excite. . . . But all excitement is, from psychal necessity, transient. It cannot be sustained through a poem of great length. In the course of an hour's reading at most, it flags, fails; and then the poem is, in effect, no longer such."[80] This fear of flagging excitement was precisely the reason that Rossetti revised his first scheme for *Rose Mary*: "I had originally meant to intercept the stanzas with a running and very varied burden," he wrote Hake, "but I found the poem was too long and intricate for such treatment, as the mind was overtaxed with a double current of ideas."[81]

But the very methods of composition that Rossetti advocated and practiced were hardly conducive to long — or great — poems. Nit-picking perfectionism rarely leads to the creation of an epic. There were other factors limiting his poetic productivity: ill health, for one, and more important, the greater demands of painting, to which he had to yield because painting paid as poetry did not. Rossetti gave this latter as the reason why he, like Coleridge, had written so little poetry. Of Coleridge, Rossetti said that he conceived "the leading fact of his career" to be "the sad fact of how little of it was devoted to [poetic] work." Rossetti continued: "The last is such as I (alas!) can sympathize with, though what has excluded more poetry with me (mountains of it I

don't want to heap) has chiefly been livelihood necessity."[82]
There are mountains. . .and mountains. Great as were
Rossetti's talents, great also were his limitations. He was
not destined to tower among the Alps of literature.

The most important result of Rossetti's personal ideal
of "perfection," in short, was perhaps the poems he did *not*
write. Yet the work he did produce did not emerge unscathed.
On the whole, his paintings seem to have suffered from less
skillful revising than his poems. Several owners, indeed,
became so incensed at alterations Rossetti made in their
pictures that they refused to let him get his hands on any
others. William Sharp describes a number of paintings
bought by a Mr. George Rae, and continues: "Of these,
Rossetti subsequently requested for 'improvement' the last
named ["Chapel before the Lists"], but the result was so
unsatisfactory that Mr. Rae wisely resisted many after-re-
quests to retouch the others."[83]

In contrast, the major alterations in many of his poems,
such as *The Blessed Damozel* and *Sister Helen*, are indubitable improvements. P. F. Baum cites the revisions of *The
Blessed Damozel* as of "special interest as a study of the
poet's search for perfection."[84] Yet the Beryl-Songs in *Rose
Mary* are without doubt an addition for the worse, as (to my
taste at least) is the intrusion of Cousin Nell in the revised
version of *Jenny,* with such gauche lines as:

> My cousin Nell is fond of love.
> And she's the girl I'm proudest of.

The last two stanzas added to *Upon the Cliffs: Noon* (retitled
The Sea-Limits) overload a relatively simple poem and in-
troduce an idea not prepared for in the original two stanzas.
The Cloud Confines would have been badly damaged had
Rossetti retained the two new stanzas that he wrote in 1873.
Any number of changes of words and lines in *The House of*

Life are of debatable value. Rossetti's fussy and incessant revising drew this attack in 1869, according to brother William: "Swinburne objects much to Gabriel's continual revising of his old poems, and thinks indeed that Gabriel's whole system of verse-writing is becoming somewhat over-elaborate."[85]

The ideal of perfection that Rossetti set for the poet, leading from "searching self-criticism" through "continual revising" to "lifelong dissatisfaction" clearly did not end in perfection. On the contrary, this ideal worked as a limiting factor on the gifts that Rossetti thought essential to the poet, gifts that he himself had in abundant measure.

NOTES

[1]*L & M,* II, 112.
[2]Mills, p. 128.
[3]*D & W,* II, 798.
[4]*L & M,* I, 304.
[5]*Collected Works,* I, 489.
[6]Skelton, pp. 85-6.
[7]*Collected Works,* I, 489.
[8]*Ibid.,* p. 499.
[9]*Ibid.*
[10]*Ibid.,* p. 490.
[11]*D & W,* II, 798.
[12]*Collected Works,* I, 521.
[13]*Ibid.,* p. 496.
[14]*Ibid.,* p. 454.
[15]Baum and Ghodes, eds., *Letters of William M. Rossetti* (Durham, 1934), pp. 6-7.
[16]*D & W,* I, 45-6.
[17]*Ibid.,* II, 806-7.
[18]J. C. Troxell, *Rossetti's Sister Helen* (New Haven, 1939), p. 14.
[19]Caine, p. 126.
[20]*D & W,* II, 721.
[21]*Ibid.,* p. 777.

[22]*Ibid.*, p. 807.

[23]*Ibid.*, p. 812.

[24]B. Chamneys, *Coventry Patmore* (London, 1900), II, 232-3.

[25]Quoted in *The London Times*, May 11, 1928.

[26]Holman Hunt, I, 105.

[27]W. M. Rossetti, ed., *The Poems of Dante Gabriel Rossetti* (London, 1904), II, 218.

[28]*D & W*, III, 1003.

[29]*Ibid.*, pp. 972-3. For easier reference, this and each succeeding version of the last five lines of the final stanza will be numbered consecutively in parenthesis: (1), (2), etc.

[30]*Ibid.*, pp. 989-90.

[31]*Ibid.*, p. 989.

[32]*Ibid.*, p. 990.

[33]*Ibid.*

[34]*Ibid.*, p. 999.

[35]*Ibid.*, p. 1003. (The italics are mine.)

[36]*Ibid.*, p. 1005.

[37]*Ibid.*, p. 990.

[38]In 1873, he actually wrote two additional stanzas for this poem — fortunately later discarded.

[39]Caine, p. 144.

[40]*Ashley Catalogue*, IV, 115.

[41]*D & W*, II, 859.

[42]*Ibid.*, p. 873.

[43]Ingram, p. 83.

[44]D. G. Rossetti, *John Keats, Criticism and Comment* (London, 1919), pp. 16-7.

[45]*D & W*, II, 821.

[46]*Ibid.*, p. 798.

[47]W. M. Rossetti, *The Poems of Dante Gabriel Rossetti*, II, 227.

[48]Caine, p. 195.

[49]Gilchrist, p. 136.

[50]Baum, "The Bancroft Manuscripts," p. 49 and p. 51.

[51]Italics added in this and the next sonnet to indicate changes between 1870 and 1881 versions.

[52]*D & W*, II, 734.

[53]Grylls, p. 185.

[54]Burne-Jones, I, 149.

[55]Scott, II, 136.

[56]*Collected Works*, I, 459.

[57]*D & W*, IV, 1470. Rossetti here was speaking of his painting, but the quotation applies equally well to his poetry.

[58]*Collected Works,* I, 507.

[59]*Ibid.,* pp. 500-01.

[60]*D & W,* II, 581.

[61]*Collected Works,* I, 510.

[62]E. B. Burgum, "Rossetti and the Ivory Tower," *Sewanee Review,* XXXVII (October, 1929), p. 435.

[63]*L & M,* II, 112.

[64]W. M. Rossetti, *Ruskin: Rossetti: Preraphaelitism,* pp. 205-6.

[65]Sharp, p. 321.

[66]*Ibid.,* p. 378 and p. 361.

[67]Caine, p. 144.

[68]Mills, p. 128.

[69]*Ashley Catalogue,* VII, 15.

[70]Mills, pp. 138-9.

[71]Skelton, p. 89.

[72]Caine, p. 248.

[73]*D & W,* III, 1040.

[74]*Ibid.,* II, 773.

[75]Caine, p. 243.

[76]D. G. Rossetti, *Keats,* pp. 20-21.

[77]*L & M,* I, 421.

[78]Caine, pp. 264-5.

[79]*D & W,* III, 1164.

[80]E. A. Poe, *The Complete Works* (New York, 1903), V, 167-8.

[81]*D & W,* III, 1005.

[82]Caine, p. 165.

[83]Sharp, pp. 153-4.

[84]Baum, *The Blessed Damozel,* p. xxi.

[85]W. M. Rossetti, *Rossetti Papers,* p. 407.

V
Rossetti and the Poet, II

A Shakespearian sonnet is better than the most perfect form,
because Shakespeare wrote it.

Rossetti to Hall Caine, approx. 1880[1]

The chief gifts that Rossetti believed a poet must have were imagination, invention, "primary vital impulse," "fundamental brainwork," originality and, of course, technical ability. Except for the last, however, analysis of Rossetti's criticism shows that all of these gifts were so closely interrelated as to be almost one and the same thing—the one attribute that most characterized the boy Rossetti, and that most governed his choice of favorite authors: *imagination.*

THE IMAGINATION OF THE POET

A Coleridge could theorize about imagination, dividing it into "primary" and "secondary," and distinguishing both from "fancy." But Rossetti was no Coleridge. "Facts," he once wrote crisply, "and descriptions of facts are in my line, but to talk *about* a thing merely is what I could never well manage."[2] What Rossetti meant by "imagination," therefore, is best arrived at by discovering what he meant by invention, fundamental brainwork, and the rest.

To begin with, it is apparent that to Rossetti, poetry and imagination were almost synonymous. In his lexicon, poetry is most often simply "imaginative work," and poets "men of imagination," as when he asserts that "the men of imagination in England have always been a persecuted sect,"[3] and that "the three greatest English imaginations are Shakespeare, Coleridge, and Shelley,"[4] and when he refers to English poetry as "England's theatre of imagination."[5]

That Rossetti himself had great powers of imagination cannot be questioned. The testimony of those who knew him is impressive. Coventry Patmore tells of Rossetti's "extraordinary faculty for seeing objects in such a fierce light of imagination as very few poets have been able to throw upon external things."[6] William Rossetti attributes his brother's collapse in 1872 in part to his "too active and unappeased imagination."[7] Burne-Jones called Rossetti's generous interest in other men's ideas "part of his enormous imagination."[8] Sharp speaks of the "irresistibly imaginative groove in which his thoughts moved."[9] Hall Caine goes so far as to say that "the poet never existed, perhaps, who, while at work, lived so vividly in the imagined situation."[10] And Watts-Dunton goes even further:

> So powerful (that is to say, so childlike) was Rossetti's imagination, so entirely did it dominate an intellect of unusual subtlety, that [invented] stories interested him just as much as real adventures, and though he knew them to be gossamer fictions woven at the moment of telling, he would be as much affected by an unhappy catastrophe as though they had been incidents of real life, and would sometimes beg for the catastrophe to be altered.[11]

To pile up proof about Rossetti's extraordinary imagination is not to define the word as it applies to him. But from these quotations emerges one fact with which to begin building a definition: Rossetti's imagination enabled him to put himself into other men's ideas, to live in an imagined situation, to see gossamer fictions as real adventures. Paull Franklin Baum has called attention to Rossetti's "power to dramatize an imaginary 'moment.'"[12] The creation of characters and situations that—though fictional—seem movingly real is commonly called "invention." Invention, then, is the means whereby imagination makes itself manifest: imagination is the faculty, invention the process. This is the relationship between the two that Rossetti saw when he wrote of Burne-Jones:

> He has oceans of *imagination,* and in this respect there has been nobody like him since Botticelli. If, as I hold, the noblest picture is a painted poem, then I say that in the whole history of art there has never been a painter more greatly gifted in *invention.*[13]

This probably is why Rossetti speaks of "invention" rather than of imagination as his best quality.[14] To say that invention should be coupled with originality may seem redundant, yet Rossetti made a great point of his originality. In 1851 he boasted that his religious subjects were "indeed altogether original in inventions."[15] In 1869 he carefully assured Swinburne that the story of a contemplated poem, *The Doom of the Sirens,* was his "own invention."[16] He would go to any lengths to preserve this originality, as when—in the course of writing *The King's Tragedy*—he wrote Shields: "Helps wrote a tragedy called *Catherine Douglas.* I have avoided seeing it in order that I might be able to say it is unknown to me in case any of his treatment should co-incide with mine."[17]

Interrelated with the imagination, invention and originality that Rossetti demanded of the poet were "primary vital impulse" and "fundamental brainwork." Essential to this primary impulse was the poet's own "anguish and ardour."[18] The emotion necessary to the poetic process was not Wordsworth's emotion "recollected in tranquility," however, but rather emotion that racked the heart even as one wrote. He described his method of composition to Caine: "I lie on the couch, the racked and tortured medium, never permitted an instant's surcease of agony until the thing on hand is finished."[19] Of the sonnet *Without Her*, he said, "I cannot tell you at what terrible moment it was wrung from me."[20] Sometimes preceding, sometimes accompanying, the emotion of creation was what Rossetti called "fundamental brainwork," of which invention was a part.

That Rossetti related "fundamental brainwork" to the process of invention is shown in a letter to Scott, in which he discusses having his pictures lithographed: "If one could do something with one's inventions (much the best quality I have as a painter) one might really get one's brain into print before one died."[21] It is necessary to realize all that Rossetti meant by "brain" to avoid misinterpreting his statement to Caine: "I would not be too anxious, were I you, about anything in choice of sonnets except the brains and the music."[22] For here "music" means all of technique; "brains" means all of imagination, invention, originality, primary vital impulse, and fundamental brainwork. Further analysis of what Rossetti had to say about fundamental brainwork and originality will make this clear, and further illuminate what he meant by "imagination."

THE FUNDAMENTAL BRAINWORK OF THE POET

"Fundamental brainwork" is probably the best known of Rossetti's critical dicta, and often, it would seem, the only one. Taken out of context, it can be made to appear as an insistence upon intellectuality in poetry. Then when Rossetti's own work is examined and intellectuality is found to be conspicuous by its absence, Rossetti stands accused of either empty boasting or utter nonsense. For who could expect the young Rossetti, who loved all things imaginative — and disliked all things dogmatic, philosophical, and scientific — to grow into a painter and poet who put cold intellect above warm imagination?

The fact is that what Rossetti actually did was to make imagination and intellect ("brains") amount to the same thing, just as he had imagination and invention, and invention and brains. A logician, indeed, would be forced by the poet's premises to come to the same conclusion: if imagination is "invention," and invention is "brains," then obviously imagination is brains. Rossetti's premises represent fuzzy thinking, true. But that is just the point. He was not a clear or precise thinker, and his "fundamental brainwork" is not a demand that the poet be one. As Rossetti said, he could deal with facts, but not talk *about* them. The sonnet *From Dawn to Noon* is a frank confession that the processes of orderly thought were a mystery to him:

> Even so the thought that is at length fullgrown
> Turns back to note the sun-smit paths, all gray
> And marvelous once, where first it walked alone;
> And haply doubts, amid the blenching day,
> Which most or least impelled its onward way, —
> Those unknown things or these things overknown.

Such a way of "thought," if the word is at all justified, is more imaginative than intellectual. Rossetti's confusion of intellect and imagination is obvious when he says: "I am ashamed to belong to a profession in which the possession of *intellect* is rather a disqualification than an advantage. The men of *imagination* in England have always been a persecuted sect."[23]

William Sharp said that Rossetti had "but one aim in art — to have something to say first, and then say it beautifully."[24] Here are the "brains" and the "music" again — the two major elements that run through so much of Rossetti's own criticism. For example, he wrote of "some striking tales. . .better sometimes I thought in idea than in execution."[25] Often the "brains" is thus expressed as "thought" or the main "idea," and "music" as execution. So of a Watts-Dunton sonnet he said "the main idea [is] unquestionably grand and valuable," but it "lacked subtlety of execution."[26] Blanco White's sonnet *Night and Death* was "difficult to overrate in *thought* — probably in this respect unsurpassable, but easy to overrate as regards its workmanship."[27]

Fundamental brainwork in his own peculiar sense of the term must be understood when Rossetti praises "mind" or "intellect" or "mental qualities." Witness his statement about Leighton's paintings: "As for purely intellectual qualities, expression, intention, etc., there is little as yet of them; but I think that in art richness or arrangement is so nearly allied to these that where it exists (in an earnest man) they will probably supervene."[28] Witness, too, his sincere appeal to Swinburne that his poems permit "many men. . .to profit by your mind,"[29] and his assertion that *Ben Nevis* was perhaps Keats's "most thoughtful" poem.[30] Rossetti has the same connotations in mind when he speaks of Deverell's paintings as having "a true interest for those who can discover mental qualities in art,"[31] or when he praises Blake's "mental resources"[32] or his "depth of thought."[33] These "mental resources," remember, had nothing to do with Blake's metaphysics: *Tiriel* was "too heavy," and therefore Rossetti refused even to read it. Once, in fact, Rossetti "dealt firmly" with a man who dared to discuss metaphysics in his presence.[34] Rossetti's "brains" had no room for abstract speculation.

This is exactly what Rossetti said about fundamental brainwork in his letter to Caine:

> You have too great a habit of speaking of special octave,
> sestette, or line. Conception, my boy, *FUNDAMENTAL
> BRAINWORK,* that is what makes the difference in all art.
> Work your metal as much as you like, but first take care
> that it is worth working. A Shakespearian sonnet is better
> than the most perfect form, because Shakespeare wrote
> it.[35]

Once more there is the twofold division, the ore (the conception, the brainwork), and the working of it (the execution,
the form). And, as always, there is the insistence that the
"brains" must come before the "music": *first* "take care that
it is gold," and *better* "than form. . .because Shakespeare
wrote it."

Rossetti found two kinds of brainwork possible. First
and highest was that in which "the work has been all mentally 'cartooned,' as it were, beforehand, by a process intensely conscious but patient and silent — an occult evolution
of life."[36] This kind of conception Rossetti tried to achieve in
his own poetry, but it was difficult. He even feared that "of
this order of poetic action, — the omnipotent freewill of the
artist's mind, — our curbed and slackening world may seem
to have seen the last."[37]

The second and lower order of conception Rossetti described as "devoted and ardent, but less building on assured
foundations than self-questioning in the very moment of
action or even later."[38] This involved only partial "cartooning"
at best, with patching or "remoulding" afterwards to bring
the poem nearer to the ideal of perfection. Generally, Rossetti
seems to have attempted the first order of perfect "cartooning
beforehand," and then — mistrusting his success — resorted
to the second by revising.

Interestingly enough, at their best Rossetti's major revisions amounted to a second go-round for the first and highest kind of fundamental brainwork, where the initial conception of the poem is re-examined, and significantly changed.

For some poems, the result was definite improvement. Two such are *The Blessed Damozel* and *Sister Helen*. The former is of special interest, for despite Rossetti's statement to Caine about *The Blessed Damozel*, "which I wrote (and have altered little since) when I was eighteen," the poem in truth underwent numerous revisions.[39] In his excellent analysis of these revisions, P. F. Baum points out that Stanza 18 was the only stanza never changed in any way.[40] There is no need to repeat Baum's conclusions here, but a series of changes that involve the lover on earth are useful in showing how Rossetti continued his fundamental brainwork even after a poem had been published.

The Blessed Damozel was first published in the PRB *Germ,* in 1850. For its next appearance in print, in the *Oxford and Cambridge Magazine* in 1856, Rossetti added the following stanza reflecting the lover's thoughts:

(Ah sweet! Even now, in that bird's song,
　　Strove not her accents there,
Fain to be hearkened? When those bells
　　Possessed the mid-day air,
Strove not her steps to reach my side
　　Down all the trembling stair?[41]

In the 1856 version, this stanza was placed before Stanza 17.[42] But in the 1870 *Poems*, this stanza was moved to become Stanza 11, an excellent change. Now, instead of being introduced early in the poem and then being ignored until nearly the end, the lover is presented at almost equal intervals throughout the poem: in Stanzas 4, 11, 17 and (the last stanza) 24. Moreover, after the 1850 publication, Rossetti permanently cancelled two stanzas that Baum describes as "so disconcerting as to interfere with the general tone of the poem."[43] Again it is the lover talking:

(Alas! to *her* wise simple mind
　　These things were all but known

Before: they trembled on her sense,—
  Her voice had caught their tone.
Alas for lonely heaven! Alas
  For life wrung out alone!

Alas, and though the end were reached?
  Was *thy* part understood
Or borne in trust? And for her sake
  Shall this too be found good?—
May the close lips that knew not prayer
  Praise ever, though they would?)[44]

As Baum points out, these stanzas reflected serious doubts. The lover is distrustful of her prophecy of reunion in heaven. He is not sure that this reunion would be best for *her*. He was not religious on earth; could he be so after death? Baum was right. The loss of these lines was a gain.

Sister Helen also was frequently revised between its first publication in the *Dusseldorf Annual* in 1854 and Rossetti's final version in the 1881 *Poems*.[45] Pertinent here are two stanzas that Rossetti added in 1869, and eight added in 1879. In August of 1869, he wrote a new stanza to open the poem, "as Scott said the impression of what was going on was not perfectly distinct."[46] Similarly "valuable for elucidation" was the addition in September of the stanza (18 in the final version):

'But he calls for ever on your name,
              Sister Helen,
And says that he melts before a flame.'
'My heart for his pleasure fared the same,
              Little brother.'
        (O Mother, Mary Mother,
Fire at the heart, between Hell and Heaven.)

This gives the first explanation of Sister Helen's hatred: "My heart for his pleasure fared the same."

Much more important were the stanzas added in 1879, for these gave a whole new dimension to the poem, "to humanize Helen, besides lifting the tragedy to a yet sterner height."[47] What Rossetti did was to introduce a whole new character, Keith of Ewern's bride, who comes in her turn to beg, vainly, that her husband be spared. In the original, there was no suggestion that Ewern had married. Now the three days that Sister Helen has been melting her waxen man are not any old three days, but the three days since her lover married another woman. She is not only a woman spurned, but a woman spurned for a triumphant bride. Sister Helen's rejection of the various pleas *is* humanized, and the tragedy lifted to a sterner height.

Rossetti's insertion of this new and vital addition to his original conception of the poem is most skillful. After Keith of Eastholm's appeal to Sister Helen, the wedding is first referred to in what became Stanza 14 of the final version:

'Three days ago, on his marriage morn,
                  Sister Helen,
He sickened, and lies since then forlorn.'
'For bridegroom's side is the bride a thorn,
                  Little brother?'
      (O Mother, Mary Mother,
Cold bridal cheer, between Hell and Heaven!)

Then, in six consecutive stanzas following the petitions of Keith of Westholm and Keith of Keith, Rossetti inserts the plea of the bride, beginning with

'A lady's here, by a dark steed brought,'

and ending with the bitter lines,

'They've caught her to Westholm's saddle-bow,
                  Sister Helen,
And her moonlit hair gleams white in its flow.'

'Let it turn whiter than winter snow,
                Little brother!'
          (O Mother, Mary Mother
Woe-withered gold, between Hell and Heaven!)[48]

Finally, in what became Stanza 39, there is a last, poignant glimpse of the despairing bride:

'Flank to flank are the three steeds gone,
                Sister Helen,
But the lady's dark steed goes alone.'
'And lonely her bridegroom's soul hath flown,
                Little brother.'
          (O Mother, Mary Mother,
The lonely ghost, between Hell and Heaven!)

As Rossetti told Caine, "the gain is immense."[49] And as he wrote Janey Morris, "in fact, once thought of, I cannot think how I never did it before."[50] To my mind, the addition of this episode to *Sister Helen* was Rossetti's most brilliant application of further fundamental brainwork to his first basic conception of a poem.

Donald Stauffer has described the two ways in which poets may arrive at a basic conception to embody in verse. They may either "begin with a proposition which they proceed to illustrate," or "begin with a specific experience which they proceed to interpret."[51] Rossetti used both methods. Usually he began with a specific experience (real or imagined) or emotion. "I hardly ever do produce a sonnet except on some basis of special momentary emotion," he wrote Scott. "But I think there is another class admissible also—and that is the only other I practice, viz. the class depending on a line or two clearly given you, you know not whence, and calling up a sequence of ideas."[52]

From a proposition to illustrate ("sequence of ideas")

came sonnets like *The Dark Glass* and *The Choice.* But so often, as many of the sonnets in *The House of Life* suggest, the inspiration was "special momentary emotion." As Watts-Dunton said, Rossetti's imagination was too powerful for his intellect to predominate for long. Rossetti admitted this when he said of *Soothsay,* another poem of the illustrative order, "such like verses do not interest me much."[53] He acknowledged "rather a grudge against the three sonnets called *The Choice.* "[54]

His longer poems for the most part also stem from a "momentary emotion," aroused by the fierce imagination that could make "gossamer fictions" affect him "as though they had been incidents of real life." *The Blessed Damozel,* he told Caine, grew from his desire to reverse Poe's *Raven,* and show the longings of a maid in heaven for her lover on earth.[55] The structure of *The Burden of Nineveh* suggests that the poem was evoked by Rossetti's momentary glimpse of, and reaction to, the carrying of the idol into the British Museum. The dramatic situations of *The White Ship, The King's Tragedy, Eden Bower, Troy Town,* and *Rose Mary* all certainly came before whatever interpretation Rossetti gave them. Watts-Dunton describes this aspect of Rossetti's fundamental brainwork, saying "Rossetti's imaginative conceptions came to him. . .in actual pictures which he afterwards translated into words."[56]

The actual experience, the fact, the "concrete" as brother William put it, were the food on which Rossetti's conception fed, not abstract or theoretic propositions.[57] Rossetti censured Hake for attempting the latter: "But we fear that too great and probably organic abstraction of mind interferes continually with the projection of his thoughts."[58] To Rossetti, abstract thinking meant only confusion and obscurity. Therefore he advised the young writer John Payne "never to write except to embody a conception which you feel sure to be a "separate and distinct one."[59] One wonders where the "separate and distinct" conception was when Rossetti was wading through the morass of the final stanza of *The Cloud Confines*.[60]

Rossetti's creative process, his personal kind of fundamental brainwork, was an established routine by 1869. First would come the emotional impulse or dramatic situation that impelled him to write. Then came the brainwork that provided the details with which to set forth the emotions or situation. Next (for the narrative poems at least) came actual "cartooning" upon the heels of this mental cartooning. This usually consisted of making a prose synopsis of the story to be told.[61] Then came the actual writing of the poem. All this can be thought of as Rossetti's attempt to achieve that epitome of fundamental brainwork "when the work has been all mentally cartooned. . .beforehand." After the first draft of the poem came the lower order of brainwork, where books were searched through for the precise word wanted, where lines were polished and repolished, and sections were added or subtracted as the poet's confidence waxed and waned.

Evidence for the preliminary cartooning is available for many of the longer poems, even if the testimony of William Rossetti and Scott were not sufficient to prove that this was Rossetti's usual practice.[62] Of *Eden Bower*, completed in 1869, Sharp says that it was "thoroughly matured in [Rossetti's] mind before the first stanza was written."[63] Reporting the completion of *Eden Bower*, Rossetti himself suggested his method when he wrote: "I have been working towards, but not yet at, other new things."[64] In 1871 he was more explicit: "I have made a complete prose version [of *Rose Mary*] beforehand, and so get on with it easily."[65] In 1881 he twice wrote to Caine about similar preparations for poems never completed. Of one to be called *Orchard Pit* he wrote: "I am now thinking of writing another ballad-poem . . . . I have a clear scheme for it."[66] Of the other he said: "I have a complete scheme drawn up for a ballad, to be called *Michael Scott's Wooing.*"⁶⁷ (Prose synopses of both appeared in the 1886 edition of his *Works.*)

Rossetti's process of fundamental brainwork cannot be called completely successful. Without doubt he was wise in insisting that a poet have a clear conception in mind before attempting to write a poem. And for a long narrative poem, a prose synopsis of events should make for a clearer, firmer, more dramatic structure. But Rossetti's own practice of incessant revision shows that the "system," as Swinburne scornfully called it, did not really achieve the perfection the poet sought. Perhaps, too, William Bell Scott was to some degree right in asserting that Rossetti's use of prose versions ruined his "impulse and invention."⁶⁸ Rossetti admitted "inevitably level work" in the early stages of *The King's Tragedy*, and stretches of *The White Ship* and *Rose Mary* are equally "level." Rossetti also confessed of *Rose Mary* that "there is so much incident that it is necessarily much more of a regular narrative poem than is usual for me, and thus lacks the incisive concentration of such a piece as *Sister Helen.*"⁶⁹ (For *Sister Helen* and the other long poems written before 1869, it would seem from Scott's testimony, Rossetti had not first written "complete" prose versions beforehand.)

Scott may also be right in suggesting that Rossetti's preliminary prose versions sometimes even prevented his ever doing the subject in poetry. The creative impulse may well have spent itself on the elaborately detailed prose, leaving little incentive for what would inevitably be a somewhat routine task of transforming prose to verse. There is an interesting parallel here, at any rate, to the innumerable sketches or designs for paintings that got no further, mere promises of great pictures that were never produced. Maybe, too, Rossetti's faith in his powers of execution failed him, once he had his basic conception outlined. Whatever the correct explanation, Rossetti did design in detail a number of poems that never passed from prose to poetry—poems that might have done much to bolster his reputation. Among these were *Orchard Pit, Michael Scott's Wooing, The Doom of the Sirens,* and the conclusion of *The Bride's Prelude.*

THE ORIGINALITY OF THE POET

Originality sets itself, often defiantly, against convention. It was inevitable that such a boy as the young Gabriel Rossetti should, as he matured, become a cheerleader in the revolt against the dicta of "Sir Sloshua" Reynolds, blast most Eighteenth-Century writers as "the usual array of nobodies," and adore the likes of Blake, Keats, Coleridge, and Shelley. Although he insisted on originality in a poet, he realized the price one must pay: "Invention absolute is slow of acceptance, and must be so. This Coleridge and others have found. Why make a place for what is neither adaptation nor reproduction? Let it hew its way if it can."[70] Hew away Rossetti did, proclaiming, "I was one of those whose little is their own."[71] He placed originality foremost among the distinctions of the sonnet: "Special originality and even *newness* (though this might be called a vulgarizing word) of thought and picture in individual lines. . .seems to me the very first qualification of a sonnet."[72]

Yet Rossetti did not advocate newness for its own sake alone. Of Ebenezer Jones's poems, he said: "I was little more than a lad at the time I first chanced on them, but they struck me greatly, though I was not blind to. . .the ludicrous side of their wilful 'newness,' "[73] Considering his general disdain for the Eighteenth Century, Rossetti's belief that "poetry should seem to the hearer to have always been present to his thought, but never before heard"[74] is curiously like Pope's "What oft was thought but ne'er so well expressed," and Johnson's comment on the ideas of Gray's *Elegy:* "He that reads them here persuades himself that he has always felt them."

Rossetti created his own style not simply to be different, but because his "enormous imagination" could express itself in no other way. As Watts-Dunton said:

> Another misconception in connection with Rossetti is that his art represents a school. . . . The Rossetti note is a note of originality, the note of artistic creation. He invented his own style in poetry as surely as Shelley invented his; he invented his own style in painting as surely as Titian invented his; he invented his own new type of female beauty as surely as Leonardo invented his.[75]

Part of the Buchanan attack that stung was the "little charge. . .which this minstrel in mufti brings against *Jenny*, namely one of plagiarism"—plagiarism, of all things, from Buchanan himself![76] The charge was absurd. William Rossetti was correct when he said that his brother was "more than uncommonly free from plagiarism, conscious or unconscious."[77]

Nonetheless—another manifestation of his self-mistrust, perhaps—Rossetti was acutely sensitive to even the suspicion of plagiarism, as when he refused to read Helps's *Catherine Douglas* while working on the same subject in his own *The King's Tragedy*. When his sister-in-law, William's wife Lucy, sent a copy of the manuscript of *The White Ship* to her father, Ford Maddox Brown, Rossetti warned her:

> I was most happy that it should be sent to your Father, but think it very needful it should not be shown to others. I find the ideas and even phrases of poetry get so soon caught up that a thing shown in MS. is actually liable to charges of plagiarism when it appears, owning to what it has already furnished to others.[78]

Even though Brown was his best friend, the poet was still uneasy, and followed this up with a note to Brown himself:

Lucy also told me that she made a copy of my poem, the *White Ship,* and sent it you. I want just to say, dont show it about at all, though I dare say you would not. I have such experience of the matter and phraseology of MS. being caught up before the original gets published, that I feel a little anxiety on this point.[79]

As far back as 1850 Rossetti was aware of the risk of imitation an original poet must face:

I think that when a poet strikes out for himself a new path in style; he should first be quite convinced that it possesses sufficient advantages to counterbalance the contempt which the swarm of his imitators will bring upon poetry.[80]

Worse than the contempt that imitators might bring, however, was the possible accusation that the *originator* was the plagiarist, should the imitations be published before the real thing. It is not hard to see Rossetti himself as the "initiatory" man when he writes of Blake:

In each style or the art of a period, and more especially in the poetic style, there is often some one central initiatory man, to whom personally, if not to the care of the world, it is important that his creative power be held to be his own, and that his ideas and slowly perfected materials should not be caught up before he has them ready for his own use. Yet, consciously or unconsciously, such an one's treasures and possessions are, time after time, while he still lives and needs them, sent forth to the world by others in forms from which he cannot perhaps again clearly claim what is his own, but which render the material useless to him henceforward. . . . It is no small provocation, to be sure, when the gazers hoot you as outstripped in your race, and you know all the time that the man ahead whom they shout for, is only a flying thief.[81]

Whoever Rossetti's own "flying thieves" may have been, the fact is that Morris and Swinburne had already published, while a number of Rossetti's best poems lay buried in his wife's grave.

In his diction, Rossetti strove always for originality—both to avoid the conventional, and to eliminate "echoes" of his own work or that of others that might smack of plagiarism. Basically, his was really a rather simple, even plain, poetic vocabulary.[82] What makes Rossetti's language uniquely his is the order and interplay of the words, and his habit of "spicing" his lines, as it were, with choice and rare words ("stunners," he called them) that he often culled from old books in the British Museum. He was quick to pounce upon conventional phraseology. As early as 1849 he was telling his brother brusquely, "the word *rustling* is rather old, and the last line a trifle awkward," and "something newer, I think might be done" with a stanza or two.[83] He scolded Christina that some of her verses "smack rather of the old shop."[84] He called his own use of "Dreamland" in *Love's Nocturne* "a rather hackneyed phrase," and was distressed because he couldn't find another to replace it.[85] When Swinburne suggested that "stood confessed" in the line from *Troy Town,*

There the arrow stood confessed

was a "burlesque" and "slang," Rossetti objected: "I am disturbed. . . . Do you take into consideration that I mean absolutely that Cupid does see his arrow there? Thus it ceases to be a mere conventional metaphor."[86] All the same, Rossetti worked away on the line until he could report to Swinburne triumphantly: "I fancy I've hit it—'Marked his arrow's burning crest.' "[87]

Rossetti was as anxious not to echo himself as he was not to imitate others. He was troubled because *Soul's Beauty* had the phrase, "This is the Lady Beauty," and *Mary's Girlhood* "This is that blessed Mary." (He considered changing the latter to "'Tis of that blessed Mary," but ultimately kept both phrases as they originally were.)[88] He even said that he would rather have a line seem "too violent" than repeat a meaning.[89] He reacted strongly when Scott suggested that two of his sonnets had the same basic image:

> I cannot at all perceive that I have a habit of using images a second time, and think that any impression to that effect must result from hardly making due allowance for the general theme of the series. I do not know where you would find an instance in point, certainly it does not seem to me that there is any more than a generic likeness between the two called *The Dark Glass, Through Death to Love,* or any likeness in either to any sonnet previously written by me. Certainly there is a reference in both to love and death, but the keynote of one 'Not I myself,' etc., is a very special and quite individual theme, and I cannot see that the word 'Glass' occurring in the title of the one and the body of the other is worth thinking about.[90]

There is some truth in Scott's charge. Here are the sonnets:

The Dark Glass

Not I myself know all my love for thee:
   How should I reach so far, who cannot weigh
   To-morrow's dower by gage of yesterday?
Shall birth and death, and all dark names that be
As doors and windows bared to some loud sea,
   Lash deaf mine ears and blind my face with spray;
   And shall my sense pierce love,—the last relay
And ultimate outpost of eternity?

Lo! what am I to Love, the lord of all?
   One murmuring shell he gathers from the sand,—
   One little heart-flame sheltered in his hand.

Yet through thine eyes he grants me clearest call
And veriest touch of powers primordial
   That any hour-girt life may understand.

Through Death to Love

Like labor-laden moonclouds faint to flee
   From winds that sweep the winter-bitten wold, —
   Like multiform circumfluence manifold
Of night's flood-tide, — like terrors that agree
Of hoarse-tongued fire and inarticulate sea, —
   Even such, within some glass dimmed by our breath,
   Our hearts discern wild images of Death.
Shadows and shoals that edge eternity.

Howbeit athwart Death's imminent shade doth soar
   One Power, than flow of stream or flight of dove
   Sweeter to glide around, to brood above.
Tell me, my heart, — what angel-greeted door
Or threshold of wing-winnowed threshing-floor
   Hath guest fire-fledged as thine, whose lord is Love?

    In both sonnets, the inability to know is compared to
looking through a dark glass, or "some glass dimmed by our
breath." In one, the idea is further developed by "loud sea"
and "lash deaf mine ears and blind my face with spray,"
and in the other by "inarticulate sea." The "ultimate outpost
of eternity" of one is not too different from the "shoals that
edge eternity" of the other. In both Love triumphs over all
else: "Love, lord of all" and "[heart] whose lord is Love."
    But recurring images abound in Rossetti's poetry. The
sea as a symbol of Life and Time, as in *The Sea-Limits*, also
occurs in Sonnets 55, 73, 79, 97, and 99 of *The House of
Life*. Images of water, lilies, fire, hair, etc. are used again and
again. Not that such use of recurring symbols is necessarily

detrimental to good poetry. Critics like Caroline Spurgeon
and G. Wilson Knight have shown that this practice was an
essential element in Shakespeare's art. What Donald Stauffer
says of Yeats is applicable in a way to Rossetti:

> He consciously cultivates a new method of rendering his
> poetry intense in its complex allusions: he retains unique
> symbols, but he repeats them so frequently, in poem after
> poem, that they acquire a life of their own that goes far
> beyond the bounds of any one particular lyric.[91]

The symbols that Rossetti used most frequently are not
unique in themselves, as Yeats's are, but Rossetti makes
them peculiarly his own by limiting their connotations. The
water image of the first stanza of *The Blessed Damozel*—

> Her eyes were deeper than the depth
> Of water stilled at even—

has a life far beyond the bounds of this poem for those who
recall any number of similar images, such as these selected
at random from *The House of Life*:

> Weary water of the place of sighs (Sonnet 3)

> Image of thine eyes in any spring (Sonnet 4)

> the difficult deeps of Love (Sonnet 5)

> where wan water trembles in the grove (Sonnet 9)

These lines suggest the limits of Rossetti's water images.
Water, for him, is usually mysterious, deep, weary, listless,
shadowy, inscrutable, rather than filled with wild, roaring,
surging power and uncontrolled energy, as in *The Dark Glass.*
    When it came to detecting echoes of others in his own
work, Rossetti was extremely alert—even when they might

only *seem* to be echoes. Thus he wrote Allingham about *Sister Helen*:

> The family name used in it was originally 'Keith.' This I altered because of Dobell's ballad, *Keith of Ravelston* which bears also on faithless love and supernaturalism. (I may add, however, that D.'s ballad was never published till some years after mine had been originally in print, but still I hate coincidences of this kind.) Thus I have changed it to 'Holm' which is objected to, now, from I think a quarter worth considering as not being a well-sounding territorial name.[92]

The "quarter worth considering" was Swinburne, and Rossetti asked him, "Would 'Neill' do better?. . .I don't think I can revert to Keith."[93] After consulting with Allingham, Rossetti wrote Swinburne, "I have chosen *Weir* which I think not amiss. Neill he said wouldn't do, being merely a patronymic."[94] What was the upshot of all this to-do? "I have stuck 'Keith' back in despair, though 'Hearne', 'Lyle', and 'Carr' occurred to me, which I believe would have been free from objection, but the sound seemed inferior."[95]

Several letters written to his brother in 1869, while Rossetti was readying his poems for their first major publication, are dotted with queries touching on possible charges of plagiarism, usually coupled with a quick denial. He asked William about the advisability of appending a note to *My Sister's Sleep*, explaining that he had used its metre *before* Tennyson made it famous in *In Memoriam*, and did include such a note in the 1870 *Poems*. It also upset him that both poems dealt with Christmas Eve: "I remember too there is some *Xmas Eve* business in I [n] M [emoriam] but what I cannot remember."[96] ("Some Xmas Eve business"! How it would have pained Mr. Tennyson to learn that Rossetti couldn't "remember" the three Christmases that are so central to his great elegy.)

Possibly because he had read Browning so thoroughly in his youth, Rossetti had particular trouble with apparent Browning echoes. "A very vexatious point" arose in connection with the first *The Choice* sonnet—so vexatious that Rossetti considered omitting all three of these sonnets from *The House of Life.* The idea of the line,

> They die not,—for their life was death,—but cease

was "identical," he said, with one at the close of Browning's *In a Gondola:*

> The Three, I do not scorn
> To death, because they never lived.

"I know that I had never then read that poem," Rossetti complained, "and that on first reading it this annoying fact struck me at once, but then this is not known to the world. The point is just what is wanted and not possible to alter."[97] It was not altered.

"There is a similar case in the *Nocturn*," Rossetti went on. " 'Lamps of an *auspicious* soul' stood in my last correction (made long ago) 'pellucid' which is much finer. But lately in the *Ring and Book* I came on *pellucid soul,* applied to Caponsacchi, and the inevitable charge of plagiarism struck me at once as impending whenever my poem should be printed."[98] Rossetti altered *auspicious* to *translucent* in the 1881 *Poems.* But he stuck firm on yet another echo: "There is also in the *R[ing] and B[ook]* 'pail frail wife', which interferes in the same way with the 'pale frail mist' of my *New Year's Burden,* also of course written long before. But this I left."[99]

Rossetti was more than usually sensitive to charges that he imitated Browning. He must have been stung by the review of his 1870 *Poems* in *The Nation,* which made the assertion that *Jenny* and *A Last Confession* were imitations of

Browning, who had "done the same sort of thing so long, and so much better."[100] The comparison, although perhaps to be expected, was unfair. W. C. DeVane, while showing that they were "intimate (in the Browningesque manner)" has demonstrated that both poems were unmistakably "Rossetti's own."[101]

As unfair as impugning Rossetti's originality by calling his execution imitative would be disparaging his subject matter as derivative. Source-hunting is a harmless game, but Rossetti himself has spoiled the fun for most hunters. As he freely admitted *The Blessed Damozel's* debt to Poe's *The Raven*, so in his letters he tells us that the story of *The Staff and Scrip* came from *Gesta Romanorum*, *The White Ship* and *The King's Tragedy* from old chronicles, and *Jan Van Hunks* from *Henkerwyssel's Challenge*. Of *The White Ship*, Rossetti told his mother when he sent her the manuscript, "Every incident, including that of the boy at the end, is given in one or another account of the event."[102]

The only important justification for source-hunting, surely, is not where the poet finds his materials, but what he does with them. In discussing, in addition to Poe, the influences of Dante, Philip Bailey's *Festus*, and others upon *The Blessed Damozel*, P. F. Baum states emphatically: "It is a strange parentage. . .which in no wise derogates from the extraordinary originality of Rossetti."[103] J. R. Wahl pays similar tribute to Rossetti's use of *Henkerwyssel's Challenge* for his *Jan Van Hunks*, the "grotesque ballad," as William Rossetti calls it, in which Van Hunks refuses his children's plea for help, and loses his soul to the devil in consequence. Rossetti, says Wahl, "seized upon the central dramatic situation, and trimmed that of all irrelevancies. . . . In their place Rossetti gives us a series of remarkably successful 'inventions,' each of which symbolizes and develops the major irony which underlines the poem."[104]

In an excellent study of the sources of *The King's Tragedy*,

Dwight and Helen Culler provide another analysis of the magic of Rossetti's fundamental brainwork. They demonstrate that for this ballad Rossetti used four major sources, of which King James's own *King's Quair* was most important for inspiration, and Shirley's *The Dethe of the Kynge of Scotis* most important for materials. Rossetti's handling of his sources, they found, ranged all the way from an almost direct versification of Shirley in four lines to an amazing amalgamation of all four sources. Most striking was Rossetti's new conception of the character of the king, whom the poet changed from a lustful, tyrannical, unfaithful man of action to a resigned, brave, faithful, sensitive lover-poet. In addition, Rossetti built up and "ennobled" the slight supernatural element in his sources, and toned down their cruelty, animalism and sensationalism.[105]

These changes were original with Rossetti, his "invention," the product of his fundamental brainwork. They were, in a word, the fruits of his imagination, produced with their effect on the reader and the ideal of perfection in mind. They demonstrate in action, that is, Rossetti's conception of the poet as shown in these last two chapters.

NOTES

[1]Caine, p. 249.
[2]Gilchrist, p. 134.
[3]*L & M*, I, 414.
[4]Caine, p. 148.
[5]*Ibid.*, p. 185.
[6]*L & M*, I, 436.
[7]*Ibid.*, p. 304.
[8]Burne-Jones, I, 137.
[9]Sharp, p. 31.
[10]Caine, p. 269.
[11]Watts-Dunton, p. 419.

[12]P. F. Baum, ed., *Dante Gabriel Rossetti, An Analytical List of Manuscripts* (Durham, 1931), p. 14.

[13]Carr, p. 67, (The italics are mine.)

[14]*L & M*, I, 283; and Scott, II, 156.

[15]*L & M*, II, 93.

[16]*D & W*, II, 770.

[17]*Ibid.*, IV, 1850 See *inf.* pp. 124 ff. for a fuller discussion of Rossetti and originality.

[18]See Rossetti's *The Song-Throe.*

[19]Caine, p. 220.

[20]*Ibid.*, p. 221.

[21]Scott, II, 156.

[22]Caine, p. 248.

[23]*L & M*, I, 414. (The italics are mine.)

[24]Sharp, p. 120.

[25]W. M. Rossetti, *Ruskin: Rossetti: Preraphaelitism*, p. 205.

[26]*Ashley Catalogue*, IV, 134-5.

[27]Caine, p. 251.

[28]Hill, p. 124.

[29]*Ashley Catalogue*, VII, 6.

[30]D. G. Rossetti, *Keats*, p. 19.

[31]W. M. Rossetti, *Rossetti Papers*, p. 506.

[32]*Collected Works*, I, 464.

[33]*Ibid.*, p. 460.

[34]Burne-Jones, I, 129.

[35]Caine, p. 249.

[36]*Collected Works*, I, 500.

[37]*Ibid.*

[38]*Ibid.*

[39]Caine, p. 125.

[40]Baum, *The Blessed Damozel*, p. xxi.

[41]I am accepting the conclusion of J. A. Sanford that the so-called 1847 version in the Morgan manuscript, which contained this stanza, is spurious. See J. A. Sanford, "The Morgan Manuscript of Rossetti's 'The Blessed Damozel,' " *Studies in Philology*, XXXV (July, 1938), 471-86. See *inf.*, p. 236.

[42]Stanzas are numbered according to the final, 1881 version.

[43]Baum, *The Blessed Damozel*, p. xvi.

[44]*Ibid.*, p. 28.

[45]J. C. Troxell collates some 14 versions in her useful *Rossetti's Sister Helen* (New Haven, 1939).

[46]*D & W*, II, 721.

[47]Caine, p. 128.

[48]These are Stanzas 30-35 in the final version.

[49]Caine, p. 126.

[50]*D & W*, IV, 1686.

[51]D. Stauffer, *The Nature of Poetry* (New York, 1946), p. 128.

[52]Scott, II, 150.

[53]*Ibid.*, p. 151.

[54]*L & M*, II, 219.

[55]Caine, p. 284.

[56]Watts-Dunton, p. 408.

[57]*L & M*, I, 408.

[58]*Collected Works*, I, 494.

[59]T. Wright, *The Life of John Payne* (London, 1919), p. 46.

[60]See *sup.*, pp. 90-95.

[61]For shorter poems, especially the sonnets, Rossetti's first draft may be said to have served as his cartoon. "My sonnets are not generally finished." he said of *Lost on Both Sides*, "till I see them again after forgetting them, and this is only two days old." (*D & W*, II, 207.)

[62]W. M. Rossetti, *Rossetti Papers*, p. 393; and Scott, II, 159.

[63]Sharp, p. 363.

[64]*Ashley Catalogue*, VII, 15-16.

[65]Scott, II, 157.

[66]Caine, p. 274.

[67]*Ibid.*, p. 265.

[68]Scott, II, 159.

[69]*Ibid.*, pp. 157-8.

[70]*Collected Works*, I, 511.

[71]W. M. Rossetti, *Some Reminiscences of William Michael Rossetti* (New York, 1906), I, 211.

[72]Caine, pp. 110-11.

[73]*Collected Works*, I, 478.

[74]*Ibid.*, p. 511.

[75]Watts-Dunton, p. 408.

[76]*Collected Works*, I, 485.

[77]W. M. Rossetti, *Rossetti as Designer and Writer*, p. 136.

[78]*D & W*, IV, 1825.

[79]*Ibid.*, p. 1826.

[80]*Collected Works*, I, 407. (From his unfinished *St. Agnes.*)

[81]*Ibid.*, p. 467.

[82]See *inf.*, pp. 211-222 for a discussion of Rossetti's diction.

[83]*L & M*, II, 64-5.

[84]*Ibid.*, p. 120.

[85]*Ibid.*, p. 215.

[86]*D & W*, II, 805.

[87]*Ibid.*, p. 809.

[88]*L & M*, II, 216.

[89]*Ibid.*

[90]*D & W*, III, 985.

[91]Stauffer, p. 171.

[92]*D & W*, II, 795-6.

[93]*Ibid.*, p. 792.

[94]*Ibid.*, p. 805.

[95]*Ibid.*, p. 810.

[96]*Ibid.*, p. 732.

[97]*Ibid.*, p. 726.

[98]*Ibid.*

[99]*Ibid.*

[100]"Dante Gabriel Rossetti's Poems," *The Nation*, XI (July 14, 1870), 29-30.

[101]W. C. DeVane, "The Harlot and the Thoughtful Young Man," *Studies in Philology*, XXIV (July, 1932), 463-84.

[102]*D & W*, IV, 1763.

[103]Baum, *The Blessed Damozel*, p. xiv.

[104]Wahl, p. 15.

[105]Dwight and Helen Culler, "The Sources of 'The King's Tragedy,' " *Studies in Philology*, XLI (July, 1944), 427-41.

VI

Rossetti and the Poem: Spirituality, Emotion, Beauty

*This is that Lady Beauty, in whose praise
Thy voice and hand shake still.*

Soul's Beauty

Just as Rossetti proclaimed what a poet should be, so with equal assurance he declared what a poem should be. A poem should, above all else, be possessed of spirituality, intense emotion, and beauty. And who would quarrel with that—except those who have read Rossetti's own poems and found the spirituality "fleshly," the emotion "Ivory Tower," and the beauty "sound superior to sense." Once again there is the twofold explanation of the discrepancy: first, the disparity between aim and achievement; and second, a confusion (on Rossetti's part as well as the critics') as to what he meant by spirituality, emotion, and beauty. As always, the best course would seem to be to see what he said about each, and then to examine what he did.

SPIRITUALITY

A rough rule of thumb for the critic might be: when in doubt, be omniscient. But no such gift is needed to suggest that Rossetti never had any desire to write a *Lead Kindly Light* or a *Paradise Lost.* On the other hand, there is ample evidence that all his life he wanted his poetry to be thought "spiritual." As a boy, he quickly purged lines that his pious family found "indecent." As a young Pre-Raphaelite, he lived a pure and moral life, filled (said Holman Hunt) with "spiritual dreams." His first successful work in both painting and poetry was sufficiently religious to give rise to charges of "popery." In 1848, in Sonnet I of *Old and New Art,* he praised St. Luke, "who first taught art to fold her hands and pray." Twenty years later the same sense of dedication is expressed in *Newborn Death II:* "And art, whose eyes were worlds by God found fair."

It must be remembered that for Rossetti the spiritual involved an emotional superstition rather than any formal religion.[1] But he seems to have thought one amounted to the other, as when he asked Dixon, "Do not my works testify to my Christianity?"[2] To him, *Jenny* was "a sermon, nothing less."[3] It was Caine's lecture on Rossetti's poetry, asserting that the poet was "prompted by the highest of spiritual emotions," that first drew Rossetti to the younger man. Says Caine:

> Rossetti. . .invariably shrank from classification with the poetry of aestheticism, and aspired to the fame of a poet who had been prompted primarily by the highest of spiritual emotions, and to whom the sensations of the body were as naught, unless they were sanctified by the concurrence of the soul.[4]

Rossetti heartily agreed, writing to Caine: "Your estimate of the impulses influencing my poetry is such as I should wish it to suggest, and this suggestion, I believe, it will have always for a true-hearted nature."[5] Rossetti had not then met his young admirer. In token of his appreciation he added, "I daresay you sometimes come to London. I should be very glad to know you."

The same emphasis on spirituality, in terms of highest praise, is found in Rossetti's own comments about the works of others. He praised the "genuine human and spiritual sympathy" in the poems of Dr. Hake,[6] and said of the painter Samuel Palmer, "Such a manifestation of spiritual force absolutely present. . .has certainly never been united with native landscape power in the same degree."[7] He had similar encomia for the likes of Wells, Gilchrist, and Mrs. Alice Meynell, a friendly critic who sent Rossetti "a most genuine little book of poems containing some sonnets of true spiritual beauty."[8] Blake is lauded for his "spiritual quality,"[9] Shelley for "impregnating landscapes with spiritual power,"[10] and the Early Italian poets for their "spiritual beauty."[11]

Rossetti had every right to feel that he was being consistent and honest about his artistic *aims* when he denied Buchanan's charge that he extolled "fleshliness as the distinct and supreme end of poetic and pictorial art."[12] He might take a "wider view than some poets or critics" as to the kind of material "admissible within the limits of art." This he admitted. "But," said he, "to state that I do so to the ignoring or overshadowing of spiritual beauty is an absolute falsehood."[13]

Could it be, however, that Rossetti was answering his own doubts as well as Buchanan—that in too many poems there was, as Buchanan claimed, the suggestion "by inference that the body is greater than the soul?" Even in the earliest version of *The Blessed Damozel* Professor Baum saw a hint of a "conflict too strong for [Rossetti's] power of will," a conflict from which he sought "an easy escape, and spirit succumbed to body."[14] In any case, one can easily imagine the conflict that ensued when the piously raised and moral poet —

at age twenty-eight—ran full-tilt into the abundant charms of Fanny Cornforth. She became his mistress, a "little elephant" whose trunk he continued to fill with gold to his dying day. Coarse, voluptuous, greedy, dear "Fan," upon whom he depended as late as 1881 to "get me a good *blotting book* with a pocket in it and made to lock up."[15]

But the family always frowned on Fanny. Short months before his death, Rossetti was writing her: "Such difficulties are now arising with my family that it will be impossible for me to see you here till I write again."[16] And persisting throughout their long liaison, there was that other part of Rossetti that Fanny could never touch, the part that sought a complete union of soul and body, first with Elizabeth Siddal, whom he married, and then with Janey Morris, whom he could not. One feels that with Rosssetti, the soul never completely succumbed to the body—except, perhaps, temporarily. Rather, it was as if the soul, yielding again and again to the body's demands, never ceased trying to make the body itself "spiritual." For if the sexual act could somehow be made the expression of the soul, then the soul, by yielding to the body, would have triumphed. Body and soul would be one.

Analysis of the sonnets of *The House of Life* bears out this theses (without, I think, resorting unduly to another critical rule of thumb—when in doubt, wax biographical). The keynote is struck in Sonnet 5, *Heart's Hope:*

> Thy soul I know not from thy body, nor
> Thee from myself, neither our love from God.

It is echoed in 45, *Secret Parting:*

> And as she kissed, her mouth became her soul

and 50, *Willowwood II,*

> the soul-wrung implacable close kiss

and 57, *True Woman II*,

> she welcomes all command
> Of love, — her soul to answering ardors fanned.

All of these are from Part I of *The House of Life*, which though titled "Youth and Change" is really a ringing of the changes on love. Of the sixty sonnets that make up Part I, fifty-five actually use the word *love*, and the other five are love-sonnets. And of the sixty, thirty-five also use the word *soul*, and six others use such equivalents as *spirit* or *sacred*. Soul and love, then, are linked in an astonishing total of forty-one of the sixty sonnets. Lest it be argued that "soul" and "love" do not necessarily add up to soul = body, permit me one more statistic. In twenty-seven of the forty-one sonnets where soul and love are linked, the love described is unmistakably physical.

This linking of soul with physical ecstasy could be successful, as in *Love-Sweetness*, which Rossetti quoted in defending himself against Buchanan:

> Sweet dimness of her loosened hair's downfall
>   About thy face; her sweet hands round thy head
>   In gracious fostering union garlanded;
> Her tremulous smiles; her glances' sweet recall
> Of love; her murmuring sighs memorial;
>   Her mouth's culled sweetness by thy kisses shed
>   On cheeks and neck and eyelids, and so led
> Back to her mouth which answers there for all: —

> What sweeter than these things, except the thing
>   In lacking which all these would lack their sweet: —
>   The confident heart's still fervor: the swift beat
> And soft subsidence of the spirit's wing,
> Then when it feels, in cloud-girt wayfaring
>   The breath of kindred plumes against its feet?

Without Her grows most poignant as the sense of spiritual loss succeeds the pangs of physical loss:

> What of the glass without her? The blank gray
>   There where the pool is blind of the moon's face.
>   Her dress without her? The tossed empty space
> Of cloud-rack whence the moon has passed away.
> Her paths without her? Day's appointed sway
>   Usurped by desolate night. Her pillowed place
>   Without her? Tears, ah me! for love's good grace,
> And cold forgetfulness of night or day.
>
> What of the heart without her? Nay, poor heart,
>   Of thee what word remains ere speech be still?
>   A wayfarer by barren ways and chill,
> Steep ways and weary, without her thou art,
> Where the long cloud, the long wood's counterpart,
>   Sheds doubled darkness up the laboring hill.

But alas, sexual ecstasy does not always lead to a spiritual heaven, as sonnets like *The Kiss* and *Supreme Surrender* illustrate. Buchanan was cunning in picking out *Nuptial Sleep* for special abuse, for here the soul literally gets drowned:

> At length their long kiss severed, with sweet smart:
>   And as the last slow sudden drops are shed
>   From sparkling eaves when all the storm has fled,
> So singly flagged the pulses of each heart.
> Their bosoms sundered, with the opening start
>   Of married flowers to either side outspread
>   From the knit stem; yet still their mouths, burnt red,
> Fawned on each other where they lay apart.
>
>
> Sleep sank them lower than the tide of dreams,
>   And their dreams watched them sink, and slid away.
> Slowly their souls swam up again, through gleams

Of watered light and dull drowned waifs of day;
Till from some wonder of new woods and streams
He woke, and wondered more: for there she lay.

Rossetti might argue, as he did, that "all the passionate and just delights of the body are declared. . .to be as naught if not ennobled by the concurrence of the soul at all times." He could go on to insist that *Nuptial Sleep* was "one stanza, embodying, for its small constituent share, a beauty of natural function, only to be reprobated in art if dwelt on (as I have shown that it is not here) to the exclusion of those other higher things of which it is the harmonious concomitant."[17]

Perhaps even for us, however, let alone the Victorians, sexual passion is too powerful to stand as a "small, constituent share" of anything. It apparently was too powerful for Rossetti, too. His intended effect was to *embody* the spiritual; his actual effect was all too often erotic or sensual, with "soul" only a vague word lost amid "bosoms sundered" and mouths that "fawned," and lovers clinging "breast to breast." Too often it was body's beauty, not soul's beauty, that triumphed, leaving "round his heart one strangling golden hair." Fanny's hair was golden.

Rossetti thought he saw the triumph of "spiritualism" in Blake:

> I would specially direct attention to the exquisite beauty
> of the female figures. Nothing proves more thoroughly how
> free was the spiritualism of Blake's art from any ascetic
> tinge. These women are given to us no less noble in body
> than in soul; large-eyed, and large-armed also; such as a
> man may love with all his life.[18]

But Rossetti's women are more often convincingly "large-armed" and noble in body than noble in soul, like Helen of Troy with breasts like "apples meet for his mouth," and Lilith urging the snake to "Grip and lip my limbs as I tell thee." Large-armed indeed is the "beloved" in *The Song of the Bower*:

> What were my prize, could I enter thy bower,
>   This day, tomorrow, at eve or at morn?
> Large lovely arms and a neck like a tower,
>   Bosom then heaving that now lies forlorn.
> Kindled with love-breath, (the sun's kiss is colder!)
>   Thy sweetness all near me, so distant today;
> My hand round thy neck and thy hand on my shoulder,
>   My mouth to thy mouth as the world melts away.

William Rossetti suggested that the woman in question was Elizabeth Siddal. But as Oswald Doughty points out in his biography of Rossetti, the physical description is far more appropriate to Swinburne's identification of her—Fanny, "the bitch."[19]

Still, Rossetti insisted that his aims were noble, in the longer poems as well as the sonnets, however short of the goal his achievement might be:

> It is no part of my undertaking to dispute the verdict. . .
> on my own measure of executive success; but the accu-
> sation cited above is not against the poetic value of certain
> work, but against its primary (and by assumption) its
> admitted aim. And to this I must reply that so far, assured-
> ly, not even Shakespeare himself could desire more arduous
> human tragedy for development in art than belongs to the
> themes I venture to embody, however incalculably higher
> might be his power of dealing with them.

Rossetti then proceeds to disclose his intentions:

> What more inspiring for poetic effort than the terrible Love
> turned to Hate,—perhaps the deadliest of all passion-
> woven complexities,—which is the theme of *Sister Helen*,
> and, in more fantastic form, of *Eden Bower*—the surround-

ings of both being the mere machinery of a central universal
meaning. What, again, more so than the savage penalty
exacted for a lost ideal, as expressed in the *Last Confession*;
— than the outraged love for man and burning compen-
sations in art and memory of *Dante at Verona*;—than
the baffling problems which the face of *Jenny* conjures
up; or than the analysis of passion and feeling attempted
in *The House of Life,* and others among the more purely
lyrical poems? I speak here, as does my critic. . .of *aim*
not of *achievement.*[20]

This eloquent statement of aims is Rossetti's most direct
defense of his poetry. It is his major claim to the highest
"spirituality." There is no need to dispute its sincerity. But
his simply was not a mind that moved from "a central universal meaning" to the "mere machinery" with which to
illustrate it. Quite the contrary. His high "themes" were
dominated by imagination, not intellect. It is the emotional
effect of his poems that captivates the reader. One well remembers the hate of Sister Helen and Lilith, the passion of
A Last Confession, the yearning of the Blessed Damozel,
the love, remorse, frustration and despair in *The House of
Life*—but not very clearly the "central universal meaning"
for which their "mere machinery" was ostensibly designed.
The reason is simple. Rossetti wanted intense emotion in
his poems as ardently as he desired spirituality. In a man
of his make-up, the two aims were bound to conflict. . .and
emotion bound to triumph.

EMOTION

It would be hard to overemphasize the importance of
emotion in poetry to Rossetti. His basic approach to a poem,
even when it was not itself moving, was emotional. He confessed to Caine: "All poetry, that is really poetry, affects me
deeply and often to tears. It does not need to be pathetic

nor yet tender to produce such a result."[21] Caine describes
Rossetti reading *Without Her* aloud: "He had read it with
tears of voice, subsiding at length into suppressed sobs and
intervals of silence."[22]

When dealing with other poets, emotional effect was one
of the first things Rossetti seized upon to praise, as "best
where most impassioned, as all poetry is and must be."[23]
He loved Blake's first *Chimney Sweeper*, "which touches
with such perfect simplicity the true pathetic chord of its
subject."[24] Nothing, he said, so "simple and touching" as
Coleridge's "O Sleep! it is a gentle thing" had ever been written.[25] When his wife Lizzie made a few pathetic attempts
at writing poetry, he praised her for her "great merit of
feeling."[26] Even Hake's mediocrities shone with "tender
thought for human suffering."[27] Swinburne's *Mona Lisa*
rated high as one of his "finest pieces of execution and emotion."[28] Morris' *Earthly Paradise* won approval for going
"deeper into the treatment of intense personal passion than
he has yet done."[29]

To Rossetti, poetry without emotion was no poetry at
all. Both parts of *The House of Life* begin with sonnets that
state this emphatically. Introducing the whole sequence is
the sonnet on the sonnet, with its injunction:

> Look that it be,
> Whether for lustral rite or dire portent,
> Of its own arduous fulness reverent.

Part II opens with *Transfigured Life* and *The Song-Throe*.
In the former, a poem and its author are compared to a
growing child and its parents. Just as part of each parent is
a part of the child, yet the child (transfigured by life) becomes
a separate man or woman, so the poet's emotions (joy and
pain), the "very parents of the poem," are part of the poem,
but are transfigured by art into a new and different thing,
the poem (song) itself:

So in the Song, the singer's Joy and Pain,
    Its very parents, evermore expand
To bid the passion's fullgrown birth remain,
    By Art's transfiguring essence subtly spann'd

The Song-Throe says there is no magic charm for the poet except his own tears. Only the inspired response to his own pain can produce a poem that can pierce a reader's heart:

By thine own tears thy song must tears beget,
    O Singer! Magic mirror thou hast none
    Except thy manifest heart; and save thine own
Anguish or ardor, else no amulet.
Cisterned in Pride, verse is a feathery jet
    Of soulless air-flung fountains; nay, more dry
    Than the Dead Sea for throats that thirst and sigh,
That song o'er which no singer's lids grew wet.

The Song-god—He the Sun-god—is no slave
    Of thine: thy Hunter he, who for thy soul
    Fledges his shaft: to no august control
Of thy skilled hand his quivered store he gave:
But if thy lips' loud cry leap to his smart,
The inspir'd recoil shall pierce thy brother's heart.

Yes, Sidney wrote long before Rossetti, " 'Fool,' said my muse to me, 'Look in thy heart and write.' " Yet for Rossetti, this very process was itself emotional. P. F. Baum has said that Rossetti's "deliberate method of composition [is] the opposite of impulsive outpourings of emotion."[30] This is true and untrue: true if one looks only at the lesser order of brainwork that involved searching for "stunning" words, revising and revising, polishing and repolishing; not true if one recalls the poet as a "racked and tortured medium, never permitted an instant's surcease of agony."[31] It may even be that the elaborate system of composition that Rossetti devised was in fact an attempt to escape the agony, as he did escape it with his painting. He told Caine that his painting "in early years tormented me more than enough. Now I paint by a set of unwritten but clearly-defined rules."[32]

In contrast, the emotion that went into the creation of his poems is told again and again in Rossetti's own words. *Lost Days,* he said, might be his favorite sonnet "if I did not remember in what too opportune juncture it was wrung out of me."[33] Of *Rose Mary* he said, "the physical prostration ensuing [its composition] had been more than he would care to go through again."[34] *The King's Tragedy,* too, racked him: "It was as though my life ebbed out with it,"[35] *Hand and Soul* left him "entirely broken."[36] And to Christina he bleakly wrote: "With me, sonnets mean insomnia."[37]

All this makes one wonder at critics, such as E. B. Burgum, who suggest that Rossetti failed as a poet because he had emotional experiences only in youth, and—when Time had erased these—had no new emotions to write about, but only vague memories:

> *Woodspurge* was the explanation of [Rossetti's] failure quite generally in other works. . . . An intense emotion, the poet says, seeks distraction in irrelevant particulars. When the emotion fades, those irrelevancies are all that the memory can conjure up into specific form. The poem records impressively what may happen in the emotional lives of many sensitive persons. It is doubtless the record of what took place in Rossetti's own life.[38]

First, Mr. Burgum misses the true power of *Woodspurge.* The emotional impact—for poet and reader alike—comes from the very realization that a past emotional experience has left no more important memory than the fact that the flower of the woodspurge has "a cup of three." What could be more poignant—or more immediate? The *source* of the emotion is in the past; the emotion itself is vibrantly of the present.

More important, however, is the implication that youth once past, Rossetti had no new emotional experiences. Mr. Burgum uses as his chief "evidence" that Rossetti lacked immediacy of emotion the sonnets of *The House of Life.* Now, by Professor Baum's estimate, some 75 of the 103 sonnets in this sequence were written during the years 1868-71. How in the world could a poet who had, right at this time, recovered the manuscripts of his poems from the grave of a wife who had committed suicide, who had one mistress and loved another man's wife, who was planning to publish yet was deathly afraid of the public, who thought he was going blind, who fought sleepless nights with chloral and alcohol—how could such a man have any lack of emotions?

Analysis of the sonnets shows that fifty-three indisputably treat of immediate or timeless emotions. Twenty others derive their immediacy of emotion (as does *Woodspurge*) from recalling past crises. Thirteen sonnets voice the fear that present happiness will end. And the remaining seventeen gain a special kind of emotional immediacy from both looking to the past and anticipating the future.

As examples of sonnets dealing with immediate emotional experiences, *Nuptial Sleep, The Kiss, Supreme Surrender, Autumn Idleness,* and *Silent Noon* will serve. As with *Bridal Birth,* the time is *now:*

> Now, shadowed by his wings, our faces yearn
> Together

Timeless in their themes are sonnets like the sonnet on the sonnet, *Transfigured Life,* and *The Song-Throe,* all of which deal with poetry.

Of the next group—the twenty that gain an immediacy from recalling the past—*Without Her* is a striking example.

Others include *Life in Love, Parted Love, The Landmark,* the *Willowwood* group, and *Life the Beloved.*

There are thirteen sonnets in which the emotion is one of dark foreboding that present joy may flee, as in *Winged Hours:*

> What of that hour at last, when for her sake
>   No wing may fly to me nor song may flow;
>   When, wandering round my life unleaved, I know
> The bloodied feathers scattered in the brake,
> And think how she, far from me, with like eyes
> Sees through the untuneful bough the wingless skies?

This seizing a vicarious emotion, as it were, from the future by anticipating grief yet to come is also prominent in *Lovesight, The Morrow's Message,* and both parts of *Newborn Death.* *The One Hope,* the final sonnet of *The House of Life,* contrasts "vain desire and vain regret" with the possibilities of afterlife:

> Shall Peace be still a sunk stream long unmet, —
>   Or may the soul at once in a green plain
>   Stoop through the spray of some sweet life-fountain
> And cull the dew-drenched flowering amulet?

The fourth group of sonnets, numbering seventeen in all, sweep up all of the poet's life—past, present, and future—through memory, realization, and anticipation of emotions. Of these, *Last Fire* portrays the moment of serenity when bliss is still a warmly remembered memory, and forebodings of the future, though dark, are still too vague for anguish:

> Love, through your spirit and mine what summer eve
>   Now glows with glory of all things possess'd
>   Since this day's sun of rapture filled the west
> And the light sweetened as the fire took leave?
> Awhile now softlier let your bosom heave,

As in Love's harbor, even that loving breast,
All care takes refuge while we sink to rest,
And mutual dreams the bygone bliss retrieve.

Many the days that Winter keeps in store,
    Sunless throughout, or whose brief sun-glimpses
    Scarce shed the heaped snow through the naked trees.
This day at least was Summer's paramour,
Sun-colored at the imperishable core
    With sweet well-being of love and full heart's ease.

The Soul's Sphere remembers the "infinite images" of the past, and wonders what they portend,

                                    Whether it forecast
    The rose-winged hours that flutter in the van
    Of Love's unquestioning unrevealed span, —
Visions of golden futures: or that last
Wild pageant of the accumulated past
    That clangs and flashes for a drowning man.

A Dark Day similarly questions whether today's gloom brings "Fresh storm, or be old rain the covert bears." In *Memorial Thresholds*, the poet stands outside a door that must lead him into eternity,

Even with one presence filled, as once of yore:
Or mocking winds whirl round a chaff-strown floor
    Thee and thy years and these my words and me.

Whether the poet's emotion stems from the immediate experience only, or from the contrast of the present with the past, with the future, or with both past and future at once, the sonnets of *The House of Life* deal with emotion still throbbing at the moment of creation. Rossetti's diction, imagery and "thought" may be vague and obscure at times, which may make the emotion seem more remote and "Ivory Tower" than it was. Part of the fault lay in his "system" of composition, and part in yet a third essential of a poem that Rossetti tried to pile upon spirituality and emotion: beauty — beauty that often became, in Baum's words, "a cloud of gorgeous phrasing that disguised his meaning."[39]

BEAUTY

At times Rossetti asserted the need for beauty in art so forcefully that he sounded like a veritable high priest of Art for Art's sake. In his review of Maclise's paintings he wrote: "Of course, as in all cases of clear satisfaction in art, the gift of beauty, and no other, is at the bottom of it."[40] With equal emphasis he said of poetry that any form of the sonnet was justified, so long as it did not "lessen the only absolute aim — that of beauty."[41] In the sonnet *Soul's Beauty* Rossetti pays his utmost tribute to Beauty:

> This is that Lady Beauty, in whose praise
>   Thy voice and hand shake still, — long known to thee
>   By flying hair and fluttering hem, — the beat
>   Following her daily of thy heart and feet,
>   How passionately and irretrievably,
> In what fond flight, how many ways and days!

Even though this tribute has been used to "prove" Rossetti's complete acceptance of Art for Art's sake, his pronouncement that beauty was the "only absolute aim" must — like all his sweeping pronouncements — be balanced with other equally sweeping pronouncements, such as those about spirituality and emotion. In his lexicon, it was imagination — not "beauty" — that was the synonym for poetry. And it was invention that he considered his best quality, not execution or perfection of form.

With the realization of what Rossetti meant by beauty,

any apparent paradox or contradiction vanishes. Really, the word should be plural, not singular, as when he said it was the *beauties* in a poet's work for which the critic must first look. As the title of the sonnet indicates, in his tribute to Lady Beauty he means *soul's* beauty. That he held this paramount is shown by his terming "an absolute lie" Buchanan's implication that he was guilty of deliberate "ignoring or overshadowing of spiritual beauty." Nonetheless, matching *Soul's Beauty* there is *Body's Beauty*, even as in the "spiritualism" of Blake's art there was the "exquisite beauty of the female figures. . .no less noble in body than in soul."

There were also the beauties of execution as well as of theme and subject matter. Rossetti praised Swinburne's "splendour of execution."[42] In Hake's poems he found "beauty" of imagery.[43] Blake had "exquisiteness" of metrics as well as "beauty of expression."[44] But such beauties were secondary, Rossetti implied, in denying that he was one of those who would "wish to create form for its own sake." Citing the "inspiring" themes that he sought to embody, he said sardonically:

> To assert that the poet whose matter is such as this aims chiefly at "creating form for its own sake," is, in fact, almost an ingenuous kind of dishonesty; for surely it delivers up the asserter at once, bound hand and foot, to the tender mercies of contradictory proof.[45]

If in his execution Rossetti did get carried away by his devotion to his Lady Beauty, it was certainly not because he thought that execution *was* that Lady. It was rather that in trying to adorn her worthily, he often (and typically) overdid the job.

NOTES

[1]See *sup.*, pp. 6-11.
[2]Caine, pp. 39-40.
[3]*Ibid.*, p. 226.
[4]*Ibid.*, p. 104.
[5]*Ibid.*, p. 105.
[6]*Collected Works*, I, 493.
[7]Sharp, pp. 301-2.
[8]Caine, p. 261.
[9]*Collected Works*, I, 445.
[10]Caine, p. 147.
[11]*Ibid.*, p. 203.
[12]Buchanan, p. 32.
[13]*Collected Works*, I, 485-6.
[14]Baum, *The Blessed Damozel*, p. iv.
[15]*D & W*, IV, 1916.
[16]*Ibid.*, p. 1942.
[17]*Collected Works*, I, 482.
[18]*Ibid.*, p. 471.
[19]Doughty, *Dante Gabriel Rossetti*, p. 263n.
[20]*Collected Works*, I, 486-7.
[21]Caine, p. 222.
[22]*Ibid.*, pp. 221-2.
[23]Hill, p. 256.
[24]*Collected Works*, I, 460.
[25]Caine, p. 165.
[26]W. M. Rossetti, *Rossetti Papers*, p. 511.
[27]*Collected Works*, I, 493.
[28]*Ashley Catalogue*, IV, 117.
[29]Skelton, pp. 85-6.
[30]Baum, *The House of Life*, p. 10.
[31]See *sup.*, p. 113.
[32]Caine, p. 218.
[33]*Ibid.*, p. 237.
[34]*Ibid.*, p. 218.
[35]*Ibid.*, p. 269.
[36]*Ibid.*, p. 134.
[37]W. M. Rossetti, *Rossetti as Designer and Writer*, p. 171.
[38]Burgum, pp. 442-3.
[39]Baum, *The House of Life*, p. 3.
[40]*Collected Works*, II, 509.

[41]*L & M.* I, 417.
[42]*Ibid.,* p. 199.
[43]Hake, p. 250.
[44]*Collected Works.* I, 464 and 458.
[45]*Ibid.,* p. 487.

VII

Rossetti and the Poem: From Here to Obscurity

I am rather aghast for my own lucidity.
Rossetti to Hall Caine, 1880[1]

"Overdoing" may well have been Rossetti's greatest weakness. So often, as if not sure he had achieved what he wanted, he gave a work another lick or two. . .or three. . .or four. The qualities in a poem that Critic Rossetti most admired included simplicity, subtlety, completeness, brevity, compression, clarity, forcefulness — and moderation. When Poet Rossetti tried to achieve all these, however, he frequently wound up with a quality he detested: obscurity.

The fault would seem to lie not in the qualities themselves, but in the extremes of each which the poet sought to attain. The *epitome* of both simplicity and subtlety involves a conflict taxing the powers of a Shakespeare. So does the utmost of completeness and brevity, compression and clarity. And how could Rossetti, of all people, achieve the ultimate in forcefulness, with moderation? In seeking the absolute, he proved only that nothing exceeds like excess.

SIMPLICITY AND SUBTLETY

From the beginning, Rossetti highly valued simplicity. One of the qualities of the ballads he loved as a boy was their simplicity of diction, form, and theme. Simplicity was a key aim of the Pre-Raphaelite Brotherhood. Though Hunt seems to have disagreed, Rossetti extolled his own *My Sister's Sleep* as "simpler and more like nature."[2] Rossetti continued to cherish simplicity in others. He praised Keats for growing "choicer and simpler."[3] One reason that Coleridge's line on "sleep" had moved him deeply was that it was "so simple" as well as so touching. Blake was hailed for his "perfect simplicity,"[4] and Browning for "pure simple diction."[5] When Caine repeated to Rossetti J. A. Symonds' comment that poems like *Rose Mary, The King's Tragedy,* and *The White Ship* lacked the sinewy simplicity of primitive ballads, Rossetti replied that he had given proof of his ability to achieve this in *The Staff and Scrip* and *Stratton Water.*[6]

But simplicity alone was not enough. Rossetti came to regard *My Sister's Sleep* as a rather "spoony affair," and was reluctant to include it in his 1870 *Poems.*[7] Art's "transfiguring essence," says his sonnet, *Transfigured Life,* must "subtly" span the poet's joy and pain. Martin's translation of Dante's *Vita Nuova* dissatisfied Rossetti because it missed the "subtler side of the original."[8] Similarly, Rossetti found in Watts-Dunton's sonnets "a certain want of complete subtlety in execution."[9] Nolly Brown was chided for "deliberateness and obviousness."[10] On the other hand, "poor blind gifted" Philip Marston, as Rossetti once described his young poet-friend, must have mightily cherished Rossetti's description of some of his poems as "worthy of Shakespeare in his subtlest lyrical moods."[11]

For Rossetti, a poem could be too simple; apparently it could not be too subtle. When a Browning or a Blake became overly subtle, Rossetti did not use the word "subtle" at all, but called him "obscure," which is semantics at its best.

For obscurity is exactly what resulted when Rossetti's avowed love of simplicity was overwhelmed by his desire for subtlety. A case in point is his *Cloud and Wind,* one of those sonnets criticized for having no immediate emotion to express.[12] The sonnet is one of the group that contrasts present love with forebodings of the future. The emotion, as such, is true, immediate, and moving. Simply put, the octet asks: "Which would be worse, your dying first or I? If you die, I can follow you. But what guarantee have I that I won't rue rushing to join you in death, that after death I won't lose you forever in dark, empty eternity?" The sestet then takes up the alternative of the poet's dying first, with the equally gloomy prospect of either an afterlife of watching his living, weeping lover, or complete oblivion.

Thus put, the meaning of the sonnet seems simple and clear enough. But look what Rossetti did to the octet:

> Love, should I fear death most for you or me?
>   Yet if you die, can I not follow you,
>   Forcing the straits of change? Alas! but who
> Shall wrest a bond from night's inveteracy,
> Ere yet my hazardous soul put forth, to be
>   Her warrant against all her haste might rue?—
>   Ah! in your eyes so reached what dumb adieu,
> What unsunned gyres of waste eternity?

The language itself is basically simple, save for such words as "inveteracy" and "gyres," which the poet may have thought stunning. But E. B. Burgum, who criticized the poem, was correct in attacking its "blur of images." I cannot agree that the fault was a lack of true emotion. It seems to me that what happened was that Rossetti took a simple, true emotion, and put his "system" to work overpacking the lines with "subtle" ideas that are really little more than underdeveloped images, thus obscuring the emotional effect.

The first of the images, "forcing the straits of change,"

which basically means "if I die," repeats what the poet has already said simply in the first two lines. But "forcing" adds the idea of suicide, "straits" provides a voyage image, and "change" points out the obvious fact that death is different from life. "Wrest a bond from night's inveteracy" means basically "get a guarantee," but with "wrest" (as with "forcing") the poet has suggested a struggle, "night" implies the darkness of death, which runs through the whole sonnet, and "inveteracy" adds the idea of the unchanging, eternal unyieldingness of death, which would make the struggle futile. "Hazardous" soul suggests the peril that awaits the soul; "puts forth" picks up the "straits" image of death as a voyage. "Warrant" repeats "bond," and "all haste might rue" implies again both the peril and the futility of seeking reunion in death. "Eyes so reached" completes the voyage-image. "Dumb adieu" presents the futility of death again: the poet has reached his lover in death only to be separated once more. "Unsunned" is another reference to the darkness of Death, and "gyres" summons up the infinite circles (and perhaps changes) of "eternity," which is "waste" largely because empty and futile.

The subtlety of this octet is suggested by the number of "ideas" that Rossetti has forced into the six lines that follow the simple opening two-line statement. In these six lines death is made all of the following: a voyage (three times); a change, but itself unchanging and unyielding; a darkness (twice); a peril to the soul (twice); eternal (twice); a hasty act of the soul; a separation; a turning (changing?) universe; an emptiness and loss; and so a futile hope. Here are a dozen aspects of death in the six lines, and this analysis has hardly been exhaustive. Rossetti's images can thus be clarified, and the inner consistency that he saw in them revealed. But the reader may well ask if the result is worth the effort.

Based on a simple emotion, the six lines will not support a dozen or more undeveloped images. So loaded, the initial emotion sinks, to be recovered only by the patient reader who is willing to dredge beneath the "subtle" obscurities for the flake of gold with which Rossetti began the sonnet. In three lines of one of the *Willowwood* sonnets, on the other hand, Rossetti captures instantly and simply for the reader the whole emotional value which he buried in *Cloud and Wind:*

> And her face fell back drowned, and was as gray
>   As its gray eyes; and if it ever may
> Meet mine again I know not if Love knows.

> (*Willowwood* IV)

Here is the triumph of simplicity over subtlety—and obscurity.

COMPLETENESS AND BREVITY

Cloud and Wind also illustrates the conflict of two other qualities that Rossetti esteemed in a poem: completeness and brevity. All the "ideas" he wished to embody in this poem could not possibly be embodied in so brief a form as the sonnet. Both completeness and brevity, of course, are highly desirable. It is one of the glories of poetry that it can suggest in one line more than pages of prose can express. But suggestion is not the kind of "completeness" that tries to state every possible connotation of a word or image, every ramification of an idea or emotion that occurs to the poet. It hints at the infinite. There are limits of completeness beyond which the poet should not go; there is a saturation point that calls for a compromise between completeness and brevity.

Completeness was one of the aims of Rossetti's fundamental brainwork, the kind of well-shaped fullness where "from the chaos of incident and reflection arise the rounded

worlds of poetry, and go singing on their way."[13] Of Blake's
Two Songs he wrote: "It is, indeed, one of the finest things
Blake ever did, really belonging, by its vivid completeness,
to the order of perfect short poems—never a large band, even
when the best poets are ransacked to recruit it."[14] One of
Marzials' poems stood out, he said, as "so much more of a
whole than almost any of the others."[15] The best of Davies'
work were his "full toned and complete things."[16]

As well as complete, however, Rossetti insisted that a
poem be brief as possible: "I hate long poems." A sonnet
must have "arduous fulness," says the sonnet on the sonnet,
but it must be (though Rossetti himself forgot this now and
then) a "moment's" monument, not a biography. Burne-Jones
explains Rossetti's preference for short poems:

> Like many people, he could not bear the length and quiet-
> ness of an epic. He wanted to keep a poem at boiling point
> all the way through, and he did it to that degree that it
> went into ether with fervent glowing heat before he had
> done with it. The short form of his poems helped him to
> do this. As soon as the pot went off the boil, he'd take it
> from the fire.[17]

Although in his revisions Rossetti often made additions to
a poem, as in *The Blessed Damozel, Sister Helen,* and *Jenny,*
he strove constantly for brevity. As he wrote Skelton:

> This point of size is just the thing that I think last finish
> concerned in rigorously limiting. Thus a good deal has been
> excluded altogether from my volume, and among other
> things included, some had originally been written to twice
> their present length.[18]

Typical were the cuts he made in *The Burden of Nineveh,*
"for the great end of condensation."[19]

Condensation is the only feasible way to try to resolve

the conflicting aims of completeness and brevity. Rossetti confessed to a prejudice in this direction when, in criticizing a poem of O'Shaughnessy's, he said: "You will perhaps think that I am rather testing your work by a personal hobby when I say that this poem particularly and some others seem to me as if they would have greatly gained by being cast in a much more concentrated form."[20] Among the most concentrated of forms is the sonnet. Hence his fondness for the sonnet, which he called "this condensed and emphatic form."[21] But even in his longer poems he tried to be both complete and brief, and regretted that *Rose Mary* lacked the "incisive concentration" of *Sister Helen.*[22] His aversion to poets who "wrote too much," discussed earlier, stemmed in part from the feeling that overproduction was the fatal foe of concentration. He once wrote William Davies:

> Even if I did not paint [i.e. had more time for poetry] I should never be a redundant poet. To write as much as one *can* write leads either to meandering narrative, empty declamation, or mere jagged jargon. . . . Self-scrutiny and self-repression will bear a very large part in the poetic 'survival of the fittest.'[23]

One great result of his fundamental brainwork and constant revision, Rossetti insisted to Caine, was the ultimate in condensation:

> One benefit I do derive as a result of my method of composition; my work becomes more condensed. Probably the man does not live who could write what I have written more briefly than I have done.[24]

If no man could have written more briefly than Rossetti, any number might have written more clearly than he did in *Cloud and Wind.* In achieving compression in this sonnet, Rossetti also achieved indubitable obscurity.

OBSCURITY

Rossetti wrote of Blake's *My Spectre*, "I do not understand it a bit better than anybody else, only I know better than some may know that it has claims on poetry apart from the question of understanding it."[25] He was rarely that tolerant of obscurity. In spite of its "high poetic beauty," Blake's *The Mental Traveller* "seemed at first a hopeless riddle" to Rossetti, and he was on the point of omitting it from the Gilchrist *Blake* as "incomprehensible."[26] Only William Rossetti's exposition of the poem made Gabriel change his mind. He found the first series of *Songs of Innocence and Experience* far superior to the second, because "the five years intervening between the two had proved sufficient for obscurity and the darker mental phases of Blake's writings to set in and greatly mar its poetic value."[27] In one slashing sentence, Rossetti once hit at the lack of clarity of both Ford Madox Brown and Browning, declaring that Brown's sonnets "present a few obscurities of which Browning alone might perhaps serve as an introductory horn-book."[28] He took Caine to task for lacking "distinctness."[29] He censured Hake for his want of "clear-headedness."[30] The second part of Coleridge's *Christabel,* he said, "hints at infinite beauty, but somehow remains a sort of cobweb."[31]

Rossetti's eagerness to make his own work as clear to the reader as possible has already been noted.[32] This was the reason for many of his revisions. He rewrote the beginning of *Love's Nocturne*, for example, because he had been "worrying about what [William Rossetti] said of the obscurity of the opening of this poem."[33] When Caine told Rossetti that the second and third lines of his sonnet *John Keats* "wanted a little clarifying," Rossetti replied, "I am rather aghast for my own lucidity," and promptly changed the offending lines.[34]

Lost on Both Sides got a similar going over when Rossetti had to agree with Allingham that the last lines of the sonnet were "certainly foggy."[35] The original conclusion was indeed foggy, for Rossetti, after describing the rival hopes that dwelt (and warred) *within* his soul, ended with:

> So *from* that soul, in *mindful* brotherhood,
> (When silence may not be) sometimes they throng
> Through high-streets and at many dusty inns.[36]

Rossetti first altered the lines to

> So, *in* that soul, —a *mindful* brotherhood, —
> (When silence may not be,) they wind among
> Its bye-streets, knocking at the dusty inns.[37]

This is better, but the published version (1870 *Poems*) is clearer yet:

> So *through* that soul, in *restless* brotherhood,
> They roam together now, and wind among
> Its bye-streets, knocking at the dusty inns.

There is a definite gain in the word "through," which fits the image of roaming and winding better, in the excision of the somewhat vague "When silence may not be," and in the change of "mindful" brotherhood to "restless" brotherhood.

In looking over his sonnet *Thomas Chatterton,* he discerned a like lack of lucidity. He meant to say that if Chatterton had lived longer and produced more, his tomb would have become a literary shrine. As he wrote Watts-Dunton:

> I reflected that my meaning in the line
>
> 'Even to that unknown shrine else deified'
>
> was not that it would have been deified if known, but would have been so except for the interruption of his work

by the death he chose. Thus I find my first scribble where
the 'unknown' was an amendment on 'secret' 'sacred' and
'inmost'. I propose now that the line run

'Even to that inmost shrine else deified'.[38]

Having run through "inmost" to "sacred" to "secret" and
back to "inmost," the line still doesn't convey what Rossetti
meant. The final version, as it appeared in the 1881 *Ballads
and Sonnets,* does:

Even to that shrine Time else had deified.

Rossetti's one-time plan to write an "explanation" of
The House of Life—a service brother William finally rendered—is further proof that he worried about obscurity in
his poems, as well he might. In striving for the extremes of
simplicity and subtlety, of completeness and brevity, he
was demanding more than was in his (or perhaps any poet's)
power to achieve.

FORCEFULNESS

So much has been written about the "dreamy unreality"
of Rossetti's poetry that it may come as a surprise to learn
that this was a quality that he scarcely mentioned, except
for such tolerant, half-amused observations as that about
the young poets of the *Oxford and Cambridge Magazine*
who lived in "Dreamland." Instead, what he discussed was
forcefulness and "vigor" and "robustness." All these were
good; the lack of them was bad. This is why Rossetti delighted in the "kind of oracular power" that Blake had of
"giving vigorous expression to abstract or social truths."[39]
Wells's portrait of Potiphar's wife was "perfectly astounding
for vigour."[40] Keats's *Otho the Great*, said Rossetti, "affords
perhaps the clearest proof of the quality of robustness left

by Keats."[41] Even though he apparently cared little for Milton's longer poems, he admired the sonnets, and thought the one on *Tetrachordon* "a very vigorous affair indeed."[42]

For the lack of vigor, Rossetti had commensurate disapproval. For him, Tennyson's *Maud* lacked "go."[43] He had scant praise for William Morris' "deliberateness,"[44] and was far happier when his friend was "brisk and vivid."[45] Wordsworth's "tentativeness," he wrote Caine, was no "good accompaniment in music."[46] He had acclaimed Nolly Brown's *Gabriel Denver* as the "most robust literary effort of any imaginative kind" ever written by one so young.[47] But he saw in the youth's *The Black Swan* "a certain torpidity that to me is painful."[48] Equally painful was Leigh Hunt's "detestable flutter and airiness."[49]

Collected together thus, Rossetti's comments on forcefulness and vigor certainly suggest that whatever he may have achieved, he never aimed at producing "dreamy" poetry —a "forceful" dreaminess being a rather improbable ideal, to say the least. *Sister Helen*, singled out by Rossetti himself for its "incisive concentration," is a prime example of the vigor he could achieve. So is *A Last Confession*, which in fact he had to make "less emphatic" because the whore's laughter at the end was misleading to the reader. *The White Ship* and *The King's Tragedy* are others notable for forceful treatment, as are many sonnets of *The House of Life*. Balancing the dreaminess, say, of the *Willowwood* sonnets are such "robust" pieces as *Nuptial Sleep* and *Vain Virtues*, whose vigor so outraged Buchanan.

In truth, there was danger in being too forceful, as Rossetti realized when he toned down the conclusion to *A Last Confession. Rose Mary*, he wrote Scott, was "so consumedly tragic that I have been obliged to modify the intended course of the catastrophe to avoid an unmanageable heaping up of agony."[50] But inherent in the effort to control forcefulness was yet another conflict: moderation vs. reticence. He pronounced moderation to be "the highest law of poetry."[51] He despised reticence. A poet cannot, Rossetti insisted, yield completely to creative ecstasy, "treating material as product, and shooting it all out as it comes."[52] He must strive, as Keats did, to become ever "choicer and simpler."[53] Without moderation came the floods of material that (in Rossetti's eyes) obscured even the genius of Morris. Without moderation came the "reckless, defying vaunt" that was all that kept Chatterton from being "an absolute and untarnished hero."[54] "Intense and oft-renewed effort," said Rossetti, would have eliminated Ebenezer Jones's "wilful 'newness' " and his tendency to deal "recklessly with those almost inaccessible combinations in nature and feeling."[55] And self-discipline would have overcome Swinburne's "principal fault. . .abundance."[56] A like restraint would have prevented the inartistic handling of sex that Rossetti deplored in both Keats and Swinburne.

Without moderation, in sum, the achievement of the ideal of perfection seemed to Rossetti impossible:

> I think then that the pouring forth of poetical material is the greatest danger against which an affluent imagination has to contend, and in my own view it needs not only a concrete form of some kind, but immense concentration brought to bear on that, also, before material can be said to have become anything else.[57]

To repeat what Rossetti said in his letter to Davies, "self-scrutiny and self-repression" were vital. While admitting to his American friend, Professor Charles Eliot Norton, in 1870 that he knew a few of his poems, notably *Jenny,* would "raise objections," Rossetti said, "I only know that they have been written neither recklessly nor aggressively (moods which I think are sure to result in the ruin of Art)."[58] But in this controlling of reckless or aggressive impulses, as

P. F. Baum has pointed out, Rossetti had no use for hypocrisy or false modesty. Professor Baum errs, however, in going on to say: "So much for reticence! The word is not in Rossetti's vocabulary."[59] The word was in Rossetti's vocabulary—and it was a bad word, representing his chief objection to Wordsworth: "A reticence almost invariably present is fatal in my eyes to the highest pretensions on behalf of his sonnets. Reticence is but a poor sort of muse."[60] Hake was found equally guilty of "a singular native tendency to embody all conceptions through a remote and reticent medium."[61]

Ironically, much as he despised the word, Rossetti himself often achieves an effect curiously akin to reticence. If reticence be a reluctance to speak out, openly and freely, then its end result differs very little from the effect produced by Rossetti's obscurity. There is precious little open and free communication of emotion in *Cloud and Wind*, thanks to its "completeness," its oversubtlety, its "blur of images." *Supreme Surrender* has been criticized as "so overloaded with ornamental amorous conceits that its real motive and purpose are at first reading apt to be obscured."[62] In Rossetti's defense, it must be said that the fault lies chiefly in the octet; the sestet is direct enough. Any number of other sonnets might be cited as instances of a kind of remoteness or obscurity that has the effect of reticence, such as *Love's Lovers, Through Death to Love, The Monochord,* and *Memorial Thresholds.*

Sometimes the fault is an overextension of a basic image to the point of overwhelming the emotion the image was supposed to symbolize, as in *Death's Songster,* where a description of Ulysses' experiences with Helen and the Trojan horse, and with the Sirens, takes up twelve of the sonnet's fourteen lines. *Hero's Lamp* seems to be a lament that lifelong happy love is impossible. Yet despite Rossetti's "helpful" footnote summarizing the myth of the lamp dedicated to Anteros after the deaths of Hero and Leander, this reader for one gets so lost among the "Sestian Augurs" and "Avernian Lake" that he longs for the relative simplicity of Donne's "Go and catch a falling star."

   The Birth-Bond has something very like the "As. . . , so. . ." formula of an epic simile, though the image is homely rather than Homeric:

   Have you noted, in some family
      Where two were born of a first marriage-bed
      How still they own their gracious bond, though fed
   And nursed on the forgotten breast and knee?—
   How to their father's children they shall be
      In act and thought of one goodwill; but each
      Shall for the other have, in silence speech,
   And in a word complete community?

   Even so, when first I saw you, seemed it, love,
      That among souls allied to mine was yet
   One nearer kindred than life hinted of.
      O born with me somewhere that men forget,
      And though in years of sight and sound unmet,
   Known for my soul's birth-partner well enough!

So much image to say, "When I first saw you, love, I knew we were kindred spirits." *Venus Victrix* is not unlike a conventional, "literary" Elizabethan love-sonnet, in which the beloved is compared (most favorably, of course) to Juno, Pallas, and Venus. The comparison takes up most of the poem, and even ever-loyal brother William had to confess that "I think the charge of some obscurity may properly attach to the close of this sonnet."[63]

   In sonnets like these, and in scattered passages in much of Rossetti's poetry, there is an insulation between the poet's emotion and the reader, through which the "infectious electricity" that Rossetti wished to produce could not pass.[64] It is hard to believe that this was intentional, as the editors of *The Nineteenth Century and After* aver: "From some of the sonnets in *The House of Life* it is difficult or impossible to wrest a logical meaning; but it is not to be inferred that this is due to confusion of thought; the obscure inapprehensibility is deliberately contrived to convey a sense of the stress of an unresolved emotional conflict."[65] How could Rossetti the Critic, who inveighed so frequently and forcefully against obscurity, or Rossetti the Poet, who revised so often and so agonizingly to make clear his meaning, deliberately contrive to be inapprehensible? That he was guilty of "confusion of thought" now and then is fair enough. But the greatest contributor to his obscurity appears to be the extremism that marked him all his life—an extremism that made it impossible for him to find a successful compromise between the demands of the body and the soul, of the emotional and the spiritual, of simplicity and subtlety, of forcefulness and moderation. In these conflicting demands lay Rossetti's insoluble dilemma. It was but the shortest of steps from here to obscurity.

NOTES

[1]Caine, p. 174.
[2]*D & W.* I, 45.
[3]Caine, p. 170.
[4]*Collected Works,* I, 460.
[5]Scott, II, 138.
[6]Caine, p. 165.
[7]*D & W,* II, 722.
[8]W. M. Rossetti, *Ruskin: Rossetti: Preraphaelitism,* p. 300.
[9]*Ashley Catalogue,* IV, 134-5.
[10]Ingram, p. 83.
[11]*D & W,* IV, 1624-25n.
[12]Burgum, p. 441.
[13]Benson, p. 173.
[14]*Collected Works,* I, 461-2.

[15]Scott, II, 195.

[16]*L & M*, I, 362.

[17]Burne-Jones, II, 264.

[18]*D & W*, II, 822-3.

[19]*L & M*, II, 209.

[20]*D & W*, II, 907.

[21]Caine, p. 110.

[22]Scott, II, 157-8.

[23]*D & W*, IV, 1857. See *sup.*, pp. 103-6.

[24]Caine, p. 221.

[25]Gilchrist, p. 136.

[26]*Collected Works*, I, 463.

[27]*Ibid.*, p. 460.

[28]W. M. Rossetti, *Preraphaelite Diaries and Letters*, p. 37.

[29]Caine, p. 260.

[30]*Collected Works*, I, 506.

[31]Caine, p. 155.

[32]See *sup.*, pp. 87-95.

[33]*L & M*, II, 215.

[34]Caine, p. 174.

[35]*D & W*, I, 212.

[36]*Ibid.*, p. 207. (Italics in all three versions are mine.)

[37]*Ibid.*, p. 213.

[38]*Ibid.*, IV, 1762.

[39]*Collected Works*, I, 464.

[40]C. Wells, *Joseph and His Brethren* (Oxford, 1908), p. xxiv.

[41]Hake and Compton-Rickett, *Watts-Dunton*, I, 226-7.

[42]Caine, p. 238.

[43]M. L. Howe, "Rossetti's Comments on Maud," *Modern Language Notes*, XLIX (May, 1934), p. 291.

[44]*Ashley Catalogue*, IV, 115-6.

[45]Compton-Rickett, p. 316.

[46]Caine, p. 241.

[47]Ingram, p. 83.

[48]Caine, p. 216.

[49]*Ibid.*, p. 179.

[50]Scott, II, 157.

[51]*Collected Works*, I, 511.

[52]Caine, p. 169.

[53]*Ibid.*, p. 170.

[54]*Ibid.*, p. 189.

[55]*Collected Works,* I, 478.

[56]Skelton, pp. 80-1.

[57]*D & W,* II, 914.

[58]*Ibid.,* p. 838.

[59]Baum, *The House of Life,* p. 31.

[60]Caine, p. 241.

[61]*Collected Works,* I, 491.

[62]T. Bayne, "The Poetry of D. G. Rossetti," *Fraser's Magazine'* n.s., XXV (March, 1882), p. 379.

[63]W. M. Rossetti, *The Poems of Dante Gabriel Rossetti,* II, 234.

[64]Ingram, p. 84.

[65]S. C. Chew and R. D. Altick, *The Nineteenth Century and After* (New York, 1967), pp. 1425-26.

VIII

Rossetti and the Poem: Theme and Subject

My mind is a childish one, if to be isolated in Art is child's-play.
Rossetti to Hall Caine, 1880[1]

It was all well and good for Rossetti the Critic to advise a poet, as he did Hall Caine, to "work your metal as much as you like, but first take care that it is worth the working." But what was the metal — the themes and subject matter — that he thought worth the working? A critic like Ruskin, who was only a critic, could peremptorily rank subjects in art in the order of their greatness or "nobility":

    I.   Sacred Subjects.

    II.   Acts or Meditations of Great Men.

    III.   Passions and Events of Ordinary Life.

Yet even Ruskin had to concede that the artist's choice of a subject must be not only sincere, but also wise:

It happens very often that a man of weak intellect, sincerely desiring to do what is good and useful, will devote himself to high art subjects because he thinks them the only ones on which time and trouble can be usefully spent, or, sometimes, because they are really the only ones he has pleasure in contemplating. But not having intellect enough to enter into the minds of truly great men, or to imagine great events as they really happened, he cannot become a great painter; he degrades the subjects he intended to honour, and his work is utterly thrown away, and his rank as an artist in reality lower, than if he had devoted himself to the imitation of the simplest objects of natural history.[2]

The crux, then, is for the artist, be he painter, poet or whatever, to find the metal that *HE* can work successfully. His themes may be as lofty as man ever attempted, but he is at once limited by his choice of subject matter and his powers of execution. This Rossetti tacitly admitted when he said, in replying to Buchanan, that "not even Shakespeare himself could desire more arduous human tragedy for development in art than the themes I venture to embody, however incalculably higher might be his power of dealing with them."[3]

As William Michael Rossetti said, Gabriel did not have to "cudgel his brains" for the idea of a poem.[4] A glimpse of the sea at Hastings could produce an *Even So.* An illustration of a flower was enough to inspire *Woodspurge.* The sight of a winged Assyrian bull being hoisted into the British Museum inspired *The Burden of Nineveh.* Poe's *Raven* suggested *The Blessed Damozel.* Random reading induced the likes of *The Staff and Scrip, The King's Tragedy, The White Ship,* etc. Often, indeed, it would seem that as he read, Rossetti almost automatically thought of a work's possibilities as a subject for art. As he and Janey Morris read Plutarch together at Kelmscott, it struck him that "there is one subject in Plutarch not done by Shakespeare and quite worthy of him—Pompey the Great. Some one should go in for it as a play."[5] Rereading Merivale's *Roman Empire,* he came across the story of a Roman wife who, when her husband was commanded by Nero to commit suicide, stabbed herself first and said, as she handed the dagger to her husband, "It does not hurt." Said Rossetti, "it struck me as really fit for a fine picture, and I don't know but I may paint it."[6]

This was the kind of subject that appealed to Rossetti from his earliest youth. From the first, he doted on the romantic, the chivalric, the medieval, mysterious, and supernatural. In 1855 he was writing Allingham: "I must confess to the need, in narrative-dramatic poetry. . .of something rather 'exciting,' and indeed I believe something of the 'romantic' element, to rouse my mind to anything like the moods produced by personal emotion in my own life."[7] He suggested that Allingham produce "more stories of deeper incident and passion."[8] He advised Edmund Gosse, then a young, unknown poet:

> It seems to me that all poetry, to be really enduring, is bound to be as *amusing* (however trivial the word may sound) as any other class of literature; and I do not think that enough amusement to keep it alive can ever be got out of incidents not amounting to events, or out of travelling experiences of an ordinary kind, however agreeably, observantly, or even thoughtfully treated.[9]

For Rossetti, "thoughtful treatment" was no substitute for a powerful story. He said of Hake's *Madeline,* "it seems to me *Madeline* must have been conceived in a mood more susceptible to certain structural aims than to the passion of its story as a piece of human nature, which it has to be in order to interest the world."[10]

"Fine opportunities and intense situations" were what appealed to Rossetti in his own choice of subject matter, as in *The Doom of the Sirens,* which he never got around to writing,[11] and "a story with. . .good emotions and surprises in it," as in *Rose Mary.*[12] What he sought, for his sonnets as well as his narrative poems, was the "momentous," the intense, dramatic situation that would give full play to his imagination, and produce the "arduous fulness" that could turn a sonnet into a moment's monument. Hence his admiration for Coleridge: "The sense of the momentous is strongest in Coleridge; not the weird and ominous only, but the value of monumental moments."[13] In Walter Pater's view, "to Rossetti. . .life is a crisis at every moment."[14]

In this emphasis on the necessity for intense experiences for poetry, Rossetti does come close to Pater's famous statement: "To burn always with this hard, gemlike flame, to maintain this ecstasy, is success in life." The themes and subjects that he admired most in the works of others, and used most often in his own poetry, agree in the main with Pater's assertion that "Great passions may give us this quickened sense of life, ecstasy and sorrow of love, the various forms of enthusiastic activity, disinterested or otherwise, which come naturally to many of us. Only be sure it is passion—that it does yield you this fruit of a quickened, multiplied consciousness. Of such wisdom, the poetic passion, the desire of beauty, the love of art for its own sake, has most."[15]

But this does not place Rossetti in the Art-for-Art's sake camp, or with the Decadents who justified sensation for sensation's sake. He meant it when he said that the principal of Art for Art's sake was one third so essentially wrong that it negatived the whole.[16] For him, as we have seen, a poem must have spirituality as well as emotion and beauty. And for Rossetti—as not for the Decadents—there were strict taboos as to permissible subject matter. One such was Christ, whom the Pre-Raphaelite Brothers had named—along with Shakespeare—as one of the only two names deserving top place in the list of "immortals" that they drew up.[17] Rossetti could not condone Swinburne's treatment of the "pale Galilean." He even doubted that the life of Christ was a fit subject for poetry. When William Sharp wrote him that he was thinking about writing such a poem, Rossetti replied:

> Strange to say, I can conceive no higher Ideal than the Christ we know; and I judge it to be very rash to lower in poetry (to the apprehension of many beautiful minds) that Ideal, by any assumption to decide a point respecting it which it is not possible to *decide,* whichever way belief or even conviction may tend.[18]

The treatment of sex was another subject on which Rossetti had strict reservations, as was illustrated by his efforts to tone down his own treatment of the subject in order to avoid offending the reader. But Rossetti's dislike of the sordid went deeper than that. William Michael Rossetti was right when he wrote of his brother, "at no period of his life did he relish the sight of anything repellent or degrading."[19] Rossetti sincerely felt that *Jenny* was "rightly within Art's province" because it was "written neither recklessly nor aggressively."[20] He defended *Nuptial Sleep* as dealing with "a beauty of natural function" that, in context with the whole *House of Life,* did not exclude "those other higher things of which it is the harmonious concomitant."[21] Even so, he must have had his doubts about the sonnet from the start, for in 1869—two whole years before Buchanan singled the poem out for attack—Rossetti cautioned his brother "you had better remove it" if William were planning to show proofs of Gabriel's poems "en famille."[22] Rossetti condemned his own *Dennis Shand* "because it deals trivially with a base amour (it was written *very* early) and is therefore really reprehensible to some extent," and refused to publish it in his lifetime.[23] He criticized *The Bride's Prelude,* which he never finished: "My most fundamental objection to *Bride's Prelude* is that the story is unelevated and repulsive."[24] When he

finally decided to include the fragment of this poem in his
Poems, 1881, his excuse to Watts-Dunton was extremely
lame: "On reading the *Bride's Prelude* again in type, I think
you will agree with me that its picturesqueness is sufficient
to make it pass muster, though it has no other quality to
recommend it. Besides I dont [*sic*] see how it can be spared,
as the space *must* be filled."[25] Filling space with a poem he
thought unelevated and repulsive in subject was hardly worthy—or typical—of a poet who, when told that Scott had
lent a copy of his poems to a clergyman, replied: "there may
be things here and there in the book which might rather
ruffle the nap of 'The Cloth,' though not a line that is vile,
by God!"[26] The volume that the "reverend gentleman"
happened to be reading, however, did not include *The Bride's
Prelude.*

More in keeping with Rossetti's general attitude was
his reaction to Keats's *Sharing Eve's Apple,* expressed in a
letter to Henry Buxton Forman, who was working on an
edition of Keats's poems: "I don't on reflection like it at all.
It would certainly do Keats's fame no credit. You said yourself that it is 'rather vulgar,' and ought Keats to seem so
through that being printed which he never meant except as
a private pleasantry?"[27] Forman apparently agreed, for
Rossetti was soon writing him: "I am glad that you have
made up your mind not to print *Eve's Apple.* Of course I do
not consider that sexual passion, if nobly expressed, should
be excluded from poetry for any reason except that of not
restricting its circulation. But here we have a poet, conspic-
uously noble in essential tone of mind, yielding by some
freak of the moment in private to a triviality which gives no
idea of his true nature."[28] (Forman, however, did print the
poem in 1895.)

Where he could find some mitigating quality, Rossetti
could qualify his condemnation of unworthy subjects, as
when "picturesqueness" helped *The Bride's Prelude* pass

muster. His opinion of Browning's *The Ring and the Book* was that "there was perversity in the choice of subject, though of course redeemed by superb treatment."[29] But he found no such excuse for an illustration for *The Bride of Lammermoor*: "The subject, however, is a repulsive one, unredeemed by any lesson or sympathetic beauty."[30] In forthright fashion he described Byron's *Don Juan* as "immoral and harmful."[31] Rossetti's comparison of Flaubert's *Salammbo* and Victor Hugo's *Notre Dame de Paris* is especially revealing:

> It [*Salammbo*] is a phenomenal book, and could only have emanated from a nation on the brink of a great catastrophe. The line of demarcation between this and *Notre Dame de Paris,* published some thirty years before, is very singular to remark. Hugo's book astounds one with horrors, but they seem called up more for the purpose of evoking the extremes of human pity, and for the author's own luxury in that passion, than for any other aim. Flaubert, on the contrary, is not only destitute of pity, but one could not judge from his book, teeming as it does with inconceivable horrors, that such an element existed or ever had existed in human nature. . . . The only thing that deadens the agony of mutual destruction throughout to the reader is that it is perfectly impossible to feel the least preference for one character over another. . . . It seems the work of a nation from which mercy has been cast out, and which was destined soon to find none.[32]

Here, surely, speaks no lover of sensation for sensation's sake alone.

With the foregoing qualifications in mind, it is safe to say, in summary, that for a subject to appeal to Rossetti it must have something exciting, passion of story, fine opportunities for development, intense situations, and above all something of the "momentous." Where specifically, then, did he find all these when he came to choose subjects for his own poetry? To a remarkable degree, he found them in a relatively few areas of all the vast sweep that encompasses human experience, despite his statement to Swinburne that "the variety in my work, of which you in your generosity make so much, depends, I suspect, on their [*sic*] being tentative efforts in different directions."[33] In fact, Watts-Dunton said of Rossetti that "throughout his life he had taken an interest in only four subjects — poetry, painting, medieval mysticism, and woman."[34] If one takes a few liberties with Watts-Dunton's list — notably, to expand the "medieval" to include anything not of the "real" modern English world, and "mysticism" to include anything supernatural — Watts-Dunton, though too sweeping, is not far amiss. Analysis of Rossetti's major poems proves this.

Arbitrarily, I have selected twenty-four of Rossetti's "long" poems, plus the sonnets of *The House of Life,* as "major" works. If arbitrary, the limit of twenty-four is generous — much more so than is William Michael Rossetti in his 1886 edition of his brother's *Collected Works,* where he lists only ten works as "Principal Poems." Of the 364 pages in that edition devoted to Rossetti's original poetry (i.e., as distinct from his translations), 281 pages are given to those twenty-four poems and *The House of Life.* This selection of Rossetti's major poems, thus, represents 79 percent of the whole body of his original work, a rather astonishingly high proportion even for a poet who always boasted of his quality rather than quantity. Rossetti's considerable reputation as a poet rests fundamentally on these twenty-four and the sonnet sequence. Rossetti's hatred of long poems, by the way, is substantiated by his practice. Of the "long" poems he wrote (and every poem of his over fifty lines is included in the twenty-four), the longest is *Rose Mary,* with 840 lines of narrative and about 100 lines of Beryl-songs; the shortest included in the list is *Down Stream,* with forty lines.

A casual reading of Rossetti's poems leaves the impression that he found his favorite subjects in the medieval world, and in woman—most often a combination of both. Analysis of the twenty-four poems confirms this even more strongly than I would have guessed. At first glance, for instance, these twenty-four would seem to be divided equally, twelve and twelve, between a first group that are medieval (or earlier) in subject matter or tone, and a second that are "modern." Among the medieval group I include *The Bride's Prelude, Sister Helen, The Staff and Scrip, Rose Mary, The White Ship, The King's Tragedy, Ave, Stratton Water, Dante at Verona,* and *The Blessed Damozel,* with *Troy Town* and *Eden Bower* representing an even earlier time. In the "modern" group are *A Last Confession, The Stream's Secret, Love's Nocturne, Jenny, The Burden of Nineveh, Soothsay, My Sister's Sleep, The Card Dealer, The Portrait, Wellington's Funeral, Cloud Confines,* and *Down Stream.*

Further analysis, however, reveals that the real, modern English world in which Rossetti lived provided little of the stuff from which his poetry was fashioned. *The Stream's Secret* and *Love's Nocturne,* with their dreamy, unworldly atmosphere, are far from the realm that Victoria ruled. The contemporary political situation that provides the setting for *A Last Confession* has nothing to do with a Kiplingesque empire, but with the remote and savage feud between the Lombards and the Austrians. That leaves only nine poems in the second group, and they make a scant thirty-seven of the two hundred and eighty-one pages devoted to Rossetti's major poems.

When one adds the subject of "woman" as a criterion, the second group dwindles even further. *Jenny, The Portrait,* and *Down Stream* qualify indubitably. *My Sister's Sleep* and *The Card Dealer* (who is a woman, Fate, dealing the cards of life and death) may perhaps be included by a liberal interpretation of Watts-Dunton's "woman." That leaves only four poems of the original twenty-four that do not fit the two most important—the medieval and woman—of Watts-Dunton's quartet of subjects. These four are *The Burden of Nineveh, Cloud Confines,* and *Soothsay,* all reflections on life; and *Wellington's Funeral,* Rossetti's only major treatment of a contemporary English political topic. And even these four can be reduced to two when Rossetti's own deprecation of *Wellington's Funeral* and *Soothsay* is noted. *Wellington's Funeral,* he wrote Thomas Woolner sardonically, was written "*de rigeur. . .*which I keep as a monument of the universal influence of public frenzy even on the most apathetic."[35] And he had to agree with Swinburne's stricture that it was "a flagrant example of shameless cheek and historically intolerable to me as being false to 'Fact' and therefore 'damnable.' "[36] Answered Rossetti: "I heartily concur in your objections, which are of course damning. I wrote it, I remember, to express the feeling of the nation at the moment without particularly thinking whether it was my own, which it was not to any serious extent. So the thing rightly goes rotten."[37]

Rossetti also discounted *Soothsay,* originally entitled *Commandments,* in a letter in which he described its inception: "the three verses came into my head during a walk, and I think of carrying it further, probably, only such like verses do not interest me much."[38] His very process of finishing the poem belittles it: "I have nearly doubled the aphoristic poem by grinding up prose saws of mine into verse."[39] Rossetti's feeling about *Wellington's Funeral* and *Soothsay* was sound; only an excess of generosity put them among the twenty-four "major" poems in the first place. Thus we are left with only *The Burden of Nineveh* and *The Cloud Confines* as exceptions to Watts-Dunton's broad generalization about Rossetti's subjects, and even *The Cloud Confines* has its share of woman, with its "heart of love" and "kisses snatched 'neath the ban.' "

And so by a triumph of statistics, which in cunning hands ne'er yields the flag, *The Burden of Nineveh* stands alone.[40] It (along with *Dante at Verona*) provides the only important rebuttal to Watts-Dunton's claim that "with the exception of *The White Ship*, a few of the reflective sonnets, and an occasional lyric such as *Cloud Confines,* woman is the subject of all his poems."[41] Now "all" is a dangerous word, though it is true that the great preponderance of Rossetti's poetry deals with woman, or more specifically, with love. There is no need to belabor again the fact that *The House of Life* might more properly be called the house of Love. But in both *The House of Life* and in a number of other poems both major and minor, Rossetti made some use (if only ancillary) of a variety of other subjects, including art, reflections on life, religion, domestic scenes, social and political matters, and supernatural material.

Poetry and painting were the other two subjects that, with medieval mysticism and woman, made up what Watts-Dunton called the "only four subjects" that interested Rossetti. He did not achieve the dramatic power of Browning's art poems, which he said "seem to me perfection."[42] Yet the number of Rossetti's literary works whose subject was art is noteworthy: forty sonnets and two prose stories, not to mention *Dante at Verona.* These include the sonnet on the sonnet, *Old and New Art* (three sonnets, Numbers 74, 75, and 76), *Transfigured Life* (60), *The Song-Throe* (61), *The Landmark* (67), and *Lost on Both Sides* (91)—all in *The House of Life.* All of these treat of art in general, except *The Landmark* and *Lost on Both Sides,* which deal with Rossetti's own career as poet and painter. Two prose tales that are primarily concerned with the artist are *Hand and Soul* and *Saint Agnes of Intercession.* Rossetti also wrote ten sonnets about other painters, of which the best known is *For a Venetian Pastoral*; fourteen sonnets for his own pictures; and eight sonnets honoring other poets.

It may well be that for Rossetti, life was love, as the preponderance of this theme in his poetry suggests. But he did
muse from time to time about other aspects of human life,
as *The Sea-Limits* demonstrated.[43] *The Cloud Confines*
was his major attempt to grapple with the mysteries of life
and afterlife, but *Soothsay* and *The Portrait* are other examples of his reflections on life. Three sonnets in *The House
of Life* entitled *The Choice* (Numbers 71, 72, and 73) offer
three alternatives as to how man should spend his life: "Eat
thou and drink". . ."Watch thou and fear". . .and "Think
thou and act." But, to repeat, Rossetti was hardly a reflective
poet. He said it all when he said of *Soothsay*, "such like
verses" did not interest him much.

Religion *per se* had almost as little appeal as a subject.
When he was twenty, he was preparing his painting, "The
Girlhood of Mary Virgin," for the 1849 Exhibition. But the
motive seems at best to have been momentary, if not mone-
tary. There is something deliciously naive about his description of the painting in a letter to his father's patron, a botanist
and student of Dante named Charles Lyell: "It belongs to
the religious class which has always appeared to me the
most adapted and most worthy to interest the members of
a Christian community."[44] To accompany his painting, he
wrote a sonnet, which was published in his 1870 *Poems.*

Perhaps his best strictly religious poem is *Ave*, which he
also wrote in his youth. But as he neared the publishing
of his poems in 1870, he admitted that he "hesitated much"
to print it, "because of the subject," and considered footnoting
it with a comment denying any intention of celebrating any
one religion (i.e., Roman Catholicism) at the expense of "all
faiths."[45] Swinburne snorted: "Have you struck out for good
the footnote disclaiming a share in the blessings purchased
by the blood of your Redeemer?"[46] Rossetti struck it out.
His reaction, when he came to review the proofs of another
very early work, *My Sister's Sleep,* was similar: "the thing

is very distasteful to me as it stands, and I have quite determined on all changes made in pen and ink. In pencil I indicate
a very radical change in the omission of two more stanzas
which would eliminate the religious element altogether."[47]

God is seen as sanctioning Art in the *Old and New Art*
sonnets of *The House of Life.* The title of *A Last Confession*
refers, of course, to the Catholic rite, which Rossetti uses
as the setting for this tale of love and murder. There are
clerical and religious elements in the medieval settings of
various narrative poems, notably *Dante at Verona.* And there
is always the Blessed Damozel warming the golden bar of
heaven and asking Christ the Lord "Only to live as once on
earth / With Love." *The Burden of Nineveh* is an ironic com-
mentary on the idol worshipped by pagans and the lip-service
worship of God by Victorian Englishmen, with the final,
dramatically suggested possibility that the gods of both were
one. Two short poems, *Vox Ecclesiae Christi* and *Place de
la Bastille, Paris,* question the ways of God to man.
Wellington's Funeral is a cry for peace in God's name. Yet
for all his youthful fears of the charge of "popery," Rossetti's
use of religion is relatively slight. Of God's role, now and
in the hereafter, Rossetti could only say, as in *The Cloud
Confines:*

'Strange to think by the way,
Whatever there is to know,
That shall we know one day.'

In his criticism, Rossetti occasionally pays tribute to
domestic themes and subjects, as when he says of the poems
of Joseph Skipsey, "his pictures of humble life are best. He
is a working miner, and describes rustic loves and sports, and
the perils and pathos of pit-life with great charm, having a
quiet humor too when needed."[48] Yet Rossetti felt that despite
the "matter-of-fact tendencies of the reading public," the

"simpler and more domestic order of themes has not been generally, of late years, the most widely popular. Indeed," he continued in his review of Hake's *Parables and Tales*, "these have probably had less than their due in the balance of immediate acceptance." He then proceeds to illustrate his point:

> It would be easy to point to examples, — for instance, to the work which Mr. Allingham has done so well in this field, — above all, to his very memorable book, *Laurence Bloomfield in Ireland*, — a solid and undeniable achievement, no less a historical record than a searching poetic picture of those manners which can alone be depicted with a *certainty* of future value, — the manners of our own time. Yet such a book as this seems yet to have its best day to come. Should Dr. Hake's more restricted, but lovely and sincere, contributions to the poetry of real life, not find the immediate response they deserve, he may at least remember that others also have failed to meet at once with full justice and recognition.[49]

Even so, Rossetti himself was embarrassed by the public acceptance of his one major excursion into domestic life, that "spoony affair" *My Sister's Sleep*. Just before the publishing of the 1870 *Poems* he was writing Swinburne, "I almost think I shall cut out *My Sister's Sleep* at the last moment. I feel so sure that the British fool will greet it with congenial sympathy, and do so hate to please him."[50] Now and then, as in sonnets like *Broken Music, Transfigured Life, The Birth-Bond*, and *Barren Spring*, Rossetti uses touches of domestic life for imagery, but without conspicuous success. In the first version of *The Burden of Nineveh* he had a mocking picture of Londoners viewing the statue, but realized its incongruity in the poem, and whittled the detail in the final version to:

While school foundations in the act
Of holiday, three files compact,
Shall learn to view thee as a fact
Connected with that zealous tract:
  'Rome, — Babylon and Nineveh.'

Domesticity, in short, had almost as little place in Rossetti's poetry as in own life. He told Allingham in 1867: "I loathe and despise family life."[51]

For social and political problems, Rossetti had some interest, but not much. He repeatedly ducked jury duty by getting medical excuses from his physician, and rarely voted. This coincided with his general disdain for the Victorian world about him, what he called in his sonnet to Keats "the weltering London ways where children weep." In *Saint Agnes of Intercession,* he says of the hero's painting: "The subject was a modern one, and indeed it has often seemed to me that all work, to be truly worthy, should be wrought out of the age itself, as well as out of the soul of the producer, which must needs be a soul of the age."[52] But as we have seen, Rossetti found his own age slim fare for art. At age thirty he wrote: "I am beginning to doubt, more and more, I confess, whether. . .excessive elaboration is rightly bestowed on the materials of a modern subject — things so familiar to the eye that they can really be rendered thoroughly (I fancy) with much less labor; and things moreover which are often far from beautiful in themselves, — for instance, the flowing waistcoat of a potboy on which Brown has lately been spending some weeks of his life."[53]

The "attempt to make poetry out of modern stories," Rossetti said, "(where so much is commercial in origin and mechanical in means) is, while irresistible to a wide-minded poet, hardly ever successful."[54] To Rossetti, the attempt was quite resistible. He insisted that he commonly followed "poetic painting" — rather than the "real and human" — out of preference, not lack of ability, and said that if he did exhibit his paintings, the exhibit must include "Found," because "I should wish to show, — as such a picture as *Found* though small, must do, if I succeed with it — that my preference for the ideal does not depend on incapacity to deal with simple nature."[55]

The subject of "Found," like *Jenny* a sympathetic presentation of a prostitute, indicates that Rossetti did have some awareness of social problems. But *Jenny* is, after all, his only important poetic expression of this, and its occasional moralizing dulls the dramatic and emotional effect. His attitude towards poets who would be social reformers is expressed by his scorn for Shelley's "hatching yearly universes."[56] He approved of Keats's advice to Shelley to "curb your magnanimity" as "Cheeky! — but not so much amiss."[57] "Shelley did good," Rossetti told Caine, "and perhaps some harm with it. Keats's joy was after all a flawless gift."[58] Rossetti thought Blake's second *Chimney Sweeper* greatly inferior to the first because it was "tinged somewhat with the commonplaces, if also the truths, of social discontent."[59] He had little relish for the "social and other views" in Tennyson's *Maud,* asserting that they were not in harmony with the characters of the poem, but "much more like the sort of thing the author thinks *ought* to be written, but about which the author feels lazy and thinks (as some of his readers do) nothing but a bore."[60]

Rossetti's interest in political affairs appears to have been roughly equivalent to his attitude towards religion. That is, he had little concern for the specific parties and policies that serve as the politician's sects and creeds. As his brother put it, Rossetti "had some feeling for political ideals and great movements, but. . .annoyance and disdain for noise and bluster."[61] It is almost unbelievable that a man who wrote as many letters as Rossetti did (and I have read well over 2,800 of them) would have so little to say about the tumultuous and dramatic political events that swirled about him during his lifetime. The two notable exceptions are both personal. When his brother William embarked on a series of political sonnets, Rossetti, alarmed at their revolutionary tone, wrote urgently to William's wife Lucy:

> Several of William's truest friends, no less than myself, are greatly alarmed at the tone taken in some of his Sonnets respecting 'Tyrannicide', 'Fenianism', and other incendiary subjects. It appears to me and to others that the consequences are absolutely and very perilously uncertain when an official (as William is) of a monarchical government allows himself such unbridled license of public speech.[62]

He followed this up with a note to William himself, and was greatly relieved when William abandoned the project.

The other occasion when Rossetti expressed real concern about politics involved the Franco-Prussian War, and here his interest was even more personal. When the war was declared on June 19, 1870, he wrote to his publisher, Ellis, with whom he had been discussing a reissue of his Italian translations: "I suppose all poetry will be dead as ditch water now with this blessed war."[63] He was equally if not more perturbed about the effect of the war on the sale of his paintings, writing to his friend and fellow painter Frederick James Shields:

> Of your health you do not specially speak, nor do I gather clearly whether what you say of your 'suffering' from this truly atrocious and insufferable war relates simply to what all must feel or to more direct influences of a baneful kind on your own immediate prospects. Such would doubtless be a possible result for any of us, as there is no knowing the moment at which retrenchment may be forced upon the wealthy classes of this country by the state of affairs abroad or even at home, and naturally art goes first to the wall.[64]

One should not fault Rossetti too much for reacting thus selfishly to a conflict that cost thousands of lives. Poetry and painting were his only sources of income. And he was constitutionally ill-equipped, as he confessed, to "attain to the more active and practical of the mental functions of manhood."[65] In the long letter to Caine in which this confession appears, Rossetti said:

> I must admit, at all hazards, that my friends here consider me exceptionally averse to politics; and I suppose I must be, for I never read a parliamentary debate in my life! At the same time I will add that, among those whose opinions I most value, some think me not altogether wrong when I venture to speak of the momentary momentousness and eternal futility of many noisiest questions. However, you must view me as a nonentity in any practical relation to such matters.

He went on to say:

> I had better really stick to knowing how to mix vermilion and ultramarine for a flesh-grey, and how to manage their equivalents in verse. To speak without sparing myself,— my mind is a childish one, if to be isolated in Art is child's-play. . . .[66]

This was a true and honest appraisal of his own limitations. For his unconcern about politics, Rossetti gave several reasons. First, there was his "sloth," more probably the result rather than the cause of his disinterest. Second, he thought that history had perhaps "set to a great extent a *veto* against the absolute participation of artists in politics."[67] In proof of this, he cited Michaelangelo's futile participation in politics, and asked if Coleridge had been killed in battle during the months he served as Pvt. Cumberback, "should we have been more the gainers by his patriotism or the losers by his poetry?"[68] Finally, Rossetti protested that he did not consider art as more important than the "unity of a great nation." But, he added, "it is in my power to deal with the one, while no such entity, as I am, can advance or retard the other; and thus mine must needs be the poorer part."[69]

Nonetheless, Rossetti was at times sufficiently stirred by political events to use them as subjects for poems. *After the French Liberation of Italy* and its sequel, *After the German Subjugation of France*, show Rossetti reacting powerfully against aggression and tyranny. His *Wellington's Funeral* is a plea for peace, though admittedly somewhat lacking in an honest ring. His sonnet, *At the Sunrise in 1848*, is a possibly overly "literary" expression of his enthusiasm for the European revolutionists of that year. *The English Revolution of 1848*, as William Michael Rossetti describes it, "ridicules the street-spoutings of chartists and others."[70] (Rossetti once declared that Ebenezer Jones's being "the most striking example of neglected genius in our modern school of poetry" was "a more important fact about him than his being a Chartist.")[71]

Two other brief experiments with political subjects were his sonnets *Czar Alexander the Second*, which deplores the murder of the ruler who "willed kingly freedom" for the Russians, and *On Refusal of Aid Between Nations*. In the latter, which was written about the same time as *A Last Confession*, Rossetti attacks the apathy with which England watched the struggles of Italy and Hungary against Austria, and achieves real eloquence in his denunciation of man's selfishness to man:

> Not that the earth is changing, O my God!
>   Nor that the seasons totter in their walk, —
>   Not that the virulent ill of act and talk
> Seethes ever as a winepress ever trod, —
> Nor therefore are we certain that the rod

Weighs in thine hand to smite the world; though now
Beneath thine hand so many nations bow,
So many kings: — not therefore, O my God! —

But because Man is parcelled out in men
Today; because, for any wrongful blow,
No man not stricken asks, 'I would be told
Why thou dost thus;' but his heart whispers then,
'He is he, I am I.' By this we know
That the earth falls asunder, being old.

Minor though Rossetti's political poems may be, they clearly show that his sympathies lay with truth and justice.

One final source of themes and subjects for Rossetti's poetry remains to be discussed, and this one is major: the supernatural. For the weird and supernatural he had shown a marked fondness as a boy. This predilection continued throughout his career, in his criticism, in his poetry, and in his life. During the later years, particularly after the death of his wife in 1862, he experimented considerably with spiritualism and mesmerism.[72] According to Scott, Rossetti frequently attended seances, and sometimes believed that he had succeeded in communicating with the spirit of his wife. While Rossetti was visiting at Kenkill in 1868, says Scott, a chaffinch alighted on the poet's hand and Rossetti declared, "it is my wife, the spirit of my wife." The incident is eerily reminiscent of the lines he had added to *The Blessed Damozel* in 1856, four years before he had even married Lizzie:[73]

Ah sweet! Even now, in that bird's song,
Strove not her accents there,
Fain to be hearkened?

Rossetti's fascination with the supernatural was one reason for his love of Coleridge, with all that was "weird and ominous." And of Keats, Caine asserts that "in general terms it was not so much the wealth of expression in the author of *Endymion* which attracted the author of *Rose Mary* as the perfect hold of the supernatural which is seen in *La Belle Dame Sans Merci* and in the fragment of the *Eve of St. Mark.* "[74] Much of Dr. Hake's appeal to Rossetti, too, was perhaps in this minor poet's use of supernatural material. Rossetti showed keen interest in Caine's projected study of the use of the supernatural in poetry:

> I strongly urge you to go on with your book on the *Supernatural.* The closing chapter should, I think, be on the *weird* element in its perfection, as shown by recent poets in the mass, — i.e. those who take the lead. Tennyson has it certainly here and there in imagery, but there is no great success in the part it plays through his *Idylls.* The Old Romaunt beats him there. The strongest instance of this feeling in Tennyson is in a few lines of the *Palace of Art.*[75]

Rossetti then quoted the lines he had in mind,

> And hollow breasts enclosing hearts of flame;
> And with dim-fretted foreheads all
> On corpses three-months old at morn she came,
> That stood against the wall.

Rossetti added the warning, "I won't answer for the precise age of the corpses — perhaps I have staled them somewhat." He had not staled the corpses, but he had made several unconscious changes in the text which, interestingly enough, made for added vividness. Thus, "breasts" had been substituted for "shades," and "morn" for "noon."

Watts-Dunton called Rossetti's own use of the supernatural his "wizard's wand."[76] He has a sure instinct for how the supernatural should be used. When he chanced upon a story, "The Queen of the Red Chessmen," in the *Atlantic* magazine, he asked Charles Eliot Norton who wrote it, and continued: "There seems a wild appropriateness in much of it, but it struck me that the human and the superhuman were not quite comfortably grafted on to each other."[77] Here was his key to the successful use of the supernatural, the grafting of the human and the superhuman, the natural and the supernatural. In his review of Hake's *Madeline,* Rossetti described the technique precisely:

> The scheme of this strange poem is as literal and deliberate in a certain sense as though the story were the simplest in the world; and so far it might be supposed to fulfill one of the truest laws of the supernatural in art—that of homely externals developing by silent contrast the inner soul of the subject. But here, in fact, the outer world does not once affect us in tangible form.[78]

Rossetti's most masterful use of this necessary contrast of homely externals and the inner soul of the supernatural is to be found, to my mind, in *Sister Helen.* Here the "little brother's" innocent questions and his childish reporting of the essential action of the poem create an enormous emotional impact when juxtaposed, as they are in every stanza, with Sister Helen's inexorable replies and unyielding hate and despair. The mother in *Rose Mary* serves similarly as the measure of the outer world, whereby the stature of the supernatural is manifest. In the same way, homely details give emphasis and credibility, as well as vividness, to the "otherwordly" in *The Blessed Damozel.* In *The King's Tragedy*—whose supernaturalism Rossetti intentionally built up—the refusal of the king to be swayed by a "sorcerer" echoes the reader's own doubts of the supernatural, and thus, in that paradoxical way of art, obtains the reader's willing suspension of disbelief.

Allied to Rossetti's use of the strictly supernatural was his use of what in *The Blessed Damozel* has been called "otherworldly," and his use of what might be described as "weird." The dream-world of *Love's Nocturne,* and such visions as the *Willowwood Sonnets* in *The House of Life* exemplify the former; the latter is used in *Troy Town* and especially in *Eden Bower.*

When combined with the frequent use of the medieval in his major poetry, this reliance on the otherworldly, the weird, and the supernatural re-emphasize the extent to which Rossetti departed from contemporary Victorian life for his themes and subject matter. Although he showed some passing interest in religion, reflections on life, domesticity, and social and political problems, he remains a poet not merely "isolated in art," but isolated in only a part of the broad demesne that art may properly claim for its own — the narrow yet golden realms of poetry, painting, the supernatural, and. . .woman.

NOTES

[1] Caine, p. 201.

[2] J. Ruskin, *Modern Painters* (New York, 1885), III, 44-5.

[3] *Collected Works.* I, 486.

[4] *Ibid.,* p. xxxiv.

[5] *D & W,* III, 978.

[6] *Ibid.,* p. 1068.

[7] *Ibid.,* I, 255.

[8] *Ibid.,* p. 256.

[9] *Ibid.,* III, 1246.

[10] *Ibid.,* II, 919.

[11] *Ibid.,* p. 770.

[12] *Ibid.,* p. 1005.

[13] *Collected Works.* I, 511.

[14] W. Pater, *Appreciations* (London, 1927), p. 211.

[15] W. Pater, *The Renaissance* (London, 1925), pp. 238-9.

[16] See *sup.,* p. 36.

[17] *D & W,* I, 42.

[18]*Ibid.*, IV, 1699. However, he praised Hake's "symbolic expression" of Christ. (*Collected Works*, I, 490.)

[19]*L & M*, I, 38.

[20]*D & W*, II, 838.

[21]*Collected Works*, I, 482.

[22]*D & W*, II, 715.

[23]Caine, p. 122.

[24]*D & W*. IV, 1861.

[25]*Ibid.*, p. 1880.

[26]*Ibid.*, p. 1693.

[27]*Ibid.*, p. 1880.

[28]*Ibid.*, pp. 1886-7.

[29]Gilchrist, pp. 174-5.

[30]*Collected Works*, II, 479.

[31]*L & M*, I, 100.

[32]*D & W*, III, 1115-6.

[33]*Ibid.*, II, 804.

[34]Watts-Dunton, p. 416.

[35]*D & W*, I, 133.

[36]*Ibid.*, II, 805n.

[37]*Ibid.*, p. 805.

[38]*Ibid.*, III, 986.

[39]*Ibid.*, IV, 1692.

[40]To Rossetti, *The Burden of Nineveh* also had its limitations: "The *Nineveh* I reckon on as destined probably to be the most generally popular thing in the book [the 1870 *Poems*]. I do not regard it with indifference myself, but am inclined to give the preference to the more emotional order of subject." (*D & W*, II, 759-60.)

[41]Watts-Dunton, p. 417.

[42]*D & W*, I, 277.

[43]See *sup.*, pp. 44-6.

[44]*D & W*, I, 48.

[45]*Ibid.*, II, 714. In writing his painter-friend James Smetham he would gladly correspond about Art, but not "religious enquiry and discussion," Rossetti said almost brutally, "I had better tell you frankly at once that I have no such faith as you have." (*D & W*. II, 582.)

[46]*Ibid.*, p. 714n.

[47]*Ibid.*, p. 731.

[48]Caine, p. 198.

[49]*Collected Works*, I, 508.

[50]*D & W*, II, 798. The poem was printed.

[51]Allingham, p. 166.

[52]*Collected Works*, I, 402.

[53]*D & W*, I, 335.

[54]*Ibid.*, IV, 1334.

[55]*Ibid.*, p. 1635.

[56]Caine, p. 170.

[57]*Ibid.*, p. 180.

[58]*Ibid.*

[59]*Collected Works*, I, 460.

[60]Howe, p. 291.

[61]*L & M*, I, 108.

[62]*D & W*, IV, 1865. The fact that Rossetti's own father suffered political persecution adds weight to his concern.

[63]*Ibid.*, II, 893.

[64]*Ibid.*, p. 897.

[65]Caine, p. 202.

[66]*Ibid.*, pp. 200-01.

[67]*Ibid.*, p. 202.

[68]*Ibid.*, p. 205.

[69]*Ibid.*, p. 203.

[70]*L & M*, I, 108-9.

[71]*D & W*, II, 788.

[72]Scott, II, 235; and *L & M*, I, 255.

[73]For comments, see Baum, *The House of Life*, p. xx; Doughty, *Dante Gabriel Rossetti*, pp. 394-5; and Knickerbocker, "Rossetti's *The Blessed Damozel.*"

[74]Caine, p. 167.

[75]*Ibid.*, p. 266.

[76]Watts-Dunton, pp. 414-5.

[77]*D & W*, I, 399. The author was Lucretia Peabody Hale.

[78]*Collected Works*, I, 496.

IX

Rossetti and the Poem: Execution

I have so often had to retrace my steps by the humblest verbal labor.
Rossetti to Dr. T. G. Hake, 1871[1]

Rossetti most succinctly described the role of execution in the fashioning of a poem in his sonnet *Transfigured Life*, in which he asserts that the poet's passion must be "subtly spann'd" by "Art's transfiguring essence."[2] Execution, that is, must make of the inspiring emotion a new and different thing—like to that which provoked the creative impulse, but not identical, because consciously shaped to achieve a preconceived effect. His image of a poet's working his gold (theme and subject) is another expression of the same concept. To adopt still another of his metaphors, the materials of poetry, be they ivory or ebony (joy or sorrow), are to be carved out as Day or Night (the mood) may rule. Involved in this process of "carving out" a poem from the raw materials are form, rhythm and metre, rhyme, diction, and imagery.

FORM

Poetry without form is perhaps a contradiction of terms. At least it seemed so to Rossetti, who in writing about

Whitman's *Leaves of Grass* said: "Poetry without form is—what shall I say? Proportion seems to me the most inalienable quality in a poem. From the chaos of incident and reflection arise the rounded worlds of poetry, and go singing on their way."[3] Rossetti's words are interestingly similar to Coleridge's famous phrase, "reducing chaos to multiplicity of effect." It is "immense concentration brought to bear" on "concrete form," according to Rossetti, that alone can curb the "affluent imagination."[4] "Rightness in point of form"—along with his "exquisite metrical gift"—constituted "Blake's special glory among his contemporaries."[5] Much as he admired both Browning and Charles Wells, Rossetti could not forgive them for faults of form. Although it had "much good work," he censured Browning's *Balaustion's Adventure* for its "extremely irritating structure."[6] Of *On Chaucer,* a sonnet by Wells, he said: "Certainly nothing so disjointed ever gave itself the name before."[7]

It was not that Rossetti felt that any one particular form was superior to any other, but that there must be (as he said of Blake) "rightness of form"—that is, "unity of purpose and execution."[8] Whatever form could achieve this was the best form. Therefore Rossetti attacked Caine's insistence on a "pure" sonnet form, as when he said a "Shakespearian sonnet is better than the most perfect form, because Shakespeare wrote it."[9] Of his own sonnets he said: "though no one ever took more pleasure in continually using the form I prefer when not interfering with thought, to insist on it would after a certain point be ruin to common sense." Never to deviate from strict rules of the sonnet form, he declared, "must pinion both thought and diction." Besides, he added, "a series gains rather than loses by such varieties as do not lessen the only absolute aim—that of beauty."[10]

The sonnet was, of course, with the ballad, one of the two forms that Rossetti made peculiarly his own, and he handles both with consummate freedom. P. F. Baum has provided a brief but useful analysis of the structure of the sonnets in *The House of Life.* This analysis shows that all but two of the 103 sonnets in the sequence "follow the Petrarchan or Italian model with the conventional varia-tions."[11] While holding to the basic pattern, however, Rossetti manages to achieve infinite variety even within the "conven-tional" variations. As Rossetti himself truly observed: "It would not be at all found that my best sonnets are always in the mere form I think best."[12] Rossetti's mastery of the sonnet form is exemplified in his introductory sonnet to *The House of Life,* which Donald Stauffer has called "one of the most perfectly constructed, compact, and balanced sonnets in English."[13] His analysis of this sonnet shows the poet's skill-ful "building by opposed halves," with joy and fear, ivory and ebony, day and night, Art and Time, the two sides of the coin and the two parts of the sonnet among the many formally balanced elements.[14]

In his use of the ballad form, Rossetti is even freer than in his execution of the sonnet. Only four days before he died, so stricken that he could barely talk, Rossetti spoke to Caine about his love of early English ballad literature, and of how when he first met with it as a youth, he had said to himself: "There lies your line."[15] But into this traditional form Rossetti introduced so much variety that so good a critic as R. L. Mégroz admitted the difficulty of trying to classify Rossetti's ballads.[16] Poems with "varying degrees of ballad character," Mégroz found, were *Dennis Shand, Stratton Water, Sister Helen, Rose Mary, The King's Tragedy, The White Ship, Troy Town, Eden Bower,* and *The Staff and Scrip.* Among these nine, as he says, "there is a wide range of essential poetic power, formal character, and mood."[17] Whether or not one agrees with Oswald Doughty's statement that there "is nothing really medieval in Rossetti's ballads" depends, probably, on which word is emphasized, "nothing" or "re-ally."[18] There is much that is medieval, but that a Victorian poet could be "really" medieval is a self-evident impossibility. Rossetti himself acknowledged this when he described *Stratton Water* as "professedly modern antique."[19] In Mégroz's opinion, *Dennis Shand* comes close to being a conventional ballad. *The Staff and Scrip* is too lyrical; *Sister Helen* is too psychological; *Rose Mary* too complicated; *The King's Tragedy* possibly too diffuse; and *Eden Bower* and *Troy Town,* although both employ the ballad refrain, are "personal in style. . .and esoteric in metaphor."[20]

Each of Rossetti's ballads, then, uses an approximate ballad structure, something of the ballad's dramatic quality, and treats of ballad themes of love and hate and the supernatural. But these elements are differently combined and used, and achieve strikingly different effects. Even the use of the refrain varies greatly, from the powerful incremental refrain of *Sister Helen,* which Rossetti called "the very scheme of the poem,"[21] to the monotonous repetition of "O Troy's down, Tall Troy's on fire!" and the alternation in *Eden Bower* of "Sing Eden Bower" with "Alas the hour!"

In addition to his sonnets and ballads, Rossetti proved in his use of other poetic forms that he did not "create form for its own sake," but that—as he said of the sonnet—"the question with me is regulated by what I have to say."[22] P. F. Baum, for instance, has pointed out how dramatic are Rossetti's lyrics.[23] On the other hand, *Jenny, The Bride's Prelude,* and *The Blessed Damozel* are lyrical in manner, though their form is dramatic. The fair conclusion is that Rossetti did, as he claimed, subordinate (or adapt) form to the larger aims of other poetic qualities and the desired effect on the reader.

RHYTHM AND METRE

Paralleling Buchanan's unjust assertion that Rossetti subordinated thought to form was his accusation that the poet believed "sound superior to sense." Among the basic elements that contribute to the sound of poetry are rhythm and metre, and Rossetti would seem to be substantiating Buchanan's criticism when he says, "Colour and metre, these are the true patents of nobility in painting and poetry, *taking precedence of all intellectual claims;* and it is by virtue of these, first of all, that Blake holds, in both arts, a rank which cannot be taken from him."[24] But one must remember Rossetti's habit of exaggeration when he is trying to make a given point, and also his own rebuttal to Buchanan, wherein he listed the lofty themes that he wished to embody. And again and again in this book it has been shown that — in *aim,* if not *achievement* — to Rossetti "brains" in poetry always took precedence over "music."

In no way does this deny the emphasis that Rossetti placed on the "sound" of a poem. He called Swinburne's *The Complaint of Mona Lisa* one of his "finest pieces of execution and emotion," singling out its "reverberating music" for particular praise.[25] In comparing W. B. Scott to Browning, he said that in his best moments, Scott had "more of that commonly appreciable sort of melody."[26] It is significant that Rossetti's usual word for a poet is "singer," and for a poem, "song." For him, the poetic process was a *Song-Throe.*

When he read a poem aloud, Rossetti emphasized its melody. "His voice was deep and harmonious," says brother William, "in the reading of poetry, remarkably rich, with rolling swell and musical cadence."[27] Caine gives a dramatic picture of Rossetti reading his *The White Ship:*

It seemed to me that I never heard anything at all matchable with Rossetti's elocution; his rich deep voice lent an added music to the music of the verse: it rose and fell in the passages descriptive of the wreck with something of the surge and sibilation of the sea itself; in the tenderer passages it

was soft as a woman's, and in the pathetic stanzas with
which the ballad closes it was profoundly moving.[28]

After quoting this passage from Caine's *Recollections*,
William Rossetti says:

> To this account I may add that my brother's reading of
> poetry, his own or that of others, had a certain tendency
> to the 'intoning' quality (and so had Tennyson's reading,
> in a higher degree), giving a wholeness to the entire
> composition, and bringing out the rhythmical sequence.[29]

So important were rhythm and metre to Rossetti that
despite Blake's "exquisite metrical gift," he did not hesitate
to "improve" Blake when, in helping to edit Gilchrist's *Life
of Blake,* he found him faulty.[30] In Blake's unfinished play,
Edward the Third, Rossetti found lines "marred by frequent
imperfections in the metre (partly real and partly dependent
on careless printing), which," he says blandly, "I have
thought it best to remove, as I found it possible to do so without once, in the slightest degree, affecting the originality of
the text."[31] But trying to improve the metre of a line was
with Rossetti a lifelong habit. Professor Baum pays tribute
to Rossetti's early command of metrics in his analysis of
the various revisions of *The Blessed Damozel,* saying that
"some of the most interesting stanzas metrically" are very
little changed from earlier versions. In tracing the variants
through successive versions, however, Baum finds that the
revisions show "increased mastery" as the years pass.[32]

In the interest of metre, Rossetti was even tempted on
occasion to sacrifice clarity. An example is *The Hill Summit,*
in which the last four lines of the octet (describing the "face"
of the setting sun), originally read:

> Yet may I not forget that I was 'ware,
>   So journeying, of his face at intervals, —

> Where the whole land to its horizon falls,
> Some fiery bush with corruscating [*sic*] hair.

When his friend Allingham objected that the meaning wasn't clear, Rossetti replied, "The construction of those four lines is thus: —

> 'Yet may I not forget that I was ware,
> So journeying, of his face at intervals,
> Some fiery bush with coruscating hair,
> Where the whole land to its horizon falls.' "

Rossetti continued: "Only the metre forced me to transpose. It is meant to refer to the effect one is nearly sure to see in passing along a road at sunset, when the sun glares in a radiant focus behind some low bush or some hedge on the horizon of the meadows. But it is obscure, I believe. . . . I'll try to alter it — if worth working at."[33] Alter it he did, and successfully. The final version reads:

> Yet may I not forget that I was 'ware,
> So journeying, of his face at intervals,
> Transfigured where the fringed horizon falls, —
> A fiery bush with coruscating hair.

In the main, however, Rossetti was quick to defend his metrics. Of his translations of the early Italian poets, he wrote Coventry Patmore: "Before sending you the translations, I. . .want to apprise you that all the instances of varying metre, missing rhyme, etc. are close adherence to the originals, and not carelessnesses."[34] When William Rossetti objected to the metre of the Italian poem Gabriel had written for *A Last Confession,* Rossetti asked for their sister Maria's opinion, but maintained, "of course it is meant to be a very irregular sort of antiquated Italian, and I am pretty sure quite as bad slips are continual among the earliest poets."[35] And when Dr. Hake criticized a phrase in *The Stream's Secret,* Rossetti answered: "I cannot see that the syllables 'passion of peace' make the line unmetrical; — on the contrary, I think such varieties of modulation absolutely a law in passionate lyrical poetry."[36]

Such variety consistently attracted Rossetti. He admired Swinburne's *Tristram and Iseult*: "You have made the heroic metre so much your own by characteristic use of it that it does not strike one as having been used at all before, so exceptional is the impression in your hands."[37] Of the same poet's *Super Flumina Babylonis* he said: "the metre is of the order of great discoveries."[38] He practically stunned Canon Richard Watson Dixon, a long-time friend first introduced to him by Burne-Jones, with praise, and asked eagerly: "The metre adopted in *St. John* and *La Faerie* is new to me; is it your own? It is very happily contrived."[39]

Among Rossetti's own experiments with metre, the stanza form of *My Sister's Sleep* and the variations of the standard ballad form have already been noted. *The Blessed Damozel* is another illustration of his metrical versatility. In it, says Elizabeth Jackson, "we have a kind of shifting, hesitant rhythm that is practically unique in English verse."[40] Baum points out that the metrical structure of this poem had been used earlier by Wordsworth and Hood, among others, but may have been "an extension of the ballad stanza, such as Rossetti found in *The Ancient Mariner* and *Festus.*" But as Baum concludes, "where Rossetti actually got it is another question."[41]

Rossetti experimented interestingly with metres for *Michael Scott's Wooing,* one of the poems that never got past the stage of fundamental brainwork. He tried a four-line balladlike stanza ("the metre is of my own devising"),[42] and a six-line stanza created from this quatrain and two additional lines. After outlining the story of *Rose Mary* in prose, Rossetti again experimented with various metres and stanzas. Professor Baum has made available samples of these experiments, and gives the following summary: "It would seem that at first, Rossetti planned to write the whole poem in three-line stanzas with refrains, either repeating them with each stanza, as in 'Sister Helen' and 'Eden Bower,' or perhaps at intervals, as in 'The White Ship.' But this scheme he discarded very soon as too cumbersome."[43] In the end, of course, Rossetti wound up with a five-line stanza, plus the Beryl-songs.

The wide range of metrical patterns that Rossetti used, and the skillful variations he achieved within each, however, can hardly be suggested here. If the blunt assertion that Rossetti was a master of metrics sends the reader to Rossetti's poems for proof, so much the better.

RHYME

Caine's description of Rossetti's "prolonged tension of the rhyme sounds" as he read poetry aloud suggests how much the poet delighted in rhyme. Of all his poetry, the blank verse of *A Last Confession* is his only important departure from rhymed verse.[44] Rhyming seems always to have been a challenge, or even a game, to Rossetti, from the *bouts-rimés* of his youth with William and Christina to the countless limericks he tossed off in maturity, often spurred by a name unusually difficult to rhyme. One of the favorite diversions of the young Pre-Raphaelite Brothers was to write stanzas on the "alternate system," each one writing a stanza in turn until the poem was finished.[45] *Sir Hugh The Heron*, that *chef d'ouevre* by "Gabriel Rossetti, Jr.," age twelve, had stanzas with as many as nine consecutive lines with the same rhyme. At age fifty, with the Beryl-songs of *Rose Mary*, Dante Gabriel Rossetti was playing the same game. His brother William reports:

> I have heard my brother say that he wrote them to show
> that he was not incapable of the daring rhyming and rhyth-
> mical exploits of other poets. As to this point, readers
> must judge. It is at any rate true that in making the word
> 'Beryl' the pivot of his experiment, a word to which there
> are the fewest possible rhymes, my brother weighted
> himself heavily.[46]

"The very general opinion" of these songs, says William,
"has been that they were better away; I cannot but agree with
it, and indeed the author did so eventually." Unfortunately,
William means that Gabriel agreed with the general opinion — not that the songs were put away.

The most extraordinary example of Rossetti's toying
with rhyme is undoubtedly *The Lady's Lament*, which has
five stanzas of seven lines each — with every one of the thirty-
five lines ending with a word that rhymes with "more"!
Less blatant in its exploitation of rhyme is *The Burden of
Nineveh*, which has twenty nine-line stanzas, the fifth line
of each stanza rhyming with the word "me," with the first
four lines having one common rhyme, and the last four another. *Love's Nocturne* is one of several poems with four
lines with the same rhyme in each stanza, and in *The
Woodspurge* each four-line stanza has but a single rhyme.
Poems in which three lines in each stanza have the same
rhyme are too numerous to mention. The determination of
the rhyme scheme, and even at times the rhyme-words themselves, apparently, were part of Rossetti's fundamental brainwork. For *God's Graal*, which was to be a poem about
Lancelot and Guenevere, Rossetti not only made extensive
notes, but also drew up a list of fifty "Rime Words," thirteen
ending in "—ood," and the rest in "—ude."[47] Only nineteen
lines of the poem were written, however.

Rossetti's use of rhyme has often been criticized.
Buchanan wrote a parody of Rossetti's rhyming of weak
endings, which amused the poet himself.[48] This parody,

which rhymed "sailor" with "pour," and "tell" with "binnacle," was only too deserved. Partly from his youthful translations of the early Italian poets, partly perhaps from his imitations of old ballads, and also partly, no doubt, from the comparative poverty of rhyme-words in the English language, Rossetti did fall prey to this mannerism.[49] He often permitted imperfect rhymes, such as "call-musical-footfall," "player-here," and "along-song-tongue." William's censure of his brother's rhymes in the octet to the third *Willowwood* sonnet was just:

> I cannot but consider it a grave defect in versification that the word 'willowwood' should have been treated as if it constituted a dactylic rhyme, chiming (only too imperfectly) with 'widowhood' and 'pillow could.' Clearly, the only true rhyme syllable is the final 'wood,' which, in other lines, is, with moderate correctness, rhymed with 'wooed' and 'food.'[50]

Not that Rossetti needed anyone to point out less-than-perfect rhymes. It would be more accurate to say that he had far more liberal ideas as to what was permissible in rhyme than many critics. He disliked rigid exactness in rhyme as much as he did narrow and strict regularity in form and metre. He urged variety, and especially assonance, upon Hake:

> Moreover, a rigid exactness in rhymes—without the variation of assonance so valuable or even invaluable in poetry—is apt here to be preserved at the expense of meaning and spontaneity.[51]

There is ample evidence that both as poet and critic, Rossetti paid careful attention to rhyme. While revising *Love's Nocturne,* he noticed "that in the present version there is 'whisperings' rhyming with 'rings' which is bad."[52] As

printed, the rhyme became "springs-rings." One version of
Lost on Both Sides had the rhyme "long" and "along," which
Rossetti feared was "hardly admissible."[53] It was changed
to "long-among." Rossetti agreed with his brother about a
rhyme in the sonnet *Our Lady of the Rocks:* "I also object
to *difficult* rhyming with *occult* of course most absolutely.
But the distance from rhyme to rhyme being considerable,
and alteration difficult, I have left it."[54]

Rossetti's ear was equally keen for what *he* considered
faulty rhymes in other poets. He pounced upon the "singular
defect of a misrhyme" in Keats's *A Dream,* where "bereft"
rhymed with "slept."[55] The rhyming of "water" with "shorter"
in Keats's *To Charles Cowden Clarke* also bothered him.[56]
There was a time, though, said Rossetti, when he was "rather
proud to be as cockney as Keats *could* be," and he cited his
own adaptation of Keats's epitaph, which—curiously
enough—contained the very same rhyme-sounds:

> Through one, years since damned and forgot
>   Who stabbed backs by the Quarter,
> Here lieth one who, while Time's stream
>   Still runs, as God hath taught her,
> Bearing man's fame to men, hath writ
>   His name upon that water.[57]

Criticizing W. B. Scott's poems, Rossetti pointed out
that "I ween" was "essentially the same rhyme as 'between,' "
and said, "surely the rhyme 'man' and 'one' will *not* do."[58]
(This from a man who, in his own *Eden Bower,* dared to
rhyme "no man" with "woman"!) While helping to edit
Gilchrist's *Life of Blake,* Rossetti gave Blake's rhymes a
"rather unceremonious shaking up."[59] He even ventured to
question Tennyson's rhymes, giving as an example the lines:

> I wove a crown before her,
> For her I love so dearly,
> A garland for Lenora!

"It is possible," Rossetti wrote Caine, "the laurel crown should now hide a venerable and impeccable ear that was once the ear of a cockney?"[60]

But enough of examples. It is obvious that Rossetti knew a good rhyme from a bad one. Much as the individual reader may dislike Rossetti's freedom in rhyming, therefore, one must recognize that his rhymes came from a determined policy, not from carelessness or a defective ear for the English language.

DICTION

Possibly surpassing Rossetti's fascination with rhythm and rhyme was his sheer delight in words. His love of the English language is evident in his sardonic advice to young esthetes: "Quit so poor a language as that of Shakespeare, and write entirely in French."[61] His was a sometimes exuberant, sometimes studied, exploitation of language that at times achieved magnificent effects, and at others produced flaws more serious than his less-than-impeccable rhymes. In his hands, words could be a toy—or a torture.

There is a tone of almost boyish triumph in his note to W. B. Scott about *Down Stream*: "I doubt not you will note the intention to make the first half of each verse, expressing the landscape, tally with the second expressing the emotion, even tò the repetition of phrases."[62] The result, though somewhat mechanical, is not ineffective, as a sample stanza shows:

> Between Holmscote and Hurstcote
>   The river-reaches wind,
> The whispering trees accept the breeze,
>   The ripple's cool and kind:
> With love low-whispered 'twixt the shores,
>   With rippling laughters gay,
> With white arms bared to ply the oars,
>   On last year's first of May.

On the other hand, Rossetti's sixfold playing on the word
"fare" in *Farewell to the Glen* recalls the execrable
Shakespeare sonnets on "Will":

> Sweet stream-fed glen, why say "farewell" to thee
>   Who far'st so well and find'st for ever smooth
>   The brow of Time where man may read no ruth?
> Nay, do thou rather say "farewell" to me,
> Who now fare forth in bitterer fantasy
>   Than erst was mine where other shade might soothe
>   By other streams, what while in fragrant youth
> The bliss of being sad made melancholy.
>
> And yet, farewell! For better shalt thou fare
>   (etc.)

Even heavier-handed wordplay occurs in *Chimes,* which has
seven stanzas of relentless alliteration like the following:

> Beauty's body and benison
> With a bosom-flower new blown.
>
> Bitter beauty and blessing bann'd
> With a breast to burn and brand.
>
> Beauty's bower in the dust o'erblown
> With a bare white breast of bone.
>
> Barren beauty and bower of sand
> With a blast on either hand.

When not overdone, however, Rossetti's wordplay could
achieve such striking lines as these from *Sleepless Dreams*:

> O lonely night! art thou not known to me,
> A thicket hung with masks of mockery
>   And watered with the wasteful warmth of tears?

and even better, from *The Stream's Secret*:

O wandering water ever whispering.

In his choice of words, Rossetti attempted to avoid both the shallows of "proseman's diction" and the rocks of "metaphysical involution," to be simple without being plain, or where appropriate, splendid without being pompous. He scoffed at Caine's "fancy" language:

I am sure I could write 100 essays, on all possible subjects (I once did project a series under the title, *Essays written in the intervals of Elephantiasis, Hydrophobia, and Penal Servitude*), without once experiencing the "aching void" which is filled by such words as "mythopoeic," and "anthropomorphism." I do not find life long enough to know in the least what they mean. . . .But seriously, simple English in prose writing and in all narrative poetry (however monumental language may become in abstract verse) seems to me a treasure not to be foregone in favor of German innovations.[63]

Even in the PRB's game of writing alternate stanzas of a poem, Rossetti could not countenance such diction, and laughed at poor Hunt's efforts as "metaphysico-mysterioso-obscure."[64] He quibbled about the title for the Brotherhood's magazine, as to whether it should be *The Germ: Thoughts toward Nature* etc., or *Thoughts towards:* "I think 'towards' is much better—'toward' being altogether between you, me, and Tennyson; and it is well to seem as little affected as possible."[65] He jeered at an early review written by his brother, asking William: "What do you mean by the 'enforcement of magnificence having a tendency to impair the more essential development of feeling'? This smacks villainously of Malvolio's vein."[66]

Rossetti objected to anything "of the far-fetched order—

but chiefly the cherished (not the rejected) phrases of academic writing—that is of the over fastidious and somewhat artificial order. . .savouring of the more stilted order of last-century writing."[67] When he observed Keats, in *Endymion,* abandoning simple words for such affectations as *orby* and *sphery,* his censure was swift: "All such forms are execrable, and disfigure the poem throughout."[68] Commenting on Marzials' poems, Rossetti praised one whose diction "moves freely and nobly in every word, like something that really has to be said." But he criticized another for its "puerile perversities in diction," and advised Marzials to "go over the volume and remove continually recurring words and phrases of a trivial or astoundingly concocted kind."[69]

Counterbalancing Rossetti's dislike for the concocted or affected was his disdain for the trite and oversimple. Says Caine, "he knew of no reproach of poetry more damning than to say it was written in proseman's diction. This was the key to his depreciation of Wordsworth."[70] Typical was the thorough going-over he gave his brother William's poem, *Mrs. Holmes Grey.* "The expression 'fish flapping about,' " he said, "might I think be altered to something newer." In the sixth stanza he found "the word *rustling* is rather old, and the last line a trifle common and awkward. . . . In the 33rd the 'divided into oblongs' business reads as trivial. The last line of 34th a little common. . . . Something newer, I think, might be done at the end of the 36th"—and so on throughout the poem.[71]

Allingham got the same kind of objection for a couplet that was "a trifle *too* homely,—a little in the broad-sheet style."[72] Brown's son Nolly was scored for a "certain deliberateness and obviousness of expression—amounting now and then almost to a gossiping tone."[73] Swinburne, for all his "glorious execution," was not invulnerable. The phrase "Blast thine eyes and ears" in one of his sonnets brought Rossetti's suggestion that it "might perhaps gain by the substitution (if possible) of some other word for 'blast,' which in that position recalls the more Topsaic forms of speech of daily life to some extent."[74]

Nor did Rossetti spare himself. He wrote Swinburne, "there is a line in Confession [*A Last Confession*] which I half believe to be silly about *'Tis you shall shriek in Latin'*! The passage might run — *'Shall my end be as their end? Some bell rings'*, etc. Would this be better?"[75] He admitted that "among paths etc." in *Dante at Verona* was "rather cockney as an idiom."[76] The word "Dreamland" in *Love's Nocturne* was a "rather hackneyed phrase I don't like, but it is so valuable for clearing up that I adopted it."[77]

Rossetti "hackneyed"? The word seems truly absurd when applied to a poet usually accused of "ornateness" and "affectations." But the fact is that Rossetti did want his diction to be both simply direct and subtly rich. For once, however, this is not a matter of the poet's trying to achieve conflicting extremes simultaneously. Rossetti made this clear when he qualified his description of "simple English. . . in all *narrative* poetry" as a "treasure not to be foregone" by including the parenthesis, "however monumental language may become in *abstract* verse."[78] Rossetti is clearly distinguishing between the diction he deemed best for his ballads, and that he thought best for his more personal sonnets and lyrics. Caine spells out this distinction when he says:

> If we compare the language of these ballads with that of the sonnets or other poems spoken in the author's own person, we find it not first of all gorgeous, condensed, emphatic. It is direct, simple, pure and musical; heightened, it is true, by imagery acquired in its passage through the medium of the poet's mind, but in other respects essentially the language of the historical personages who are made to speak.[79]

The diction of ballads like *The White Ship* and *The King's*

Tragedy. though artfully spiced with archaisms such as "southron," "furze," "sea-wold" and "writhen," is generally as simple and direct as could be. The sonnets and lyrics on the other hand, for all Rossetti's stated objections to the "far-fetched" and "artificial," are often marked by what Professor Baum has called "affectations and conceits."[80] It is the sonnets in particular that have led to this charge. Analysis of the diction of *The House of Life* shows why.

Four characteristics emerge from a study of the language of these sonnets. First, the words that Rossetti uses are often in themselves rather simple, or at least not exotic. But second, he laces his sonnets with "stunners," unusual, archaic or Latinate words that give them their peculiar Rossetti flavor. Third, he indulges from time to time in a play on words reminiscent of the Elizabethans. And fourth, he piles up words, frequently compound words, making for a complexity and subtlety that sometimes stop the reader in his tracks. The third *Willowwood* sonnet (51) has more or less typical examples of each:

"O YE, all ye that walk in Willowwood,
    That walk with hollow faces burning white;
What fathom-depth of soul-struck widowhood,
    What long, what longer hours, one lifelong night,
Ere ye again, who so in vain have wooed
    Your last hope lost, who so in vain invite
Your lips to that their unforgotten food,
    Ere ye, ere ye again shall see the light!

Alas! the bitter banks in Willowwood,
    With tear-spurge wan, with blood-wort burning red:
Alas! if ever such a pillow could
    Steep deep the soul in sleep till she were dead, —
Better all life forget her than this thing,
That Willowwood should hold her wandering!"[81]

Taken one by one, all but two compound words of this sonnet are ordinary enough; "tear-spurge" and "blood-wort" are the stunners. For wordplay there are "what long, what longer hours, one lifelong night". . ."last hope lost". . .and (most successfully, I think) "steep deep the soul in sleep." And for the crowded, intricate "stopper," there is the line: "What fathom-depth of soul-struck widowhood." Translated, the line would go something like this: How long must you endure the sorrow of your soul, stricken (like a widow) by the absence of its partner, now hidden, as if it were fathoms deep below the waters of Willowwood. The line typifies what Rossetti often tries to do — pack several images into a few words, leaving the reader to unscramble, reassemble, and interpret them. For the reader, the process is not easy. Here, for instance, for clear comprehension of "fathom-depth," one needs to recall the image of the first of the four *Willowwood* sonnets (49), which pictures the lover bending over the water, and imagining, as he peers into its depths as into a mirror, that he sees his beloved's face:

Then the dark ripples spread to waving hair,
And as I stooped, her own lips rising there
    Bubbled with brimming kisses at my mouth.[82]

In just about half the sonnets of *The House of Life,* Rossetti uses words that he may have thought "stunners," ranging from *osier-odored, galiot, auroral, guerdoning, malisons,* and *gonfalon* to such Latinisms as *refluent, confluence, philtred euphrasy, choral consonancy,* and the jaw-breaking *multiform circumfluence manifold.* The odd thing, though, is that more often than not, he seems to have been satisfied with one stunner to a sonnet.

Roughly a third of the 103 sonnets in the sequence have the kind of crowded, intricate line or phrase that I have called "reader-stoppers" (again, usually one in any given sonnet).

Typical are "love-sown harvest-field of sleep". . ."dawn-pulse of the heart of heaven". . ."The speech-bound sea-shell's low importunate strain". . ."close-companioned inarticulate hour". . .and "penury's sedulous self-torturing thought."

Most of the sonnets are, of course, full of the sound-devices of poetry, especially alliteration and assonance, which often seem little more than the wordplay of *Chimes*. But in some 15 of these 103 sonnets Rossetti has a special kind of word play that goes beyond this, often involving antithesis or paradox. At his worst, he is guilty of such verbal antics as "For heart-beats and for fire-heats". . ."Nay, pitiful Love, nay loving Pity". . ."Than all new life a livelier lovelihood". . . "threshold of wing-winnowed threshing-floor". . .and worst of all (to me at least) "The Song-god—He the Sun-god." But I find "lifted shifted steeps" a most felicitous phrase to describe a tortuous path. The poet's disdain for the wrong kind of fame is happily captured in the line, "Honour unknown, and honour known unsought." And all the yearning for oblivion in the *Willowwood* sonnets is summed up in that phrase, "Steep deep the soul in sleep."

Those who believe that they see a change in Rossetti from the simple and direct diction of his youth to an ornate and elaborate style in his maturity will find little corroboration from the sonnets of *The House of Life*. In the first place, most of the sonnets (85 of the 103) were written from 1868 on, and so naturally would be in his supposed "mature" manner. And even among these there are occasional gems of what might be called a rich simplicity not unlike that of *The Blessed Damozel* of 1850. One such is *Last Fire* (30), especially in the sestet:

> Many the days that Winter keeps in store,
>   Sunless throughout, or whose brief sun-glimpses
>   Scarce shed the heaped snow through the naked trees.
> This day at least was Summer's paramour,

> Sun-coloured to the imperishable core
> With sweet well-being of love and full heart's ease.

Also, most of the earliest sonnets—those written between 1847 and 1866—do not differ in their essential characteristics from the later ones.

Moreover, Rossetti's revisions of these early sonnets indicate as much a desire for greater clarity and precision as for ornateness. The revisions in *Lost on Both Sides* (91, first written in 1854) were to clear up lines that Rossetti said were "certainly foggy."[83] The opening image of *The Birth-Bond* (15, also first written in 1854) has already been cited as an example of how Rossetti sometimes overextends a basic image. It is interesting, therefore, to note that when he came to revise the sonnet, Rossetti—although he didn't condense the image—at least purged it of obscurities. In describing the special kinship shared by children of a first marriage, which sets them apart from children born to their father of a second wife, Rossetti originally wrote:

> Have you not noted, in some family
> Where two *remain from the* first marriage bed
> How still they own their *fragrant* bond, though fed
> And nurst *upon an unknown* breast and knee.[84]

The final version of these lines was:

> Have you not noted, in some family
> Where two *were born of a* first marriage-bed
> How still they own their *gracious bond,* though fed
> And nursed *on the forgotten* breast and knee?

Surely the changes (indicated by my italics) make the image clearer and more precise. "Where two *were born of*" removes the distracting and irrelevant suggestion contained in "*remain from*"—that there were other children from the first marriage who died. "*Gracious* bond," while still a bit vague, is certainly more appropriate than "*fragrant* bond." And "*forgotten* breast" is more likely than "*unknown* breast": the children, if very young when their mother died, might well have forgotten her, but they would undoubtedly have known who she was. *A Dark Day* (68, first written in 1855) is another sonnet revised in much the same way.[85]

Obviously, Rossetti treated his diction to the same studied revisions he gave other elements in his poetry. Rossetti himself put it thus: "It has so frequently occurred to myself to find. . .that the ardour of composition had caused me to overlook imperfections of mere phraseology, and I have so often had to retrace my steps by the humblest verbal labour to remedy this."[86] The process, he said, "involves in my opinion (though superficial critics might deem this an abnegation of the inspired quality in art) much of the most essential vitality of true poetic work."[87] No detail was too minute for this humblest verbal labor. As he revised for the publishing of his poems in 1870, he bombarded brother William, Swinburne, and others with questions about words and phrases.

In a single letter to William he asked of *Ave:* "I remember I had changed *arrayed* into some word more of the same latinized value as *conjoint*, but cannot remember what. Can you suggest a word?" And of *The Blessed Damozel:* "A question I wish to ask on my own hook is whether *trembling* or *tremulous* would be best. . . . The first is objectionable because of *stepping* above—but does not the second trip awkwardly? *Circlewise:* would this be better: 'They sit in circle'? I daresay you agree with the removal of *lapse* for *flight* in last stanza but one. 'And her hair lying down her back.' Is the sound awkward? Is 'And her hair laid upon' etc. better?" And of *Plighted Promise.* "I see no objection to *Luna* but none either to *Cynthia* except that people know it less as meaning the moon. Dian would answer best of all for the meaning of the passage, but I didn't like the sound so well as *Luna*."[88]

Rossetti was willing to try any number of variations before he found the one that suited him. An illuminating example of this is the refrain of the thirty-fifth stanza of *Sister Helen*, where Rossetti wanted to change "A woman's curse between Hell and Heaven" to a line that described the turning of the bride's golden hair to white, after Helen's refusal to lift the curse. In turn, Rossetti pondered the relative merits of

> woe-silvered gold between Hell and Heaven

> woe-stricken snow etc.

> woe-silvered gold etc.

> woe-withered snow etc.

before finally settling on

> woe-withered gold.[89]

Most of the refrains of *Sister Helen* underwent similar revisions, although rarely passing through so many variants. In these changes, one does see a decided move from the simple, sometimes almost banal, to the more subtle, more suggestive, and often more sinister.

Because he was so self-critical of his diction, so studied in his revisions, Rossetti must bear full responsibility for both the virtues and the vices that the individual reader may find in his use of language. His was no grace snatched beyond the reach of art, but a deliberate, conscious working toward the effects he desired. Of Rossetti's "affectations and conceits," Professor Baum says, "they are not a youthful error which he outgrew, but rather a concomitant of his love of ornateness."[90] On the whole, I must agree with this verdict, though I would add "love of subtlety and compactness," for these are often apparent where sheer ornateness is not.

In Rossetti's defense, let it be said that if he is at times too fond of verbal play, of oversubtle or overcrowded lines, of artificial archaisms, and sometimes of letting sound overrule sense — and he can be guilty of all of these — he nevertheless brought to the poetry of the Victorians a delight in the language, in its resources of color and sound and "magic," that made him a true heir of Keats.

IMAGERY

It has been said that Rossetti "often disguised his meaning under a cloud of gorgeous phrasing."[91] But more often, perhaps, primarily in his sonnets and lyrics, the cloud was one of overcrowded and overelaborate imagery. The kinds of packed, "reader-stopping" phrases and lines discussed in the section on *Diction* are frequently tremendously compressed images, as was shown with the phrase "fathomdepth." Here is another typical example from the sonnet, *Severed Selves:*

> Two souls, the shores wave-mocked of sundering seas.

In essence, the image is a simple one, and graphic. Separated lovers, the poet is saying, are like two shores separated by the seas, whose waves mock any attempt to unite them. But the image comes upon one with no preparation, and one has to pause to understand, interpret, and apply it.

At the other extreme are the images that Rossetti pursues, to rephrase Buchanan, not to the very pit of "beastliness," but of exhaustion. Rossetti explained very simply in a letter to Caine what he wanted to say in his sonnet-tribute to Coleridge: "I conceive the leading point about his work is its human love, and the leading point about his career, the sad fact of how little of it was devoted to that work. These are the points made in my sonnet."[92] But here is the sonnet:

SAMUEL TAYLOR COLERIDGE

His Soul fared forth (as from the deep home-grove
  The father-songster plies the hour-long quest),
  To feed his soul-brood hungering in the nest;
But his warm Heart, the mother-bird, above
Their callow fledgling progeny still hove
  With tented roof of wings and fostering breast
  Till the Soul fed the soul-brood. Richly blest
From Heaven their growth, whose food was Human Love.

Yet ah! Like desert pools that show the stars
    Once in long leagues, —even such the scarce-snatched hours
    Which deepening pain left to his lordliest powers: —
Heaven lost through spider-trammelled prison-bars.
Six years, from sixty saved! Yet kindling skies
Own them, a beacon to our centuries.

Many of the sonnets of *The House of Life* begin with equally involved, intricate images whose meaning and application are by no means immediately apparent and clear. Among such are *Heart's Hope* (5), *The Birth-Bond* (15), *Pride of Youth* (24), *Winged Hours* (25), *Broken Music* (47), *Stillborn Love* (55), *Transfigured Life* (60), *Inclusiveness* (63), *Known in Vain* (65), *A Dark Day* (68), *From Dawn to Noon* (80), *Lost on Both Sides* (91), *The Vase of Life* (95), and *Newborn Death* (99).

What Rossetti was attempting to do was to embody, to make vivid and concrete, the emotions that he considered the very soul of poetry, as opposed to the "last husk and bodiless damnation of style."[93] What he resented in Shelley's poetry, according to brother William, were "those

elements. . .when the abstract tends to lose sight of the concrete."[94] In making abstract emotions or reflections concrete,
we have seen, Rossetti himself often builds up his "picture"
or image to the point where it overwhelms the feeling or idea
it was supposed to convey. Yet this was certainly not his
intent. He did say that a "metaphor must of course be a picture in itself apart from the application of the symbol."[95]
But he also declared emphatically, "I believe no poetry could
be freer than mine from the trick of what is called 'word-
painting'. . . . I should wish to deal in poetry chiefly with
personified emotions; and in carrying out my scheme of
'The House of Life' (if ever I do so) shall try to put in action a
complete *dramatis personae* of the soul."[96]

Such personification runs the gamut from the simple
device of capitalizing abstractions like Love, Art, Life, and
Death to the fully drawn picture of *Soul's Beauty*. At their
best, Rossetti's images do progress from picture to metaphor
and symbol.[97] Were one so minded, he might be wryly amused
at comparing the conflicting views of Rossetti's imagery
held by two such noted Rossetti-scholars as Oswald Doughty
and Paull Franklin Baum. Both are speaking of the sonnets
in *The House of Life*. Professor Doughty finds in them an
"almost prosaically concrete imagery and sense of basic
reality in a real world, however *exalté* the emotions and sentiments they inspire."[98] Professor Baum, on the other hand,
says "his images are more commonly 'literary' or 'abstract'
pictures at one or two removes from the actual, or an imaginative fusion of different elements."[99] But I can see how,
in a way, both critics are right. The *matter* of Rossetti's
images is often prosaic and concrete: Children whose father
has remarried (15), a child's non-comprehension of death (24),
a bird singing his way from hidden woods to open daylight
(25), a mother listening to her babe's first words (47), a
child whose features combine those of both parents (60),
etc. But the *manner* of treatment is often, too, literary or

abstract. One does not feel that the children, the bird, the mother are "real."

Perhaps the conclusion that all this leads to is the profound declaration about Rossetti's imagery that might apply to any good poet — where he succeeds, he is a success; where he fails, he is a failure. As in all the other elements of Rossetti's execution, the key to his success or failure with imagery would seem to be the degree to which he could curb his natural tendency toward excess. When he could control his great fascination for form, metre, rhyme, diction, and imagery, the gold of his fundamental conception shines clear; where he could not, his metal loses its lustre.

NOTES

[1]*D & W*, III, 994.
[2]See *sup.*, pp. 147-48.
[3]Benson, p. 173.
[4]*D & W*, II, 914.
[5]*Collected Works*, I, 464-5.
[6]*D & W*, III, 977.
[7]Caine, p. 253.
[8]*Collected Works*, I, 490.
[9]Caine, p. 249.
[10]*Ibid.*, p. 248.
[11]Baum, *The House of Life*, p. 223.
[12]Caine, p. 248.
[13]Stauffer, p. 236.
[14]Rossetti wrote and illustrated this sonnet in 1880 as a present for his mother's eightieth birthday.
[15]Caine, p. 293.
[16]Mégroz, p. 259.
[17]*Ibid.*, p. 274.
[18]O. Doughty, ed., *Dante Gabriel Rossetti: Poems* (London, 1957), p. xiv.
[19]*D & W*, I, 227.
[20]Mégroz, p. 274.
[21]*Collected Works*, I, 487.

[22]Caine, p. 248.

[23]Baum, *The House of Life*, p. 10.

[24]*Collected Works*, I, 465. (The Italics are mine.)

[25]*D & W*, II, 790.

[26]*Ibid.*, I, 248.

[27]*Collected Works*, I, xxiii.

[28]Caine, p. 217.

[29]W. M. Rossetti, *The Poems of Dante Gabriel Rossetti*, I, 217.

[30]*Collected Works*, I, 464.

[31]*Ibid.*, pp. 459-60. (This is by no means an isolated example.)

[32]Baum, *The Blessed Damozel*, p. xxx. Baum accepts the so-called 1847 manuscript of this poem as authentic, as I do not, but even if one regards the 1850 version printed in *The Germ* as the earliest extant, his statement holds true — in fact, truer, for there is "increased mastery" in the "1847" version over the 1850 one, as would be expected if it were indeed of a much later vintage.

[33]*D & W*, I, 227. In the margin Rossetti asked: "Has coruscating one or two r's?"

[34]*Ibid.*, p. 342.

[35]*Ibid.*, II, 722. (Rossetti admitted that William's and Maria's Italian was better than his own.)

[36]*Ibid.*, p. 871.

[37]*Ibid.*, p. 790.

[38]*Ibid.*, p. 763.

[39]*Ibid.*, IV, 1834. (Dixon replied: "I would rather have that letter than all the laudations of all the periodicals in existence. . . . You are also the only person who has detected the stanza of *St. John* and *La Faerie*, which is a variation of my own on the old seven-versed stanza.") (*D & W*, III, 1335n.)

[40]E. Jackson, "Notes on the Stanza of *The Blessed Damozel*," *PMLA*, LVIII (December, 1943), p. 1053.

[41]Baum, *The Blessed Damozel*, p. xxvii.

[42]*Ashley Catalogue*, IV, 138.

[43]Baum, *Dante Gabriel Rossetti, An Analytical List*, pp. 61-4.

[44]The "diary" he wrote in blank verse during his continental tour with Holman Hunt in 1849, while interesting, hardly rates as "poetry."

[45]*D & W*, I, 40.

[46]W. M. Rossetti, *The Poems of Dante Gabriel Rossetti*, I, 221.

[47]Baum, *Dante Gabriel Rossetti, An Analytical List*, pp. 78-95.

[48]*L & M*, I, 299.

[49]But Baum has shown that "Rossetti's use of the weak ending in rhyme (be: eternity) is not nearly so excessive as is frequently supposed." (Baum, *The House of Life*, pp. 235-9.

[50]W. M. Rossetti, *The Poems of Dante Gabriel Rossetti*, II, 235.

[51]*Collected Works*, I, 497.

[52]*D & W*, II, 739.

[53]*Ibid.,* I, 213.

[54]*Ibid.,* II, 726.

[55]*Ibid.,* IV, 1710.

[56]G. Milner, "On Some Marginalia Made by D. G. Rossetti," *Manchester Quarterly,* V (January, 1883), p. 6.

[57]Caine, p. 170.

[58]*D & W,* III, 988.

[59]Gilchrist, p. 94.

[60]Caine, pp. 170-71.

[61]Hake and Compton-Rickett, *Watts-Dunton,* I, 156.

[62]*D & W,* III, 976. (The original title was *The River's Record.)*

[63]Caine, pp. 199-200.

[64]*D & W,* I, 40.

[65]*Ibid.,* p. 73. ("Towards" won out.)

[66]*Ibid.,* p. 92.

[67]*Ibid.,* III, 935.

[68]Milner, p. 4.

[69]*D & W,* III, 1164.

[70]Caine, p. 135.

[71]*D & W,* I, 67-8.

[72]*Ibid.,* p. 212.

[73]*Ibid.,* III, 1230.

[74]*Ibid.,* II, 772. (The reference is, of course, to William Morris' somewhat explosive manner of speech.)

[75]*Ibid.,* p. 798. (Swinburne said no, and the line stayed.)

[76]*Ibid.,* p. 773.

[77]*Ibid.,* p. 739.

[78]Caine, p. 200. (The italics are mine.)

[79]*Ibid.,* pp. 83-4.

[80]Baum, *The House of Life,* pp. 14-5.

[81]This is the sonnet to whose rhymes William Rossetti particularly objected. (See *sup.,* p. 209.) Gabriel apparently couldn't resist the challenge of trying to find four rhymes for "Willowwood."

[82]Buchanan attacked "Bubbled with brimming kisses at my mouth," and Rossetti felt it necessary to explain: "The sonnet describes a dream or trance of divided love momentarily re-united by the longing fancy; and in the imagery of the dream, the face of the beloved rises through deep dark waters to kiss the lover." (*Collected Works,* I, 483-4.)

[83]See *sup.,* pp. 164-65.

[84]*D & W,* I, 214. See *sup.,* p. 170.

[85]Compare the original in *D & W,* I, 241-2, with the final version in Rossetti's *Collected Works.*

[86]*D & W,* III, 994.

[87]*Ibid.,* p. 995.

[88]*Ibid.,* II, 724-5.

[89]Troxell, *Rossetti's Sister Helen,* p. 81.

[90]Baum, *The House of Life,* p. 15.

[91]*Ibid.,* p. 3.

[92]Caine, p. 165.

[93]*Ashley Catalogue,* IV, 134-5.

[94]W. M. Rossetti, ed., *The Works of Dante Gabriel Rossetti* (London, 1911), p. 671.

[95]*D & W,* III, 1340.

[96]*Ibid.,* II, 850.

[97]See, for instance, *sup.,* pp. 44-6.

[98]Doughty, *Dante Gabriel Rossetti: Poems,* p. xv.

[99]Baum, *The House of Life,* p. 17.

X

Lost on Both Sides

I was one of those whose little is their own.
Dante Gabriel Rossetti's "Notes"[1]

This book began with the question, "What makes a poet?" Succeeding chapters explored the various elements in Rossetti's background and character, the events of his life, his critical opinions as to what a poet and a poem should be, and his attempt to practice in his own poetry what he preached in his criticism—all of which had their part in making Rossetti the poet that he was. There remains, for this final chapter, a final question: What prevents a poet from being the greater poet that he might have been?

THE ONE ROSSETTI

Amid all the contradictions and paradoxes that abound in Rossetti's life, criticism, and poetry, the greatest is the consistency with which he clung to his inconsistencies. In so many ways, he grew up—without growing. He remained the same Rossetti from start to finish. He spent his childhood

in a literary and artistic household, unperturbed by the crowd
of his father's Italian expatriate cronies and their wild, futile
rantings over a political situation they could in no way
change. He spent his adult life still "isolated in art," still
unconcerned about the "momentary momentousness and
eternal futility" of politics. As a boy he gave lip-service to
the formal religion so vital to the women in his family—
mother, sisters, aunts—and as a man he proclaimed the
essential "Christianity" of his poetry; yet from first to last
religious orthodoxy escaped him. There was no development
in religious beliefs between the nineteen-year-old author of
The Blessed Damozel, vaguely yearning for a personal, physical afterlife, and the forty-one-year-old poet whose *One Hope*
was a "longing for accomplishment of individual desire after
death."[2]

He was a moral youth, yet plagued by a sensuality that
first found literary expression in *Sorrentino* (at age fifteen)
and *Jenny* (at age twenty). He was a moral man, shocked
by anything repellent or degrading, whose sensuality found
full physical outlet in the arms of his mistress, Fanny
Cornforth, and literary expression in poems epitomized by
Nuptial Sleep. Again there was no real development, except
of course the "progress" from imagining the sex-act to per-
forming it. As the boy shrank from his family's censure of
Sorrentino and his aunt's disapproval of his reading Shelley,
so the man recoiled from Buchanan's charge that he was the
leader of a "fleshly" school of poetry.[3] No wonder it was
Hall Caine's lecture on Rossetti, emphasizing "the moral
impulses animating his work," that first drew the two
together.[4]

This lifelong sensitivity to criticism was in sharp contrast
to the independence and disdain for authority that also
marked Rossetti as boy and man. "He was always and essentially of a dominant turn, in intellect and temperament a
leader," said brother William.[5] Yet at twenty he gave to the

PRB only its glamour and outward trappings; at forty he denied that he was "chef de l'école Préraphaélite" either by priority or merit, and at forty-five, when Francis Hueffer called him "the leader" of the movement, Rossetti's response was: "Please don't!" The dazzling personality that attracted Morris, Burne-Jones and Swinburne to the twenty-eight-year-old Rossetti retained enough of its glitter to win the devotion of such literary hopefuls as Watts-Dunton, William Sharp, and Hall Caine twenty and more years later. But Rossetti never grew to be a leader of anything.

Intuitive not logical, imaginative not intellectual, given to excesses of rapture over both the monumental and the mediocre—such was the young Rossetti, and he never changed. His favorite authors at age sixteen were still his favorites at age fifty.[6] Nor did Rossetti's manner of criticism ripen and mature. The exuberant fifty-two-year-old champion of Chatterton as an absolute "miracle" sounds like the seventeen-year-old who had just discovered Browning. At twenty-one Rossetti was calling Tennyson's *The Princess* "the finest poem since Shakespeare"; at fifty he was still draping Shakespeare's mantle on poets as disparate as Keats and Charles Wells. As they grow older, many men find their youthful love of the romantic, the imaginative, and the emotional in poetry mellowing into an admiration for the quietly reflective or the gravely profound. Not so Rossetti. He never gave up his "grudge" against Wordsworth; he never yielded to the power of Milton.

In his own poetry, Rossetti shows a similar basic consistency. For the youth and the adult alike, the sonnet and the ballad were his favorite forms, the medieval and supernatural—and woman—his favorite subjects, and emotion the effect he most successfully achieved. That the experiences of his stormy life should leave no imprint on his poetry would, of course, be incredible, especially for so personal a poet as Rossetti. With Fanny, the panting ecstasy ludicrously imag-

ined in *Sir Hugh the Heron* became fervid fact in *Eden Bower,*
Troy Town, and *Song of the Bower.* With Janey Morris,
the tone of grief, frustration and regret first sounded in *The*
Blessed Damozel and early sonnets like *Lost on Both Sides,*
Autumn Idleness, and *The Landmark* grew deeper and more
melancholy in so many of the sonnets of *The House of Life*
written from 1868 on.

Essential development cannot be found in Rossetti's
poetry, however, whatever criteria be used. The majority of
his poems were written during three different "periods,"
but these are only divisions in time, not stages in a poet's
development. The first period extended from 1847 to about
1854; the second spanned the years 1868 to 1872; the third
lasted from 1878 to Rossetti's death in 1882.[7] Analysis of
the major poems written during each of these periods reveals
his failure to grow as a poet.

The first criterion that might be used in this analysis is
quantity. If we use the same twenty-four poems previously
described—along with *The House of Life*—as Rossetti's
"major" work, in bulk alone more of his best writing was at
least initiated in his earliest period than in either of the other
two. In the *Collected Works* of 1886, the fifteen poems stem-
ming from the first period take up 107 pages; the seven major
poems of the middle period occupy 59 pages; and the two
major poems of the last period total only 39 pages. Even
when one distributes the 51 pages of *The House of Life* sonnets (some 75 percent of which were written during the
middle period) among each period, the first period proves
the most productive in quantity.

In quality, too, Rossetti's first period inspired more of
his best poems, including the first versions of *Dante at*
Verona, Jenny, A Last Confession, The Bride's Prelude,
Sister Helen, The Staff and Scrip, The Blessed Damozel,
and *The Burden of Nineveh*—eight poems that must be considered among Rossetti's most important work—as well as

the lesser "major poems," *My Sister's Sleep, Ave, Wellington's Funeral, The Card Dealer, The Portrait, Love's Nocturne,* and *Stratton Water.* In the middle period, only five poems, *The Stream's Secret, Rose Mary, Troy Town, Eden Bower,* and *The Cloud Confines* can be included among Rossetti's best; others of the period are *Down Stream* and *Soothsay.* The final period produced only two major poems, *The White Ship* and *The King's Tragedy.*

It is true that those sonnets of *The House of Life* written between 1868 and 1872 may be used to prove that Rossetti's second period was as fine in quality of writing as his first. Nor can one overlook Rossetti's extensive revisions of his earliest poems during the years 1868-70, revisions that are at times brilliant, and more often than not demonstrate a more skillful and knowing craftsmanship. But none of this adds up to what I would call real "growth" in a poet — the development of greater themes, broader subjects, deeper insights into the soul of man. In these respects, Rossetti had just about reached his limits during his first period. This is substantiated when one applies the criteria of Rossetti's own criticism to his poems from each period.

What Rossetti as critic sought in a poem was spirituality, beauty, and emotion. For his closest approach to true spirituality, *Ave, Dante at Verona, Jenny,* and *The Burden of Nineveh* are pre-eminent. All are from his first period. For beauty, *The Blessed Damozel,* even in the 1850 version, stands alone. For emotion, *Sister Helen* perhaps rises above all others, although *A Last Confession* and, in its own way, *The Blessed Damozel* easily rival the emotional impact of *Rose Mary* of the middle period, and *The White Ship* of the final years.

The poetic qualities that Rossetti the critic cherished were simplicity, subtlety, brevity, completeness, forcefulness, and moderation. He achieved all these as successfully in his first period of writing as he ever did. For simplicity there are *My Sister's Sleep* and *Jenny.* For subtlety there is *The Blessed Damozel.* For a successful combination of the simple and Rossetti's best subtlety, there are *Dante at Verona* and *Sister Helen.* And for possibly Rossetti's happiest combination of completeness, brevity, and forcefulness, with the requisite degree of moderation, there are (with revisions) *A Last Confession* and, again, *Sister Helen.*

In content, too, Rossetti achieved during his first period mastery of the subject matters that were to be his throughout his career. The medieval dominated such early poems as *The Blessed Damozel, Dante at Verona, The Bride's Prelude, Sister Helen,* and *The Staff and Scrip.* Woman, too, was central in all these except *Dante at Verona,* and was the subject of *Jenny,* first projected in 1847. In this first period Rossetti displayed as wide a range of subjects as he was ever to encompass. Art is represented by *Old and New Art,* by sonnets for pictures, and by *Dante at Verona;* the supernatural and otherworldly by *Sister Helen* and *The Blessed Damozel;* reflections on life by *The Choice, The Card Dealer,* and *The Burden of Nineveh;* religion by *Ave, A Last Confession,* and (in his lifelong wish for an afterlife) *The Blessed Damozel;* domesticity (the only important example in all his poems) by *My Sister's Sleep;* social problems (again his only major attempt) by *Jenny;* and politics by *Wellington's Funeral, At the Sunrise in 1848,* and *On the Refusal of Aid Between Nations.* Clearly, in his earliest period Rossetti found and used the poetic content that was to be his as long as he lived. In later poems he used the same types of material, a bit differently, but not necessarily more successfully. He never developed new fields or wider interests.

On the whole, the characteristics of Rossetti's execution were also pretty much established during the first period. It is true that he revised his poems again and again to improve their rhythm, diction, and imagery. But it is also true that he never outgrew either the need for such meticulous revising, or his frequent fault of pushing his execution to extremes. If anything, this fault became more evident as he "matured." The unfortunate Beryl-songs of *Rose Mary* were added during his last years. The overloaded, often obscure sonnets of *The House of Life* were mostly written during the middle period. A number of his earliest sonnets (e.g., *For A Venetian Pastoral, Autumn Idleness, A Dark Day*) match the command of form found in the 1880 sonnet on the sonnet. And *Rose Mary* of the middle period fails to equal the formal achievement of the earlier *Sister Helen*.

Finally, the originality and imagination by which Rossetti set the greatest store are also demonstrated as successfully in the earliest period as in any other. Individual tastes may vary, and there is no need to attempt to rank in order each of Rossetti's poems in terms of these qualities. It is enough that two poems written in his earliest period are unique as imaginative works. *The Blessed Damozel* and *Sister Helen* have no parallels in all English poetry, let alone in the poet's own later work.[8]

Rossetti himself recognized the difference between a poet who reaches a certain height in his youth, but then can climb no higher, and one whose career is a progress from peak to ever-greater peaks. In comparing the early deaths of Keats and Shelley, he said that Keats to the last was "getting always choicer and simpler," whereas it was "really a mercy" that Shelley had not gone on "hatching yearly universes till now" (i.e., 1879.)[9] As he explained to Caine, then twenty-six: "In original work, a man does some of his best things by your time of life, though he only finds it out in a rage much later; at some date when he expected to know no longer that he had ever done them."[10]

For one who finds Rossetti's greatest shortcoming as a poet his inability to rise appreciably above the level of his earliest work, there is something especially ironic in the possibility that Rossetti perhaps deliberately tried to leave the impression that some of his best work was of an even earlier date than it was. He told Caine that *The Blessed Damozel* was first written when he was eighteen, although William Rossetti thought that "his twentieth year, or even his twenty-first, would be nearer the mark."[11] Dante Gabriel also said the poem had been "little altered since," whereas in fact it was so frequently revised between its first publication in 1850 and its appearance in the 1870 *Poems* that only one stanza (18) remained completely unaltered.[12] Sanford even goes so far as to say that the alleged "1847" manuscript of *The Blessed Damozel*—which he rather convincingly suggests should be dated as much as twenty years later— "appears to be a deliberate attempt on Rossetti's part to substantiate the legend of his own precocity."[13]

Rossetti also told Caine that the "larger part" of *The House of Life* "was written when I was as young as you are."[14] Caine was then twenty-six or twenty-seven; by far the larger part of the sonnets were written between 1868 and 1872, when Rossetti was forty to forty-four years old. Indeed, Rossetti admitted in a letter written to Hake in 1870: "Much the greater proportion of the sonnets in *The House of Life* are. . .written lately." But he added, "I daresay you will agree with me that it is not desirable to mention in print what I say above about dates of composition."[15]

It may well be that Rossetti's purpose in disguising the dates of the sonnets was not so much to substantiate a legend of precocity as to prevent their being identified with Janey Morris, who inspired so many of these poems. In either case, the result was the same, to make even more apparent what was already evident: that much of his best work stemmed from his earliest period. The "legend of precocity," if true, serves only to emphasize the fact that Rossetti did not grow significantly as a poet as the years passed.

Janey Morris' assessment was essentially correct. She agreed with the verdict that Rossetti's best work was his

young work, but resented the "impudence" of Edmund
Gosse's statement that "his work after 1868 was worth-
less."[16] The point is not that Rossetti's early poetic powers
waned, but that they waxed no stronger, leaving the question:
Why? Part of the answer may lie in the very sources of
Rossetti's poetry. Emotion was the predominate wellspring
of that poetry, and emotion, if intense to begin with, can
hardly be expected to "develop." It is only the poet's awareness of the "central significance" of his emotions that can
develop, making it possible for a Shakespeare to progress
from a Brutus to a Hamlet, from a Titus Andronicus to a
Macbeth. This requires a depth of understanding, a power
of intellect, a broad knowledge of what makes *homo sapiens*
the creature he is, that were beyond Rossetti.

Granted that Rossetti was no Shakespeare, nor was
meant to be. Even so, I cannot shake the feeling that
Rossetti's earliest work contained the promise of greater
things to come—a promise never fulfilled. And here the answer lies, I believe, in the multitude of conflicts that confronted him, conflicts that for him, at least, defied resolution.

THE TWO ROSSETTI'S. . .AND A THIRD

LOST ON BOTH SIDES

As when two men have loved a woman well,
   Each hating each, through Love's and Death's deceit;
   Since not for either this stark marriage-sheet
And the long pauses of this wedding-bell;
   Yet o'er her grave the night and day dispel
   At last their feud forlorn, with cold and heat;
   Nor other than dear friends to death may fleet
The two lives left that most of her can tell:—

So separate hopes, which in a soul had wooed

The one same Peace, strove with each other long,
And Peace before their faces perished since:
So through that soul, in restless brotherhood,
They roam together now, and wind among
Its bye-streets, knocking at the dusty inns.

(91, *The House of Life*)

William Rossetti says of *Lost on Both Sides*: "I think it refers to my brother's aspirations for attainment as painter and poet, partially baulked as yet."[17] This is indeed the obvious application, although "baulked as yet" seems excessively mild for a feud forlorn and lost. What is startling about this poem is that this hint of ultimate failure comes so early in Rossetti's career—he was only twenty-six when he wrote it—and that it reflects so tellingly conflicts between "separate hopes" that were never to be resolved.

As early as age five, Rossetti was pursuing two "careers," scibbling a blank verse drama and painting illustrations of Shakespearian characters. By the time that he was nineteen, it would seem that he had decided on which career to follow, for he wrote W. B. Scott: "the object of my ambition is to deserve one day the name of painter, to which end I am at present a student of the Academy."[18] Yet within five months he was sending his poems to the prestigious Leigh Hunt and asking whether in Hunt's opinion he should choose poetry or painting as a career. Hunt's evaluation of his poetic ability, Rossetti wrote his Aunt Charlotte, was "so flattering that I cannot quote any part of it, lest it should seem like conceit."[19] But Hunt added a note of caution that all too prophetically suggested the dilemma posed by Rossetti's conflicting hopes: "if you paint as well as you write, you may be a rich man. . . . But I need hardly tell you that poetry, even the very best—nay, the best, in this respect is apt to be the worst—is not a thing for a man to live upon while he is in the flesh, however immortal it may render his spirit."[20]

Following this reply, Rossetti buckled down, more or less, to the (to him) irritating business of learning to be a painter. In 1851, he was saying to his aunt, "I am sure that you will agree with me that it is very necessary I should, if possible, occupy myself constantly with my real career as a painter, and put aside. . .minor employment, either in writing or designing."[21] And reminiscing with Hall Caine, he recalled that he gave up poetry "at about 25 [i.e., 1853], on finding that it impeded attention to what constituted another aim and a livelihood into the bargain, i.e. painting."[22] Despite the fact that he had already written some of the best poetry he was ever to write by 1854, in that year he said, "I believe my painting and poetry prevented each other from doing much good for a long while — and now I think I could do better in either, but can't write, for then I sha'n't paint."[23] He had just written *Lost on Both Sides*!

To his scarcely hidden regret, the matter of "livelihood" appeared now to have settled the conflict. In 1855 he was saying, "I have given up poetry as a pursuit of my own."[24] In 1860 he was still insisting: "I sincerely suspect it would be better for me to stick to painting only."[25] And in 1861 he was assuring Mrs. Elizabeth Gaskell, the novelist, "I hope that you will not fancy that I neglect my painting for any literary attempt. My sins of the latter kind are all old ones."[26] The next year they appeared to be not only old, but literally buried, when Rossetti placed the manuscript book of his poems in the coffin of his wife.

Then, in 1868, with the exhumation of the manuscripts and a great new burst of poetic output, the feud of rival hopes flared up anew, more bitter than ever. The need for livelihood, especially with his profligate ways with money, had turned Rossetti the painter into a drudge, even a hired hack, toiling away for patrons insisting on the completion of paintings they had long since commissioned. If there was pay in painting, there was pride in poetry. In poetry "at any rate," he told

Shields in 1869, "I have done no pot-boiling. So I am grateful to that art, and nourish against the other that base grudge which we bear for those whom we have treated shabbily."[27]

There was another reason why Rossetti at this time began to prefer poetry to painting, as brother William recorded in his diary: Gabriel "seems more anxious just now to achieve something permanent in poetry than painting—in which he now considers that at any rate two living Englishmen, Millais and Jones, show a higher innate executive power than himself."[28] By 1870, the year of the publication of his *Poems,* Rossetti was declaring: "My own belief is that I am a poet (within the limit of my powers) primarily, and that it is my poetic tendencies that chiefly give value to my pictures: only painting being—what poetry is not—a livelihood—I have put my poetry chiefly in that form. On the other hand, the bread-and-cheese question has led to a good deal of my painting being pot-boiling and no more—whereas my verse, being unprofitable, has remained (as much as I have found time for) unprostituted."[29]

The poet's feud with the painter grew even more intense. Painting "task-work," he complained in 1871, had "kept me from the other Muse, who, I believe, after all is my true mistress."[30] And in the same year: "I wish I could live by writing poetry. I think I'd see painting d——d if one could."[31] In 1871 came the bitterest blast of all: "I have often said that to be an artist is just the same thing as to be a whore, as far as dependence on the whims and fancies of individuals is concerned."[32] By now, however, there was no turning back. Poetry, alack, has "no such nourishing savour about it as painting can boast, but is rather a hungry affair to follow."[33] As Rossetti summed it all up to Caine in 1880, "what has excluded more poetry with me. . .has chiefly been livelihood necessity."[34]

Suppose, however, there had been no such conflict in Rossetti, no twin talents that called for a choice between making money by painting and serving the one true muse of poetry? He might well have become a more prolific poet — but would he have become a greater one? There is reason to wonder, for warring within Rossetti's soul were not merely Rossetti the painter and Rossetti the poet, but two Rossetti's who, at every turn, were so drastically diverse that biographers and critics can (and have) made him seem two completely different and separate identities.

Rossetti was an Italian, immoral and irreligious, arrogant and money-grasping, moody and aloof, and fickle to his friends. As a critic, he was given to wild excess, brooking no opposition to judgements based on intuition and prejudice alone, and heralding the genius of a host of nobodies. He was a painter who toyed with poetry, a leader of a school that scorned the public and prized imagination over intellect, sensation and beauty over spirituality, and execution over subject matter and meaning.

Rossetti was an Englishman, moral and mystic, sensitive and generous, bluff and outgoing, and loyal to his friends. As a critic, he was vigorous without claiming infallibility, basing his judgements upon clear (though unformalized) principles, and quick to discover and champion the genius of a number of truly outstanding poets. He was a unique poet himself, severely handicapped by the need to make a living as a painter; no leader, he was a man who influenced others but went his own way, eager for public acceptance and prizing fundamental brainwork over unrestrained imagination, spirituality over emotion and beauty for their own sake alone, and lofty themes and subjects over execution.

Both these Rossetti's existed; they were the same man. The inevitable struggle between the two had its profound effect on both the man and his work. For they were formidable adversaries, and if now one, now the other triumphed temporarily, too often the end of the conflict was stalemate and mutual defeat.

The Italian-Englishman combination was perhaps the most compatible. To William Rossetti's eye, the appearance of his brother was "rather Italian than English," and his manner "extremely natural, and therefore unaffected in tone. . .with the naturalism characteristic of Italian blood."[35] With this, "there was a certain British bluffness, streaking the finely poised Italian suppleness and facility."[36] Hall Caine observed the same admixture when he first met the poet in 1880: "Very soon Rossetti came to me through the doorway in front, which proved to be the entrance to his studio. Holding forth both hands and crying 'Hulloa,' he gave me that cheery, hearty greeting which I came to recognize as his alone, perhaps, in warmth and unfailing geniality among all the men of our circle. It was Italian in its spontaneity, and yet it was English in its manly reserve."[37]

It seems quite possible that this combination of the Italian and English contributed much to the striking personality that so attracted, in turn, the members of the PRB, the Morris-Swinburne-Burne-Jones group at Oxford, and toward the end, Watts-Dunton, Sharp, and Caine. More in the realm of conjecture is the possibility that this same combination produced the conflicts between the moral and immoral, the irreligious and the mystic Rossetti. It can be argued that the Italian's view of morality saw nothing wrong with his liaisons with Fanny Cornforth and Janey Morris, while the Englishman with his conventional, at times almost prudish, Victorian morality found them a source of remorse and frustration. Possibly, too, the Italian was responsible for the mystic, superstitious yearning for an afterlife—a yearning that brought no such comfort as his sister Maria found in her convent. What matters more than their source are the conflicts themselves, offering as they did food for Rossetti's self-mistrust to feed upon.

The arrogant-sensitive Rossetti demonstrates this self-mistrust in action. Carried away by the emotion or conviction of the moment, he would blurt out opinions whose violence often offended his friends, only to have second thoughts that led to modification or retraction. "He was impetuous and vehement," as brother William said, "and necessarily therefore impatient; easily angered, easily appeased, although the embittered feelings of his later life obscured this amiable quality to some extent."[38] Even as late in life as his first meeting with Caine, however, his young friend noted that "if, by force of some stray impulse, he was ever led to say a disparaging word of any one, he forthwith made a palpable, and sometimes amusing, effort so to obliterate the injurious impression as to convey the idea that he wished it to appear that he had not said anything at all."[39] Toward the end, drugs and illness destroyed the sensitive Rossetti, and delusions fueled the vehemence. But by then, he was neither of the old Rossetti's; he was dead before dying.

Money-grasping Rossetti was, but not for the sake of piling up a fortune. On the contrary, had he had any inclination in that direction, he might have retired with a sizable bank account at a fairly early age, said "painting be d — — d," and spent his remaining days paying tribute to his "true Muse." In 1876, when he was only forty-eight, he made £3,725 in a single year — certainly a handsome income in an age when he and Morris could rent all of Kelmscott manor for only £60 per year. For this kind of money he often abused his patrons unmercifully, calling them "lambs at the altar of sacrifice," and gouging them for advances on paintings that were sometimes far from as near completion as he pretended.[40] If the painter were a whore, his services came high.

This is Rossetti at his least attractive. It can only be said in his defense that he was always careless, even childish, about spending money, shrewd though he might be in bargaining for it. Therefore, as he said in the year of his greatest prosperity, "I am always hard up for £50!"[41] When he did have a bit of money on hand, he was extremely generous, ever ready to subscribe to a benefit for an unfortunate artist, urging money upon Brown and others when they fell upon hard times, and lavishing gifts and money, of course, on Fanny. When he was at his lowest ebb in 1872, both physically and financially, following his attempt at suicide, he wrote Fanny: "you are the only person whom it is my duty to provide for, and you may be sure I should do my utmost as long as there was a breath in my body or a penny in my purse."[42]

The consequences on both his arts of this combination of Rossetti the avaricious spendthrift are incalculable. In painting, it forced him to turn out innumerable "pot-boilers" of which he was admittedly ashamed. It also robbed him of precious time and peace of mind that might have been devoted to poetry instead of to importunate patrons and hounding creditors. When one pictures Rossetti, fighting ill health, failing eyesight and insomnia, toiling away drearily on replicas of some once-inspiring painting, there must be a measure of sympathy for the money-grasping painter who was always hard up for £50—and a sigh for the poet who suffered thereby.

Out of such circumstances and the attendant genie bottled in chloral grew, to a large extent, the image of Rossetti the moody, aloof recluse, shunning old friends and refusing to make new ones. Certainly after the Buchanan attack and the subsequent breakdown of 1872, delusions of persecution haunted him, and increasingly "he became secluded in his habits of life, and often depressed, fanciful, and gloomy." But in recording this, William Rossetti, while saying "hitherto he had on the whole an ample sufficiency of high spirits," also admits that combined with this had already been "a certain underlying gloominess or abrupt moodiness of nature and outlook."[43] And even after the breakdown, the bluff and genial Rossetti emerged from time to time in the later years of the gloomy and depressed recluse. His first greeting of Caine proves this, supporting William's comment: "Not indeed that there were no intervals of serenity, even of brightness [after 1874]; for in fact he was often genial and pleasant, and a most agreeable companion, with as much *bonhomie* as acuteness for whiling an evening away."[44]

Both these Rossetti's, then—the genial, pleasant man of *bonhomie* and the creature of underlying gloominess and abrupt moodiness—coexisted from the start. What happened is that the latter Rossetti progressively became the dominant one, even before the breakdown. The effect on his poetry is evident: the gloom and frustration of *Lost on Both Sides* and *The Landmark* of the 1850's and *Lost Days* of the early 1860's deepen in the sonnets of *The House of Life* written between 1868 and 1873, and thereafter there is only one little burst of poetry to come, for in the words of Coleridge:

Work without Hope draws nectar in a sieve,
And Hope without an object cannot live.

In large part, this increasing dominance of the moody, gloomy side of Rossetti explains his reputation as a fickle friend, who turned on Browning, drifted away from Hunt, Millais, Ruskin, Morris, Burne-Jones and others, and (certainly with more cause) came to say of Swinburne, "I now view him as the crowning nuisance of the whole world and have no longer the slightest toleration for his abominable ways."[45] Yet Rossetti remained devoted to the often-crusty Brown, and to W. B. Scott and Dr. Hake, whose reminiscences of Rossetti were to prove less than charitable. He was not wholly at fault for the broken friendships, and even when clearly innocent, he could be manly and generous. When his old friend Frederick Sandys wrote a bitter letter renouncing their friendship because Rossetti had tactfully pointed out similarities in various designs each had done, Rossetti replied feelingly:

I myself hold that friendship should only be resigned when one friend can prove malice or deception against another. Of the first of these I know I am innocent; of the second I should have been to a certain extent guilty if I had held my tongue as soon as I felt impelled to speak. I believe myself firmly in the sincerity and single-mindedness of your friendship for me till this time, and even in all you say of your pain at the termination to which you have chosen to bring it. You say that you believe this matters little to me; but why you say so I cannot conceive. It is however some relief to know that the separation which you make between us comes at a moment when, to my joy, great success and many friends await you, and that I can on my side remain still

Affectionately yours,

D. G. Rossetti.[46]

Loyalty to his friends, ironically, has been cited as one reason for the excess and prejudice that—together with reliance upon intuition—have been called Rossetti's major shortcomings as a critic. On the mediocre verses of his friends Dr. Hake, Allingham, W. B. Scott, and Canon Dixon, he did heap lavish praise. But he was at least as generous in his "puffing" of Charles Wells and Ebenezer Jones, whom he met only once. Moreover, his enthusiasm for the works of all of these was tempered by an awareness of their faults. And if he often discovered genius where it did not exist, he just as surely discovered it where it did—notably with Blake, Keats, Browning, Morris, Swinburne, and Fitzgerald. As for intuition, rule him though it did, it was backed by definite beliefs as to what a poet, and a poem, should be.

These beliefs, it is true, often conflicted with one another, producing two Rossetti's who warred with each other in the very act of writing poetry. There was the Rossetti who hated to please the "British fool" — and the Rossetti who was "not indifferent to public recognition," who went to great lengths to make his work both intelligible and acceptable to the reader. There was the Rossetti who rated imagination and primary vital impulse among the highest gifts of a poet, and confused "fundamental brainwork" with intellect — and the Rossetti who used that brainwork for preliminary "cartooning," followed by the "agonized tattooing" of endless revisions and "humblest verbal labor" that vitiated (for all his denials) the very primary impulse he called "the inspired quality in art."[47] Always there was the Rossetti whose aim it was to embody lofty themes and subjects with spirituality — and the Rossetti whose best poems are chiefly remarkable for their emotion and beauty.

Even more at odds were the poet who wanted to be as simple as possible, as complete as possible, as forceful as possible — and the poet who wanted to be as subtle as possible, as brief as possible, and who called "moderation the highest law of poetry." The one poet insisted that the "brains" in poetry took precedence over the "music," and that sound must not be superior to sense. The other delighted in execution, calling form a poem's "most inalienable quality," and metre its "true patent of nobility." Even the poet of execution was not of a single mind and purpose, for as he denounced on the one hand the far-fetched and artificial, he allowed himself on the other excesses of diction, wordplay, and imagery that smacked of both.

Both Rossetti's, and especially both poets, might have concurred on the ideal of perfection, "the feeling of pure rage and self-hatred when anyone else does better than you do."[48] But how could "they" do their best when they could not agree on what was best? All that their vaunting about the need for "self-scrutiny and self-repression" led to was what Rossetti himself called the lesser quality in poetic execution, a "self-questioning in the very moment of action or even later."[49] The result, in short, was mistrust, born of their feuds forlorn, leaving each Rossetti to charge the other that "a poet's own opinion upon his rhymes is always the least valuable."[50]

Another man than Rossetti might have settled these feuds—though of course he would not then have been Rossetti. But suppose Rossetti *had* been able to realize and confidently face up to the myriad conflicts, to resolve those that could be resolved and shrug at the rest? Suppose he had been able to say of some stronger, more resolute Rossetti, as Burne-Jones did say: "He taught me to have no shame of my own ideas. . .to seek no popularity, to be altogether myself"?[51] What then might this new Rossetti, this "third" Rossetti who was altogether himself, have been?

He would first, I think, have decided from the start that his one true muse was poetry, and either have been content to paint only as a means of providing the poet with a livelihood, or have taken his chances simply as a poet, and said "painting be d——d" entirely. Having made this decision, he would have been unhesitating about publishing, impervious to hostile critics, and bold in seeking rapport with the reader without yielding to a yearning for popularity. Realizing that real intellectual subtlety was beyond his powers and alien to his temperament, he would have relied unabashedly on his imagination, aiming frankly at achieving intense emotional impact and beauty, assured, along with Keats, that in its own way, "beauty is truth." He would have acknowledged his basically sensual nature, and while honestly admitting that the body was not the soul, would have "nobly expressed" its "just delights" without recourse to a false mask of spirituality. He would set *Body's Beauty* and *Soul's Beauty* each in its proper perspective, instead of trying to make them identical.

This Rossetti would have depended wholly on his primary

vital impulse, improving upon his original as he could, but resorting neither to elaborate prose synopses not to nit-picking revisions. Aware of his limited interests and back-ground, he would have exploited more deeply and widely those subjects he knew best: the medieval, the supernatural, the arts, and woman and love, employing symbols simply and clearly. He would have retained his mastery of execution, while curbing his excesses. He would have been simple yet rich in diction, brief and forceful, yet controlled by a judicious moderation that eschewed both reticence and obscurity. In each poem, he would do his best within these limitations, and be confident that he *had* done his best, knowing that achieve-ment can never match aim—and then go on to other work, finishing, perhaps, *The Bride's Prelude,* and bringing to birth such aborted poems as *Michael Scott's Wooing, The Doom of the Sirens, The Orchard Pit, God's Graal,* and *St. Joan.*

Such is the poet that Rossetti might have been. Indeed, a poet very like this was Rossetti at his best, writing *A Last Confession, The Blessed Damozel, Sister Helen, The Stream's Secret*; sonnets like *Without Her, The Kiss,* and *Lovesight*; and a few minor poems like *The Woodspurge* and the self-deprecated *My Sister's Sleep.* The first-rate *The Cloud Confines* would have sprung forth spontaneously without the agony of revisions that only led back to their starting point. A more dramatic, moving *Jenny* would have emerged, purged of its uncharacteristic and mushy moral-izing. There would have been a more direct and electrically charged *Rose Mary,* stripped of its banal and artificial Beryl-songs.

The very highest poetic achievement would never have been his, for he lacked the essentials that alone can develop and grow to true greatness, the combination of powerful intellect with magnificent imagination, and deepest spiritu-ality with enormous emotional power. But had faith in him-

self given Rossetti the boldness to choose unflinchingly between each of the conflicting elements and aims that were
his, he might well have found content in his life and a
measure of lifelong satisfaction in his poetry.

Instead, he tried to embrace both sides of every conflict. Thus opposing hopes roamed through his soul in
restless brotherhood, striving with each other till the peace
each sought perished before their faces, and the poet and
his poetry were lost on both sides.

NOTES

[1]*Collected Works,* I, 512.

[2]*D & W,* II, 821.

[3]Even Buchanan came to acknowledge Rossetti's basic morality, and to
retract his attack. Dedicating his *God and the Man* to Rossetti, Buchanan
wrote:

TO AN OLD ENEMY

I would have snatch'd a bay-leaf from thy brow,
   Wronging the chaplet of an honoured head;
In peace and charity I bring thee now
       A lily-flower instead.

Pure as thy purpose, blameless as thy song,
   Sweet as thy spirit, may this offering be;
Forget the bitter blame that did thee wrong,
       And take the gift from me!

                                    (Caine, p. 293.)

[4]Caine, p. 104.

[5]*Collected Works,* I, xx.

[6]The only major exceptions were Browning and Tennyson, and he felt
that they, not he, had changed.

[7]The dates used in the ensuing discussion are based primarily on W. M.
Rossetti's *Classified Lists* of his brother's writings (London, 1906, pp. 5-48)
with the corroboration of numerous other sources. Because of Rossetti's constant revisions, the date used for most poems here represents the year in which
each was brought to substantial completion, not the year in which it reached
its final published form. The criterion of "quantity," therefore, should not be
pushed too far.

[8]I cannot agree with Professor Doughty that *Sister Helen* and *The Blessed*

Damozel have been "overpraised." They may have been overexposed. Doughty, *Poems*, p. xiv.

[9]Caine, p. 170.

[10]*Ibid.*, p. 169.

[11]*Collected Works*, I, xxix.

[12]See Baum, *The House of Life*, pp. 125-6.

[13]J. A. Sanford, "The Morgan Manuscript of Rossetti's 'The Blessed Damozel,'" *Studies in Philology*, XXXV (July, 1938), p. 471. Sanford shows that the version in this manuscript, dated "1847," is unmistakably in Rossetti's later handwriting, is superior poetically to the 1850 published version (suggesting that it included later revisions), and bears the initials "DGR," which Rossetti did not use until 1848 or 1849. A more charitable explanation might be that sometime during the 1860's, Rossetti copied out the poem for a friend, and added the year "1847" merely to indicate that the poem was *first* written in that year, not that either the manuscript itself or the version it contained was that old.

[14]Caine, p. 221.

[15]*D & W*, II, 858.

[16]Grylls, p. 239.

[17]W. M. Rossetti, *Poems* (1904 ed.), II, 240.

[18]*D & W*, I, 34.

[19]*Ibid.*, p. 38.

[20]Doughty, *Dante Gabriel Rossetti*, p. 62.

[21]*D & W*, I, 99.

[22]Caine, p. 138.

[23]*D & W*, I, 214.

[24]*Ibid.*, p. 279.

[25]*Ibid.*, p. 372.

[26]*Ibid.*, II, 429-30.

[27]*Ibid.*, p. 729.

[28]*Ibid.*, p. 745.

[29]*Ibid.*, pp. 849-50.

[30]*Ibid.*, III, 986.

[31]*Ibid.*, p. 996.

[32]*Ibid.*, p. 1175.

[33]*Ibid.*, p. 1348.

[34]Caine, p. 165.

[35]*Collected Works*, I, xxii and xx.

[36]*Ibid.*, p. xx.

[37]Caine, p. 212.

[38]*Collected Works*, I, xx.

[39]Caine, p. 270.

[40]*D & W*, I, 355.

[41]*Ibid.*, III, 1435.
[42]*Ibid.*, p. 1057.
[43]*Collected Works*, I, xix.
[44]*Ibid.*, p. xix-xx.
[45]*D & W*, III, 1270.
[46]*Ibid.*, II, 698-9.
[47]See *sup.*, p. 220.
[48]*D & W*, II, 581.
[49]*Collected Works*, I, 500.
[50]*D & W*, I, 45.
[51]Burne-Jones, I, 149

SELECT BIBLIOGRAPHY

The following is not in any sense complete, but includes only works referred to or quoted in this text. William E. Fredeman's *Pre-Raphaelitism: A Bibliocritical Study,* Cambridge, 1965, contains the most recent, most nearly complete, and best bibliography of Rossetti. Also useful is William Michael Rossetti's *Dante Gabriel Rossetti: Classified Lists of His Writings with the Dates,* London, 1906.

I. PUBLISHED WORKS
OF DANTE GABRIEL ROSSETTI

1843 — *Sir Hugh the Heron, A Legendary Tale,* (by Gabriel Rossetti, Jr.). London: G. Polidori's Private Press.

1861 — *The Early Italian Poets.* London: Smith-Elder.

1870 — *Poems.* London: Ellis.

1871 — "The Stealthy School of Criticism," *The Athenaeum,* 2302 (December 16, 1871), 792-4.

1881 — *Poems.* London: Ellis.

1881 — *Ballads and Sonnets.* London: Ellis.

1886 — *Collected Works,* ed. W. M. Rossetti, 2 Vols. London: Ellis.

1901 — *The Germ,* facsimile reprint, ed. W. M. Rossetti. London: Stock.

1904 — *The Poems of Dante Gabriel Rossetti,* ed. W. M. Rossetti. 2 Vols. London: Ellis.

1911 — *The Words of Dante Gabriel Rossetti,* ed. W. M. Rossetti. London: Ellis.

1928 — *The House of Life,* ed. P. F. Baum. Cambridge: Harvard University Press.

1931 — *Dante Gabriel Rossetti, An Analytical List of Manuscripts,* ed. P. F. Baum. Durham: Duke University Press.

1938 — *The Blessed Damozel,* ed. P. F. Baum. Chapel Hill: University of North Carolina Press.

1939 — *Rossetti's Sister Helen,* ed. J. C. Troxell. New Haven: Yale University Press.

1952 — *Dante Gabriel Rossetti: Jan Van Hunks,* ed. J. R. Wahl. New York: New York Public Library.

1957 — *Dante Gabriel Rossetti: Poems,* ed. O. Doughty. London: Dent.

II. LETTERS

Baum, P. F., ed. *Rossetti's Letters to Fanny Cornforth.* Baltimore: Johns Hopkins Press, 1940.

Doughty, O., and Wahl, J. R., eds. *Letters of Dante Gabriel Rossetti.* 4 Vols. London: Oxford University Press, 1965-67.

Hill, G. B., ed. *Letters of Dante Gabriel Rossetti to William Allingham, 1854-1870.* London: Unwin, 1897.

Rossetti, D. G. *John Keats, Criticism and Comment.* London: privately printed by T. J. Wise, 1919.

Rossetti, W. M., ed. *Dante Gabriel Rossetti: His Family Letters, with a Memoir.* 2 Vols. London: Ellis, 1895.

— — —*Praeraphelite Diaries and Letters.* London: Hurst and Blackett, 1900.

— — — *Rossetti Papers 1862-1870.* London: Sands, 1903.

— — — *Ruskin: Rossetti: Preraphaelitism,* London: Allen, 1899.

Troxell, J. C. *Three Rossettis.* Cambridge: Harvard University Press, 1937.

Wise, T. J., ed. *The Ashley Library: A Catalogue.* 11 Vols. London: printed for private circulation only, 1922-1936.

III. BIBLIOGRAPHICAL AND CRITICAL STUDIES OF DANTE GABRIEL ROSSETTI

Baum, P. F. "The Bancroft Manuscripts of Dante Gabriel Rossetti," *Modern Philology,* XXXIX (August, 1941), 47-68.

Bayne, T. "The Poetry of Dante Gabriel Rossetti," *Fraser's Magazine,* n.s. XXV (March, 1882), 376-384.

Benson, A. C. *Rossetti.* London: Macmillan, 1904.

Bickley, F. *The Pre-Raphaelite Comedy.* London: Constable, 1932.

Buchanan, R. *The Fleshly School of Poetry.* London: Strahan, 1872.

Burgum, E. B. "Rossetti and the Ivory Tower," *Sewanee Review,* XXXVII (October, 1929), 431-446.

Caine, T. Hall. *Recollections of Dante Gabriel Rossetti.* Boston: Roberts Brothers, 1898.

Carr, J. C. *Some Eminent Victorians.* London: Duckworth, 1908.

Cary, E. L. *The Rossettis.* New York: Putnam, 1900.

Culler, Dwight and Helen, "The Sources of 'The King's Tragedy,' " *Studies in Philology,* XLI (July, 1944), 427-441.

"Dante Gabriel Rossetti," *The London Times,* May 11, 1928; pp. 17-18.

"Dante Gabriel Rossetti's Poems," *The Nation,* XI (July 14, 1870), 29-30.

DeVane, W. C. "The Harlot and the Thoughtful Young Man," *Studies in Philology,* XXIV (July, 1932), 463-483.

Doughty, O. *Dante Gabriel Rossetti.* New Haven: Yale University Press, 1949.

Gaunt, W. *The Aesthetic Adventure.* London: Harcourt Brace, 1945.

— — — *The Pre-Raphaelite Tragedy.* London: Cape, 1942.

Grylls, R. G. *Portrait of Rossetti.* London: Macmillan, 1964.

Howe, M. L. "Rossetti's Comments on Maud," *Modern Language Notes,* XLIX (May, 1934), 290-293.

Hueffer, F. M. *Rossetti.* London: Longmans, 1916.

Jackson, E. "Notes on the Stanza of *The Blessed Damozel,*" *Publications of the Modern Language Association,* LVIII (December, 1943), 1050-56.

Knickerbocker, K. L. "Rossetti's *The Blessed Damozel,*" *Studies in Philology* XXXIX (July, 1932) 485-504.

Knight, L. C. *Life of Dante Gabriel Rossetti.* London: Scott, 1887.

Mégroz, R. L. *Dante Gabriel Rossetti: Painter Poet of Heaven and Earth.* London: Faber, 1928.

Milner, G. "On Some Marginalia made by D. G. Rossetti," *Manchester Quarterly,* V (January, 1883), 1-10.

Pater, W. *Appreciations.* London: Macmillan, 1927.

Rossetti, W. M. *Rossetti as Designer and Writer.* London: Cassell, 1889.

Sanford, J. A. "The Morgan Manuscript of Rossetti's 'The Blessed Damozel,'" *Studies in Philology,* XXXV (July, 1938), 471-486.

Sharp, W. *Dante Gabriel Rossetti: A Record and a Study.* London: Macmillan, 1882.

Skelton, J. *The Table Talk of Shirley.* London: Blackwood, 1894.

Stephens, F. G. *Dante Gabriel Rossetti: A Record and a Study.* London: Seeley, 1894.

Symons, A. *Studies in Strange Souls.* London: Sawyer, 1929.

Tisdel, F. M. "Rossetti's *House of Life,*" *Modern Philology,* XV (September, 1917), 65-84.

Turner, A. M. "Rossetti's Reading and His Critical Opinions," *Publications of the Modern Language Association,* XLII (June, 1927), 465-491.

Watts-Dunton, T. "The Truth About Rossetti," *The Nineteenth Century,* XIII (March, 1883), 404-423.

Waugh, E. *Rossetti.* London: Duckworth, 1928.

IV.   MEMOIRS, RECOLLECTIONS,
BIOGRAPHIES, ETC.
OF OTHERS CONTAINING SOME MATERIAL ON
D. G. ROSSETTI

Allingham, H., and Radford, D., eds. *William Allingham, A Diary.* London: Macmillan, 1907.

Burne-Jones, G. *The Memorials of Edward Burne-Jones.* 2 Vols. London: Macmillan, 1904.

Chamneys, B. *Coventry Patmore.* 2 Vols. London: George Bell and Sons, 1900.

Chew, S. C. *Swinburne.* Boston: Little, Brown, 1929.

Compton-Rickett, A. *Portraits and Personalities.* London: Selwyn and Blount, 1937.

Douglas, J. *Theodore Watts-Dunton.* New York: John Lane, 1904.

Ghodes, C., and Baum, P. F., eds. *Letters of William Michael Rossetti.* Durham: Duke University Press, 1934.

Gilchrist, H. H. *Anne Gilchrist, Her Life and Writings.* London: Unwin, 1887.

Gosse, E. *The Life of A. C. Swinburne.* London: Heinemann, 1917.

Hake, T. G. *Memoirs of Eighty Years.* London: Bentley, 1892.

Hake, T. and Compton-Rickett, A., eds. *The Letters of Algernon Charles Swinburne.* London: Murray, 1918.

――― *The Life and Letters of Theodore Watts-Dunton.* 2 Vols. London: Chapman and Hall, 1913.

Hueffer, F. M. *Ford Madox Brown.* London: Longmans, 1896.

Hunt, W. Holman. *Pre-Raphaelitism and the Pre-Raphaelite Brotherhood.* 2 Vols. London: Chapman and Hall, 1913.

Hyder, C. K. *Swinburne's Literary Career and Fame.* Durham: Duke University Press, 1933.

Ingram, J. H. *Oliver Madox Brown.* London: Stock, 1883.

Mackail, J. W. *The Life of William Morris.* 2 Vols. London: Longmans, 1899.

Millais, J. G. *The Life and Letters of Sir John Everett Millais.* 2 Vols. London: Methuen, 1899.

Mills, E. *The Life and Letters of Frederick Shields.* London: Longmans, 1912.

Rossetti, W. M. *Some Reminiscences of William Michael Rossetti.* 2 Vols. New York: Scribner's Sons, 1906.

Scott, W. B. *Autobiographical Notes.* 2 Vols. London: Osgood, 1892.

Watts-Dunton, T. "Rossetti and Charles Wells: A Reminiscence of Kelmscott," in *Joseph and His Brethren: A Dramatic Poem,* by Charles Wells. Oxford: Oxford University Press, 1908.

Wright, T. *The Life of John Payne.* London: Unwin, 1919.

Zaturenska, M. *Christina Rossetti.* New York: Macmillan, 1949.

Index

Listings for frequently mentioned persons (e.g. William M. Rossetti) do not include references that merely identify them as the source of a comment or opinion of D. G. Rossetti himself. References to Rossetti's writings are listed separately in Section II, and to his paintings in Section III.

I. GENERAL

II. ROSSETTI'S POEMS AND PROSE WORKS

III. ROSSETTI'S PAINTINGS

Date Due